A Popular History of Minnesota

A Popular History
of Minnesota

NORMAN K. RISJORD

MINNESOTA HISTORICAL SOCIETY PRESS

www.mhspress.org

The Minnesota Historical Society Press is a member of the Association of American University Presses.

Manufactured in the United States of America

10 9 8 7 6 5 4 3

♾ The paper used in this publication meets the minimum requirements of the American National Standard for Information Sciences—Permanence for Printed Library Materials, ANSI Z39.48–1984.

International Standard Book Number
ISBN 13: 978-0-87351-532-0 paperback
ISBN 10: 0-87351-532-3 paperback

Library of Congress Cataloging-in-Publication Data
Risjord, Norman K.
   A popular history of Minnesota / Norman K. Risjord.
      p.   cm.
   Includes bibliographical references and index.
   ISBN 0-87351-531-5 (alk. paper) —
   ISBN 0-87351-532-3 (pbk.: alk. paper)
   1. Minnesota—History.
   I. Title.
F606.R58 2005
977.6—dc22
                                        2004025294

Maps on pages 2, 3, and 272 by CartoGraphics, Inc.
All illustrations are from the collections of the Minnesota Historical Society.

To Barbara,
a true Daughter of the Middle Border
With Love

A Popular History of Minnesota

Preface

The idea of a relatively brief, fast-paced trip through Minnesota's past was suggested to me by Gregory Britton, director of the Minnesota Historical Society Press. It is actually the second of my books to be inspired by Greg. A decade ago, while we were on an unproductive fishing trip in northern Wisconsin, he talked me into doing a popular biography of Thomas Jefferson. Ours has been a long and very productive friendship.

Because this book is a synthesis of current scholarship rather than a tome of original research, I owe a huge debt to the many fine scholars who have pioneered the study of Minnesota's past. Among them are Anne J. Aby, Gary Clayton Anderson, Theodore C. Blegen, Kenneth Carley, Clifford E. Clark, Jr., Carolyn Gilman, Rhoda R. Gilman, Stephen R. Graubard, and William E. Lass. I am also indebted to the superb editorial staff of the Minnesota Historical Society Press and to the many excellent suggestions of its "blind" reviewers. I hope this book does justice to them all.

I owe a final note of thanks to my wife, Connie, my most resourceful editor and fearless critic.

NORMAN K. RISJORD
Madison, Wisconsin

A Popular History of Minnesota

Minnesota: Major Cities and Geographical Features

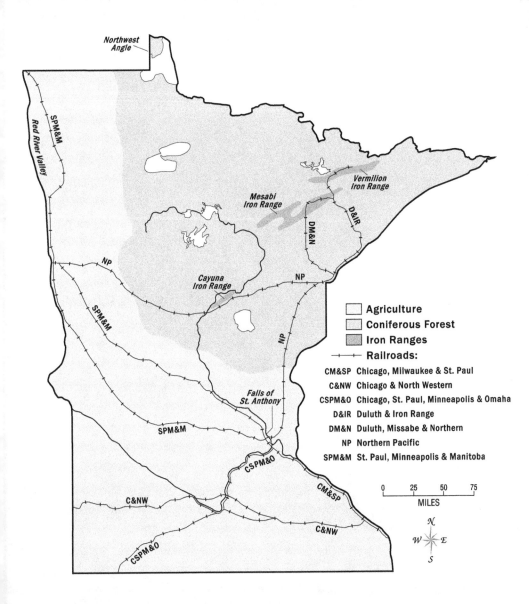

Minnesota: Resources and Railroads

1

Of Ice and Early Man

When the first settlers cleared land for farms in Minnesota in the early part of the nineteenth century, they noticed that the soil abounded with smooth, round stones of the sort usually found in streams and lakeshores. They brought an explanation for this with them from Europe: the earth had once been scoured by a great flood, described in the Book of Genesis. The Deluge had left a blanket of stony debris after its currents subsided. Farmers who dug wells found, beneath this *diluvium,* a layer of soil containing much organic matter and fossils of trees. Because this soil must have been in place before the great flood, it was called "the remains of Noah's barnyard."

In 1850 Harvard University offered a professorship to a Swiss geologist, Louis Agassiz. A decade earlier Agassiz had published a thesis arguing that a giant sheet of ice had once covered the continent of Europe. This glacier, he theorized, had deposited the smooth stones that dotted the farmland of Europe and scraped the curious striations on the rocky masses of the Swiss Alps. In the stony soils of New England Agassiz found further evidence for his glacial theory. Although he never reached Minnesota, the Harvard professor did lead an expedition along the shores of Lake Superior, where he found impressive signs of glaciation.

By the 1870s Agassiz's theory of glaciation had won general acceptance, and geologists in Minnesota began digging into the ancient history of the land. Examining soils, landforms, and sediments of nonglacial origin, they found evidence of four major expansions of glacial ice, interspersed with periods of warmer climates. The earliest, occurring about one million years ago, reached into what is now central Nebraska and was named the Nebraskan Ice Stage. The most recent, beginning about seventy thousand years ago, was named the Wisconsin Stage because of the profound impact it had on the state's topography. But the most recent glacial period might just as well have been called the Minnesota Stage, for it had an equally profound impact on the state. It not only wiped out most of the landforms created by the earlier glaciers, but it left behind the familiar topography of lakes, hilly moraines, and the water-hewn valleys of the St. Croix and Minnesota rivers.

Scientists are still not sure what caused the periods of glaciation. Possibilities include changes related to continental tectonic drift (which may have affected oceanic thermal currents or, by exposing newly formed rocks, permitted weathering to change the atmospheric levels of carbon dioxide) and changes in the earth's elliptical orbit around the sun. Because two-thirds of the land mass of North America lies north of the 45th parallel, the continent was especially vulnerable to the ice sheets. (The 45th parallel passes through the Twin Cities.) Glaciers began in mountainous areas or near polar regions when snow did not melt in summer, and they fed upon themselves. As sheets of ice spread out in a period of global cooling, they reflected the sun's rays back into space, contributing to the cooling.

The Wisconsin Stage glaciers originated in northeastern Canada, and as the snow piled up year after year and century after century it reached a depth of almost two miles. So heavy was the ice that it put a dent in the earth's crust, the remains of which are known today as Hudson Bay. When a glacier grows to about two hundred feet high, the immense weight of snow and ice causes the ice at the bottom to become flexible and, depending on the incline of the land, the mass begins to flow. New snows replenish the ice mass so the movement can continue, reaching a pace of as much as two hundred feet a year. The moving ice scoured the earth down to bedrock in many places (basalt and granite in Canada and northern Minnesota) and pushed the till of sand and rocks like a gigantic plow. The ice did not advance evenly, for it was detoured by high spots and ancient river beds. The fingers, or lobes, at the forefront of the glacier advanced, stalled, and advanced again with short-term changes in climate.

Over tens of thousands of years, several lobes of the ice sheet advanced and retreated across Minnesota, rearranging the landscape. The peak of the most recent glacial trek occurred about fourteen thousand years ago, when the Des Moines lobe swept down from the northwest, covered most of the state, and reached into central Iowa, the farthest penetration of the Wisconsin period. None of these icy projections reached southwestern Wisconsin or the southeastern corner of Minnesota, an area known today as the Driftless Region.

The Great Meltdown

South of the great ice mass in what is now Minnesota lay patches of tundra, grassland, and spruce parkland that stretched to the Ohio and Missouri rivers. Beyond the rivers, a spruce forest reached almost to the Gulf of Mexico. The deciduous forest of oak, maple, beech, and walnut that covers much of the United States today was largely confined to Florida and Texas. In the southwestern part of the continent, moist air from the warm Pacific created a land of freshwater lakes and pine forests. A land bridge across the Bering Strait between Alaska and Siberia separated the warm Pacific Ocean from the frigid waters of the Arctic. Warm Pacific currents preserved large parts of Alaska from glaciation.

About fourteen thousand years ago the earth began to warm again. The glacial lobes halted their advance and then began to melt. Short-term changes in climate of one or two hundred years turned the retreat into a stutter-step, and at each brief halt the lobes left a ridge of earth and stone, or a moraine. The Des Moines lobe, for example, deposited what is known today as the Big Stone Moraine, which essentially forms the divide between the Minnesota and Red River valleys. To the east, the retreating Superior lobe left a moraine around the western and southern sides of Mille Lacs, while furnishing the initial waters of the lake. Melting glaciers exposed till piled up into oblong hills or drumlins that paralleled their flow and conical hills or kames near terminal moraines. Rivers of water flowing in tunnels under the ice deposited sand and gravel in winding ridge-like hills called eskers.

The melting ice, together with the depressed earth's crust, created a gigantic freshwater lake that extended from Browns Valley into southern Canada. In 1879 geologists honored the originator of the theory of glaciation by naming it Lake Agassiz. Glaciers to the north and east prevented the lake from draining in those directions, and the waters built up until they eventually topped the Big Stone Moraine at the head of the Red River Valley. Spilling through the moraine, the glacial River Warren, larger than any in North America today, carved out the huge valley in which the Minnesota River now flows. As the river reached an older valley where St. Paul now stands, it formed an immense waterfall. The falls, formed by the erosion of soft sandstone under a thin layer of brittle limestone, crept northward over thousands of years, at the rate of two or three feet a year, some eight miles up the Mississippi. Now known as St. Anthony Falls, they were protected by a concrete apron in the 1860s.

About ten thousand years ago the melting of ice north of Lake Superior opened a new outlet for Lake Agassiz to the east, the lake level dropped, and the divide between the Minnesota and Red rivers was created.

As the climate warmed, the spruce forest spread across Minnesota and then was replaced by pine. Prairie grasses spread northward out of Kansas and Nebraska, reaching southwestern Minnesota about ten thousand years ago. North and east of that boundary the empire of pine and spruce held on. Animals moved in with the advance of vegetation. Some, like the Columbian mammoth, the mastodons (relatives of the elephant), and the giant sloth, had been around for millions of years, dating their ancestry to the New World's early contact with Africa. Others, like the famous wooly mammoth, originated in Siberia and came across on the Alaskan land bridge. Also prowling the forests of Minnesota were a variety of meat-eating animals—wolves, bears, and cats, large and small. Some had originated in North America; others had crossed on the land bridge. The short-faced bear, which evolved in North America, dwarfed the modern grizzly and was the largest meat-eating mammal ever to have trod the earth. Equally fearsome was an American lion twice the size and weight of the modern African lion. The saber-toothed cat, which used its extended canines to disembowel its prey, owed its ancestry to African or Asian origins and was an American relic, its ancestors in the Old World having become extinct several thousand years earlier.

All of these huge animals became extinct in North and South America within a few thousand years before and after the arrival of human hunters. Perhaps skilled early hunters contributed to the die-off. Many of the lumbering giant mammals, who had little fear of puny humans, would have made good targets. On the other hand, the same massive changes in climate that made much of North America habitable by humans may have made the area less hospitable for these large mammals.

Early Humans

The earliest reliable evidence of humans in the Americas was first uncovered at a site near the village of Clovis, New Mexico. The principal evidence for their existence is a tool, a spear point finely chiseled out of flint or chert, with a sharp point and hollowed-out ("fluted") sides so that it could be firmly affixed to a wooden shaft. Campsites and projectile points of the Clovis people, all dating from 10,000 to 9000 BC, have been found at various places in North America, especially in the Great Plains. It is likely that they began coming across the Alaskan land bridge at the beginning of the warming period. Although the land bridge had been in existence for thousands of years, the frozen tundra of Siberia discouraged Asian peoples from moving much north of the 54th parallel until the climate began to warm. About fourteen thousand years ago, at a site on the shore of the East Siberian Sea, people scavenged dead and dying mammoths swept to the sea by the Berelekh River. These people may have been the first pioneers to venture east and south along the shore of North America. In Alaska they would have found more of the same—mammoths, bison, elk, and deer—a fauna that they had been feeding upon as they crossed Asia. Interestingly, however, no Clovis spear points have been found in Siberia. The Clovis spear point seems to have been an early New World invention by the people now known as Paleoindians.

The oldest burial site in Minnesota, dated to about nine thousand years ago, is in the Big Stone Moraine near the town of Browns Valley on the headwaters of the Minnesota River. A man's skeleton, its bones stained with red ochre, was found in a gravel pit with a finely flaked stone knife and a smaller projectile point of a type known as Plano, which does not have the fluting characteristic of the Clovis implements. Plano points have been found throughout Minnesota. It thus appears that hunters of the late Paleoindian Tradition pursued both the buffalo of the prairie grasslands and the deer and elk of the northern forests.

Over the next thousand or so years people of what is called the Archaic Period developed woodworking tools such as chipped stone axes and adzes, new forms of scrapers and knives, and punches that must have quickened the process of turning animal skins into clothing. At a campsite in Itasca State Park dated to about 6000 BC, archaeologists found stone tools and the bones of bison that had been scarred in butchering. This species of bison, now extinct, was much larger than the modern bison or buffalo. It is likely that the hunters drove the animal into a swamp and then speared it as it struggled in the muck. Archaeologists also found at this site the skeleton of a domestic dog, the first evidence in Minnesota. A female skeleton of the Archaic Period was uncovered at Pelican Rapids, about a hundred miles to the north of Browns Valley. An antler tool and the shell of a salt-water clam, probably from the Gulf of Mexico, were found with the remains. This skeleton—known as Minnesota Man before being renamed Minnesota Woman in 1968—has been dated to 6700 BC.

From about 5000 BC to 1000 BC (when Egyptian and Mesopotamian civilizations were growing and thriving), people around the western Great Lakes began using copper tools. They used stone hammers to pound raw copper nuggets they found on Michigan's Keweenaw Peninsula and in glacial deposits throughout the region. Their copper spear points, knives, fishhooks, and awls were the first metal tools in the New World. One of their habitation sites in Minnesota, Petaga Point, is located on what is now the picnic ground in Mille Lacs Kathio State Park. This settlement may date to about 1500 BC.

Some time between 1000 and 500 BC people of the Woodland Tradition began to make pottery and to bury their dead in earthen mounds. One of their most common tools was a grooved hammerstone, a spherical stone encircled by a shallow groove so it could be tied to a handle with a rawhide thong. This grooved maul could be used to pound dried beef and berries together. (The pounded mixture of dried beef and berries, or pemmican, was a staple of the regional diet into modern times.) People of this tradition continued to use copper tools, but they also made great use of bones and antlers to fashion hide scrapers, awls and punches, carved dice for games, whistles made of bird bone, and barbed points for spearing aquatic mammals and fish.

At some point late in the Woodland Tradition (probably in the first centuries of the modern era) the bow and arrow made its appearance. Both hunting device and weapon, the bow and arrow was first used by the peoples of Asia. Whether it made the crossing from Siberia or was reinvented in America is a matter of conjecture. The bow and arrow enabled hunters to kill game at greater distances. The prevalence of arrow points throughout North America after this time suggest that the new technology spread rapidly among the Woodland peoples.

The pottery made by these people was at first quite utilitarian. One of the earliest excavated Woodland sites is on Grey Cloud Island in the Mississippi River bottoms near Hastings. The clay vessels found here are thick walled and flowerpot shaped. They had little decoration and no handles. They were used for cooking simply by being placed in a bed of hot coals. Later sites contain pottery of more complex construction. The Laurel people, who lived in the boundary waters area and in Ontario, made thin-walled pottery fired hard and decorated with impressions from a toothed stamp. A form of pottery, the tobacco pipe, also came into use about this time. Initially made of clay, pipes were later carved from a red stone (catlinite) found at the Pipestone quarry of southwestern Minnesota.

The mounds of the Woodland peoples were generally small, low, and round. The largest in the state, built by the Laurel people on the Rainy River, is Grand Mound, one hundred feet in diameter and forty feet high. The mounds contain human bones, shards of pottery, and occasional tools.

The Mississippian Tradition

About one thousand years ago, a new tradition reached the upper Mississippi area. Influenced by civilizations in Mexico that had built enormous pyramids in which to bury kings, people of the Mississippian culture built some large settlements with central plazas and huge earthen mounds on which they erected temples and conducted reli-

The story of a precontact hunt is inscribed on "painted rocks"
at Lake la Croix, photographed in 1935.

gious ceremonies. Leading families also lived on and buried their dead in mounds; others families lived around them. They raised crops of corn, beans, squash, and sunflowers in fields cleared in bottomlands.

Sometime around AD 1000, while the Norsemen were establishing the first European settlement on the coast of Newfoundland, the Mississippians erected a major population center at Cahokia, Illinois, near the mouth of the Missouri River. Its largest ceremonial mound stands 100 feet high (after centuries of settling and erosion) and measures 700 feet by 1,000 feet. The entire complex occupied sixteen acres. From this center smaller settlements fanned out into the area that became Minnesota and Wisconsin. Several large village sites and dozens of smaller sites near the point where the Cannon River enters the Mississippi north of Red Wing show influences of Mississippian culture, including pyramided earthen mounds and pottery. The larger settlements may have contained 600 to 800 people, who tended garden plots on terraces above the rivers and dug deep underground storage pits for the wintering of vegetables. Like the Woodland peoples, the Mississippians hunted deer and speared fish in the rivers.

In addition to the chipped stone tools of earlier cultures, the Mississippians made extensive use of animal bones and horns. Among the implements uncovered from their village sites are a hoe made from the shoulder blade of a bison, a spatula made from a rib, a turtle-shell ladle, clamshell spoons, and finely carved bone fishhooks, dice, and sewing needles. The pottery of the Mississippians is globular with flaring rims, matched handles, and smooth exterior surfaces. It was tempered with crushed clamshells and decorated with incised geometric designs.

To the north, in central Minnesota, where climate and soil were not suitable for corn, a hybrid civilization developed. The remnants of a community unearthed in Mille Lacs Kathio State Park, dated to about AD 1500, yielded Mississippian-style tools and finely decorated pottery but no deep food-storage pits. Threshing pits, on the other hand, are common, indicating that wild rice, rather than corn, was the staple vegetable food. Deer, bison, and wild rice would remain the basic elements of the regional diet long after the arrival of European settlers.

VISITING HISTORY

Evidence of the effects of the last glacial period appears in many places, from lake and river shorelines to railroad and highway cuts.

GEOLOGY

Glacial Lake Agassiz geological marker

U.S. Hwy. 2 at tourist information center near Fisher. A view of the largest lake to have ever existed, from the lakebed.

Glenwood Region geological marker

MN Hwy. 28 overlooking Lake Minnewaska near Glenwood. A view of a recessional moraine and a lake in an ice-block basin.

Gooseberry Falls geological marker

MN Hwy. 61 in Gooseberry Falls State Park near the Middle Falls. A view of lava flows from the midcontinent rift, which extended from the Lake Superior region southwest to Kansas.

Heritage and Wind Power Learning Center

Lake Benton Area Historical Society, 110 Center St., Lake Benton; 507/368-9577. Includes exhibits on the geology of Buffalo Ridge, part of the Bemis Moraine left by the Des Moines Lobe. Wind farms with over 450 turbines now stretch along the moraine, making it one of the country's largest for generating wind power.

Mystery Cave

MN Hwy. 5 at Forestville/Mystery Cave State Park west of Preston; 507/937-3251. Interpretive center and tours of Minnesota's longest cavern, carved through limestone by the South Root River, in the driftless region.

Ortonville Region geological marker

1,000 feet west of the junction of U.S. Hwys. 12 and 75, about .5 mile east of Ortonville. A view of the valley of glacial River Warren.

A R C H A E O L O G Y

Browns Valley Man historic marker

MN Hwy. 28, about .5 mile east of Browns Valley. The remains were found in the gravel pit on the plateau visible about .5 mile south of this marker.

Indian Mounds Park

Mounds Blvd., about 1.25 miles south of 7th St. E., St. Paul. Mounds built about two thousand years ago and a spectacular view of downtown St. Paul, with interpretive signs explaining both the mounds and the path of the River Warren.

Itasca Bison Kill Site historic marker

Wilderness Drive in Itasca State Park. The site of the excavation. Exhibits at the nearby Jacob V. Brower Interpretive Center (218/266-2100) include a replica of a skull from the site.

Jeffers Petroglyphs Historic Site

3 miles east of U.S. Hwy. 71 on Co. Rd. 10, then 1 mile south on Co. Rd. 2; 507/628-5591. Visitor center with exhibits; trails through natural prairie to over two thousand carvings of humans, animals, and weapons, some of them five thousand years old.

Mille Lacs Kathio State Park

Co. Rd. 26 off U.S. Hwy. 169, about 8 miles north of Onamia; 320/532-3523. Interpretive center with information on Petaga Point and many other archaeological sites, some dating to nine thousand years ago; beautiful interpretive trails.

Minnesota Woman historic marker

U.S. Hwy. 59, 4 miles north of Pelican Rapids. The remains were discovered at this point by a highway repair crew.

Pipestone National Monument

36 Reservation Ave., Pipestone; 507/825-5464. Active quarry used by American Indians; visitor center with exhibits and, in summer, carvers at work.

2

First Nations

For a hundred centuries the earliest residents of Minnesota had made their living on the land, shivering in winters and basking in summers—much like current residents of the state. While it is clear that the peoples of these cultures had a rich understanding of the resources and the character of this place, we can only guess at how they were related to each other and how they lived their lives, constructing stories based on the tools and earthworks they left behind.

But Dakota and Ojibwe people, their successors, also developed a deep knowledge of the land over centuries. These living cultures are witnesses both to ways of survival in this landscape and to spiritual points of view that grew directly from this place.

The Dakota People

The Dakota are an Eastern Woodland people, related to others of the Siouan language group: the Winnebago of Wisconsin, the Iowa and Missouri tribes, and the Assiniboin of the Red River. The term "Sioux" originated with French explorers who picked it up from the Ojibwe, an Algonkian-speaking tribe living on the shores of Lake Superior. The Ojibwe, who had battled with the Dakota, called their Minnesota neighbors *Nadouessioux*, which meant "poisonous snake," and the French abridged it to "Sioux."

Sioux is often used to refer to the people who belong to the *Océti Sakowin,* the Seven Council Fires. The three western councils speak Lakota and Nakota dialects and live near the Missouri River. The four eastern councils, living on the Mississippi and Minnesota rivers, are the Dakota, whose name for themselves means "friends" or "allies": the Mdewakanton (People of Spirit Lake), Wahpekute (Shooters Among the Leaves), Wahpeton (Dwellers Among the Leaves), and Sisseton (People of the Fish Grounds). Some traditional accounts and archaeological evidence show that the council fires originated in the Ohio River valley and moved westward between AD 800 and 1500.

A cultural and political center of the Dakotas was Spirit Lake, which whites would call Mille Lacs ("Thousand Lakes"). When the French fur trader Pierre Esprit Radisson visited the Dakota people, sometime around 1660, he traveled for seven days from Lake Superior and reached a community that he thought contained several thousand people. This may well have been at Mille Lacs.

Radisson called the Dakota people "the nation of the beefe," because buffalo were important in their diet. They sewed buffalo hides together to make tipis, snug in winter and easy to transport. Their clothes were made of deerskins and beaver pelts. The Dakotas that Radisson visited offered to trade him three hundred packs of beaver furs, which the men had gathered by trapping in the northern lakes. Radisson was sorry that he had room in his canoe for only a few. Because he was the first European the Dakotas had seen (or even heard of), the pelts must have been gathered for their own use, or for trade with the prairie tribes.

The Dakota also had semi-permanent summer residences. A frame of poles supported sides and a roof made of bark from basswood and elm trees. Houses could vary from ten to twenty feet in length, depending on the number of families they sheltered.

The social structure of each village was based on maternal relationships. A married couple often spent their first year in the lodge of the woman's parents. The home and its furnishings belonged to the wife, who had tanned and sewn the hides. She held equal status with her husband. A woman could obtain a divorce (usually for desertion) simply by moving her husband's possessions out of the lodge.

The *tiyospaye,* or extended family, was fundamental, and it ensured security for children in a society where life expectancy was short. A child's fathers included all his father's brothers and male cousins, and his father's female siblings were aunts; the pattern carried for his mother's relations as well. Brothers and sisters of the child, as well as cousins of the same generation, were all regarded as siblings, and the child was allowed to treat them in an informal, often jocular way. Some of this extended family might reside in the same camp-circle; others might be sprinkled throughout the council fires of the Dakotas. Thus, wherever a family moved it was likely to encounter relatives.

More than simply a blood relationship, the family was a civil institution, the Indian equivalent of a legal system. It was governed by

Permanent Residence, Sioux.
*Seth Eastman lived among the Dakota
and recorded numerous scenes of everyday life.*
Watercolor by Eastman, 1846–48

a code of behavior that both constrained its members and protected them. If a member suffered injury, the family was obliged to seek revenge or reparations. The reverse was also true. A person who caused harm jeopardized his or her entire family, since the family of the victim was entitled to seek retribution.

The Dakotas, like other Eastern Woodland peoples, had a seasonal subsistence cycle. When the sap began running in the spring, they spread out into the sugar bush to make maple sugar, a delicacy that was used both in spiritual ceremonies and as a daily sweetener. In summer the women planted and tended corn, squash, and beans. They gathered nuts, berries, and wild vegetables, like water lilies and wild turnips. Men hunted small animals and fished. At the end of the summer the village used dugout canoes to harvest wild rice, which grew in abundance in northern waters.

After the leaves had fallen in October, the village packed their tipis, divided into small bands, and spread in different directions for the hunt that would last until January. Heavily laded with tents, wooden utensils, blankets, and children, each band moved only a few miles in a day and then camped for a week or more at a time. When a hunter killed a deer or a buffalo, he gave a shout to attract any other hunters within hearing distance. He then shared it equally with the first three who appeared. The women dried the meat in preparation for the time, from January to March, when the village reassembled and hunkered down for the winter. In March the annual cycle of food gathering resumed as the families dispersed into the woods to make maple sugar.

Dakota culture was soon to be seriously disrupted. Radisson was the first of a succession of French explorers, traders, and missionaries who brought to the Dakota people European tools and utensils, including firearms. In addition, European colonization—the French in the St. Lawrence valley, the English in New England and Virginia, and the Dutch in New York—pushed the coastal tribes inland and created a chain reaction of pressure on the interior tribes. One of those interior nations was the Ojibwe, a large and aggressive Algonkian-speaking tribe who were living near the straits between Lake Superior and Lake Huron when French explorers first encountered them in the middle of the seventeenth century. By 1700 they had expanded westward into Wisconsin, where they collided with the Dakota. The warfare between the two peoples would go on for more than a century. Driven by strife and drawn by new ways to hunt buffalo with horses, most of the Dakota nation moved onto the Great Plains as Ojibwe bands made their way into northern Minnesota.

The Ojibwe People

The Ojibwe, like the Ottawa and Potawatomie of the western Great Lakes, trace their origin to the valley of the St. Lawrence River. Their name—first written by the French as Outchibouec, later by the Americans as Chippewa—refers to the puckered design of their moccasins. The peoples' name for themselves, Anishinabe, means simply "original man" or "first people."

All of the tribes of the western lakes came under pressure during the wars of the Iroquois in the middle decades of the seventeenth century. The Hurons were virtually obliterated; the Ottawa and the Sauk and Fox moved into Illinois and Wisconsin. Although the Ojibwe maintained a settlement at Sault Ste. Marie, where the waters of Lake Superior flowed into Lake Huron, small bands began moving westward along both the northern and southern shores of Lake Superior. By 1665 a band was living at La Pointe, now in northern Wisconsin, and their advance was being resisted by the Dakota; any attempt to move southward into the Wisconsin River valley ran afoul of the Fox.

Membership in a clan or totem, inherited from the father, provided social organization. As with the Dakota, extended families lived close together and all helped raise the children. The Ojibwe also followed a seasonal round, fishing, hunting deer, and harvesting maple sugar and wild rice in the rich lands around Lake Superior. The lakes of the region teemed with trout, sturgeon, pike, bass, walleye, and whitefish. Ojibwe women wove nets of nettle-stalk fiber of more than one hundred yards in length. In the fall and spring, when the fish moved into shallow waters to spawn, women set out the nets in huge semicircles, using floats of wood and sinkers of stone or lead. They preserved the fish by smoking them or hanging them by the tails to dry. Men speared larger fish at night, using birch bark torches to attract them to their canoes. In the winter, they speared through holes in the ice, attracting fish with decoys.

The Ojibwe made great use of the bark of the birch. Their homes, called wigwams, were made of saplings bent into rounded frames and covered with sheets of birch bark or mats woven of bulrushes. The coverings could be rolled up and carried to a new camp, where it was easy to find materials for new frames. Women made birch bark containers for winnowing baskets, for carrying and storing foods, and even for carrying maple sap and heating water.

The Ojibwe traveled in birch bark canoes that were light, strong, and easily repaired with materials at hand. Canoes are made from the outside in, and the wood, while structural, is not a frame. The builders

Ojibwe woman seated in front of traditional wigwam, 1870

Carte-de-visite by Charles Alfred Zimmerman

felled a large birch tree in July, when the bark was easy to remove. The birch bark sheets were shaped in a form, lined with thin cedar boards, strengthened with delicate ribs and crossbars, and then sewn together with root bindings and fastened to the rim. Spruce gum (sap), warmed by a torch and applied to every seam of the birch bark, made the craft watertight. The caulking cracked and loosened under the strain of paddling and portaging, and it had to be re-melted and reinforced daily. Other peoples—both Dakotas and white traders—adopted this highly efficient design.

* * *

Children gain skills in canoe construction at an Ojibwe camp, 1895.

Photo by Truman Ward Ingersoll

For both the Dakota and the Ojibwe, the plants and animals and even the rocks around them were also spiritual beings, capable of being offended and withholding their benefits. Good fortune in the hunt, methods of healing, and important dreams were attainable if one knew how to deal with the spirits. Religious ceremonies, both simple and complex, infused their daily lives with connections and meanings.

But sacred matters that have been learned by generations over centuries are not easily discussed with outsiders or summarized in a few sentences. Modern residents who feel the spirituality of places in Minnesota can simply know, however, that they are participating in an ancient tradition in this landscape.

VISITING HISTORY

Minnesota's longest-term residents celebrate their rich cultural heritage in several places around the state.

Bois Forte Heritage Center

1430 Bois Forte Rd., Tower; 218/753-6017. Small but excellent exhibit on the band's culture and history.

Goodhue County Historical Museum

1166 Oak St., Red Wing; 651/388-6024. Includes a permanent exhibit on the Dakota of Prairie Island.

Mille Lacs Indian Museum

U.S. Hwy. 169, 12 miles north of Onamia; 320/532-3632. Extensive exhibits on tribal history, culture, and sovereignty.

Pipestone National Monument

36 Reservation Ave., Pipestone; 507/825-5464. Active quarry used by American Indians; visitor center with exhibits and, in summer, carvers at work.

The Kensington Runestone

In November 1898, Olof Ohman, a Swedish immigrant who farmed near the village of Kensington, Minnesota, was clearing land with his son when the pair came upon a stone embedded in the roots of an aspen. The piece of gray rock was about two and a half feet long, sixteen inches wide, and six inches thick. On it had been chiseled runic inscriptions that, when translated, told a story of "8 Swedes and 22 Norwegians" who had embarked on a journey of exploration westward from Vinland (Greenland). Ten of their party had been killed, presumably by Indians. They had left their ships "14 days journey from this island. Year 1362."

Ohman showed the stone to some townspeople in Kensington, and a merchant solicited scholarly opinions about its authenticity. Norse language experts from the University of Minnesota recognized the runic symbols but pronounced them to be a modern forgery. They pointed out that some of the symbols were unknown in the fourteenth century. It was also noted that the stone had been found by a Scandinavian immigrant living in one of the most heavily Scandinavian counties in the state. Ohman was known locally as a fun-loving character quite capable of executing a hoax to confound scholars. There were rumors in the neighborhood that the whole thing was a prank.

Ohman himself was apparently willing to let the matter drop. He relegated the runestone to serve as a steppingstone to his barn. Nine years later Hjalmar R. Holand, a recent graduate of the University of Wisconsin who had become interested in pre-Columbian Viking explorations, appeared at Ohman's door and purchased the stone. Holand sought to have it validated by European scholars, but they too dismissed it as a hoax. They pointed out, among other things, that there was no evidence of Viking activity in North America after the Norsemen abandoned their settlement on Newfoundland in about AD 1000. Holand tried to overcome this skepticism by citing a document from the mid-fourteenth century in which King Magnus Erickson ordered one Paul Knutson to reassert control over the Viking colony in Greenland. There is no further record of Knutson or of a colony on Greenland.

Undeterred by the lack of historical evidence, Holand spun a theory that Knutson's party had reached Hudson Bay, sailed up the Nelson River to Lake Winnipeg, and from there followed the Red River into Minnesota. The theory was based entirely on guesswork and supposition, including such "evidence" as round holes found in certain Canadian rocks that supposedly indicated where the Vikings had tied up their ships. Beginning with his first book, *The Kensington Stone: A Study in Pre-Columbian American History* (1932), Holand spent a lifetime developing his thesis in books and articles. His books, well written and entertaining, were widely read, and he developed a large following of believers.

Inevitably, Minnesota boosters would see the potential in the Kensington stone. After displaying it at the Smithsonian Institution (which cautiously declared it to be an "important archeological object") in 1948, promoters brought it back to Minnesota to be exhibited as part of the 1949 Territorial Centennial. Thereafter it came into the possession of Alexandria, Minnesota, seat of the county in which the stone was found. The city began advertising itself as the "Birthplace of America," and the local Kiwanis Club raised funds to build a granite replica five times the size of the original stone. The replica was placed at the eastern entrance to the city in August 1951. In 1958, the centennial of Minnesota statehood, the Alexandria Chamber of Commerce raised funds to erect a museum to house the original stone.

Although strong defenders of the Holand thesis remain today, reputable scholars reject the thesis and regard the stone as a hoax. As such, it may reveal more about nineteenth-century American culture than it does about the Vikings. Americans of that time thoroughly enjoyed hoaxes. P. T. Barnum's American Museum in New York was famous for them. Barnum would display a curiosity and insist that it was genuine—the wooly horse, for instance, which Barnum claimed was part horse, part sheep, and part buffalo, vital to the West because you could ride it, shear it, or eat it. When public interest flagged and ticket sales declined, Barnum would publicly admit that the display had been a hoax, and everyone would return to see and discuss the fraud, insisting that they had known it all along.

Whether genuine or not, the Kensington runestone is so well known that it has a significance of its own in the public mind.

VISITING HISTORY

Runestone Museum

206 Broadway, Alexandria; 320/763-3160. Displays on the runestone and Native American history.

A replica of the Kensington runestone is on display at Alexandria, "Birthplace of America."

3

Explorers and Fur Traders

In 1661, the year in which Radisson and Médard Chouart, Sieur des Groseilliers visited the Dakota people, King Louis XIV came of age, shucked off the regents who had been governing France, and embarked upon a fifty-four-year reign. Determined to expand the power and imperial grasp of his kingdom, he moved first to take royal possession of the French claims in North America, which had been misgoverned for decades by a private fur-trading company. In 1663 the company surrendered its franchise, and New France became a royal colony under the control of the king. Louis established a two-headed government in Quebec—a governor general who would be head of state and commander of the armed forces and an intendant who had independent control of taxes, finances, and regulation of commerce.

French Explorations

The first major French-funded expedition into Minnesota was led by Daniel Greysolon, Sieur du Luth, a French-born professional soldier. Duluth's party spent the winter of 1678–79 at Sault Ste. Marie and in the spring paddled to the "bottom" (*Fond du Lac*) of Lake Superior. From there, sociable Dakotas, eager to exchange beaver and otter pelts for French goods, guided him southwest into the region of the "Thousand Lakes." In his journal he recorded the consummation of his journey in a single laconic sentence: "On the second of July, 1679, I had the honor to set up the arms of his Majesty in the great village of Nadoucioux called Izatys, where no Frenchman had ever been." The "great village" was the Mdewakanton Dakota's settlement on a level prairie at the Rum River outlet of Mille Lacs. Duluth then retraced his steps to Lake Superior and explored the north shore as far as Thunder Bay. He spent the winter of 1679–80 near the site of the later trading post of Fort William.

In 1678 the French sent another expedition to explore the Mississippi all the way to its mouth, this one lead by Robert Cavelier, Sieur de la Salle, a French-born adventurer who for some years had been trying to find financing for the exploration of the western lakes and rivers. La Salle employed a new route to the Mississippi by way of the Chicago River at the foot of Lake Michigan and the Illinois River. Illness, bad luck, and storms plagued the expedition, and in the winter of 1679–80 La Salle found himself encamped on the Illinois River somewhere around present-day Peoria. In the spring he would proceed down the Mississippi to its mouth and claim the entire basin, from the Appalachians to the Rockies, for France, naming it "Louisiana" in honor of the king.

Before departing downriver, however, La Salle decided in February 1680 to send a trio of his best men to find the source of the "great river," which had been partially explored in an earlier expedition by Jacques Marquette, a Jesuit father, and Louis Jolliet, a Canadian-born fur trader. Two of the three were experienced *voyageurs;* the third was a cleric, a friar of the Recollect Order, Father Louis Hennepin. Struggling up the Mississippi against floes of ice, in April 1680 they came upon a large Dakota war party planning a raid on the Illinois tribes. By sign language and maps drawn in the sand, Hennepin persuaded the Dakota that their quarry had gone south for the winter. The Dakota decided to return home and took the trio of Frenchmen with them—whether as guests or as captives is not entirely clear.

Shortly after the group cleared the mouth of the Minnesota River, the Indians left their canoes and proceeded with the three Frenchman on a five-day overland trek to a large Dakota village on an island in the Rum River, just below Mille Lacs. Hennepin was taken into the family of one of the village leaders and received "a robe made of ten large dressed beaver skins trimmed with porcupine quills." The Indians also took most of his trading goods—whether that was theft or a fair exchange may also have depended on one's perspective. It was still late winter, and Hennepin noticed that the Indians were short of food. "Although the women showed more tenderness and pity than the men," he later wrote, "their scant supply of fish was given to their children." In early July the men of the village went off to hunt buffalo on the prairies to the southeast, and the Frenchmen were able to leave to do some exploring of their own. They went by canoe down the Rum River to the Mississippi. A paddle of some twenty miles brought them to a splendid waterfall, which Hennepin named after his patron saint, Anthony of Padua.

In September Hennepin and his French comrades got the Dakotas' permission to go back east, after promising to return with more trading goods the following year. They traversed the Wisconsin and Fox

Father Hennepin at the Falls of St. Anthony, AD 1680
Hennepin exaggerated the height of the falls,
reporting its sixteen-foot drop to be closer to forty or fifty feet.
Chromolithograph by J. N. Marchand, 1903

rivers and wintered at Mackinac. But instead of returning to the land of the Dakota the following year, Father Hennepin sailed for France and wrote a memoir of his explorations that was published in 1683 under the title *Description de la Louisiane*. It was the first narrative Europeans had of the upper Mississippi and its people, and it was read with breathless curiosity. The work also contained a rather fanciful map of the Great Lakes and a more accurate map of the upper Mississippi from the region of Mille Lacs to the mouth of the Illinois River.

La Salle had proclaimed the sovereignty of the French king over the whole interior of the continent, but there had been no serious attempt at settlement west of Green Bay. Father Allouez's mission at La Pointe, established in 1665, was abandoned six years later due to warfare between the Dakota and the Ojibwe, and the Jesuits confined their missionary activities to Mackinac Island and Green Bay. In 1696 the French king withdrew the military garrison from Mackinac and consolidated his meager forces in Montreal. In his final years Louis XIV engaged in a disastrous European war (the War of the Spanish Succession) in which the mighty French army experienced defeat in battle for the first time in more than a century. At the 1713 peace conference in the Dutch city of Utrecht Britain demanded—and got—the cession of Newfoundland, Nova Scotia, and the lands around Hudson Bay. The days of New France were clearly numbered.

In the 1720s and 1730s the French engaged in a protracted, bloody, and debilitating series of wars with the Fox Indians of Wisconsin. The fighting closed the Fox-Wisconsin fur trade route to the west and left the Dakota peoples of the upper Mississippi isolated. French influence disappeared altogether in the region west of Lake Michigan. Ironically, as the French withdrew, a new people appeared on the shores of Lake Superior with designs on the Thousand Lakes region to the west. For years the Dakota had tried to keep the Ojibwe at bay. By 1700 the invaders stood at the very edge of the Dakota homeland.

The Arrival of the Ojibwe

Through the fur trade, the Ojibwe gained access to European goods, such as blankets and cooking utensils. The search for furs intensified their westward drift. By the end of the seventeenth century the

Ojibwe had a major settlement at the western tip of Lake Superior, and they were trapping beaver in the valley of the St. Croix River. They carried the pelts to the French post on Mackinac Island for transshipment to Montreal.

And they had begun to accumulate firearms. This gave them an immense advantage over the Dakota in warfare. The warfare between the Ojibwe and the Dakota was mostly a matter of ambushing isolated hunters, and it was punctuated with long intervals of peace. On one occasion, around 1700, the Ojibwe sent a large war party all the way to Mille Lacs, and a three-day battle ensued.

By 1730 the Ojibwe had substantial settlements on the Rainy River and on Sandy Lake near the headwaters of the Mississippi. The last great battle, according to Ojibwe tradition, occurred in 1768 at the junction of the Crow Wing and Mississippi rivers. By then, the Dakota had firearms of their own, and the fighting was deadlier than ever. The Dakota initiated the fight with a raid of several hundred warriors on the Ojibwe village at Sandy Lake; the Ojibwe summoned men from other villages and ambushed the Dakota at Crow Wing on their way home.

Even before that battle the Dakota began to move south and west out of the woodlands and onto the prairies. They were tired of perpetual warfare and perhaps attracted by the prospect of hunting on horseback. By the end of the eighteenth century about half of the Dakota people had resettled on the upper Missouri River. Those who chose to stay settled in the valley of the Minnesota River, leaving the woodlands to the north and east in the hands of the Ojibwe. Friction between the two peoples and periodic ambushes continued into the middle of the nineteenth century.

The Age of the Voyageurs

The bridge between the French explorers of the seventeenth century and the fur trading merchants and voyageurs of the eighteenth century was a Canadian-born professional soldier, Pierre Gaultier de Varennes, Sieur de la Vérendrye. After serving with distinction in the War of the Spanish Succession, La Vérendrye was placed in command of a frontier outpost on Lake Nipigon, north of Lake Superior. There he listened to Indian stories of water routes from Lake Superior to a great sea that lay far to the west. The most promising of these routes, mapped on a piece of birch bark by one of his Ojibwe friends, began at the mouth of a modest stream later called the Pigeon River. The first step was a nine-mile portage (soon named the Grand Portage) around the succession of waterfalls where the Pigeon dropped off the Laurentian Shield into Lake Superior. From the headwaters of the Pigeon a series of lakes and portages crossed the Height of Land and descended into the valley of the northwest-flowing Rainy River.

In summer 1731 La Vérendrye sent an advance detachment, including three of his four sons, to explore this route. This party reached Rainy Lake and built a small fort at its northeastern end. La Vérendrye and the main force joined them the following summer, and the explorers paddled out onto Lake of the Woods in September 1732. La Vérendrye built a small wooden palisade on its southern shore, and, as Fort St. Charles, it remained a gathering point for fur traders for the next twenty years. La Vérendrye realized that Lake of the Woods was not the inland sea described by the Indians. He and his sons continued their explorations for the next twelve years, discovering Lake Winnipeg and the Saskatchewan and Assiniboine rivers and taking side expeditions south to the Missouri River and west to the Canadian Rockies. The geographical marvel is that the Grand Portage is truly the watery crossroads of the continent. With sufficient endurance a canoeist can paddle from that point to the Atlantic, the Pacific, the Gulf of Mexico, and the Arctic Ocean without a single portage much longer than the Grand Portage itself.

The immediate consequence of La Vérendrye's voyage of discovery, however, was to open a trade route for the voyageurs, the men who paddled and portaged the route between Lake of the Woods and the Grand Portage with ninety-pound packs of beaver pelts.

The word "voyageur" originally referred to any sort of traveler or explorer, but by the mid-eighteenth century it had a more precise meaning. It referred to men who signed contracts (engagés), usually for three years, with Montreal merchants who were licensed by the government to trade with the Indians. The voyageurs did the paddling and portaging under the eye of a clerk, who was usually a son or near relative of the Montreal bourgeois who engaged them. Less experienced voyageurs, called "pork eaters" (*mangeurs de lard*), stopped at a halfway point, Mackinac or Grand Portage, and returned to Montreal in the same year. The experienced voyageurs (*hivernants*) spent the winter at a post in the interior, trading goods for furs, and returned to Grand Portage in the summer to meet with a bourgeois, renew their contracts, receive their pay, and purchase supplies. A third group, called *coureurs de bois,* were independent, unlicensed traders manning their own canoes, who confined their efforts to the lakes and rivers of Wisconsin and Minnesota.

Out of their normal context, two fur traders pose in traditional garb—
pipe included—for a studio photograph, 1880

The voyageur was as distinct in appearance and dress as a sailor or a lumberjack. By modern standards, he was not tall: European men of that era averaged about five feet six inches in height. And he had powerful arms and shoulders from paddling twelve to fourteen hours a day and carrying two—or sometimes three—ninety-pound packs across a portage. He wore his hair long and heavily greased as protection against mosquitoes and sported a gaily colored sash, a pouch of tobacco, and a pipe. Distances across portages were measured in "pipes" (about half a mile) because each rest stop involved a few minutes' smoke.

The voyageurs' canoes were marvels of engineering. The largest weighed no more than 300 pounds yet could carry up to five tons of men and furs. Three sizes of canoes were used in the fur trade. Montreal canoes, thirty-five to forty-feet long with a crew of fourteen, were used on the Great Lakes and the larger rivers. North canoes, about twenty-five feet long and capable of carrying three thousand pounds and eight men, were used on the smaller lakes and rivers because they could be carried across portages. Light canoes or Indian canoes were ten to fifteen feet long and used for hunting and speedy transportation.

Landing a loaded canoe was tricky because it was too fragile to be run up on a beach. One Great Lakes traveler described how a brigade of Montreal canoes landed at Grand Portage: "The first [canoe] makes a dash at the beach. Just as the last wave is carrying the canoe on dry ground, all her men jump out at once and support her; while her gentlemen or clerks hurry out her lading. During this time the other canoes are, if possible, heading out into the lake; but now one approaches, and is seized by the crew of the canoe first beached, who meet her up to the middle in water, and who, assisted by her own people [unload the cargo and] lift her up high and dry." Six men then hoisted the canoe onto their shoulders and carried it gently onto the land.

Because space and weight were at a premium, the diet of the voyageurs had little variety. While traversing the Ottawa River and lakes Huron and Superior they were able to carry comparatively heavy items, such as flour, dried vegetables, and salt pork. (Thus the men who returned home from Grand Portage were scornfully called "pork eaters.") The men ate two virtually identical meals a day, morning and evening. A clerk described the preparation and result when pork and dried vegetables were available:

> The tin kettle, in which they cooked their food, would hold eight or ten gallons. It was hung over the fire, nearly full of water, then nine quarts of peas—one quart per man, the daily allowance—were put in; and when they were well bursted, two or three pounds of pork, cut into strips, for seasoning, were added, and all allowed to boil or simmer till daylight, when the cook added four biscuits, broken up, to the mess, and invited all hands to breakfast. The swelling of the peas and biscuit had now filled the kettle to the brim, so thick that a stick would stand upright in it. It looked inviting, and I begged for a plate full of it, and ate little else during the journey. The men now squatted in a circle, the kettle in their midst, and each one plying his wooden spoon or ladle from kettle to mouth, with almost electric speed, soon filled every cavity. Then the pipes were soon brought out into full smoke.

Beyond the Grand Portage voyageurs carried only dried Indian corn and pemmican. Corn came to Grand Portage in sailing craft from Detroit, where Hurons and Ottawas had begun commercial farming. The corn was boiled into a thick pudding, and at least one traveler concluded that the difficulty of persuading "any other men, than Canadians, to [dine on] this fare, seems to secure to them . . . the monopoly of the fur trade." Pemmican came from the Indians and was prized for its small bulk and great nutritional value. It was made of strips of buffalo meat or venison, dried in the sun and pounded fine, then placed in a bag of buffalo or deer hide with hot grease poured in to form a mold. For eating, it was boiled in water to make soup. When available, a bit of flour and sugar were added, as well as berries, birds' eggs, and fish. "Pemmican," wrote one river-and-lake sojourner with heavy sarcasm, "is supposed by the benighted world outside to consist only of pounded meat and grease; an egregious error; for, from experience on the subject, I am authorized to state that hair, sticks, bark, spruce leaves, stones, sand, etc., enter into its composition, often quite largely."

Despite La Vérendrye's discovery of a route to the fur-bearing waters of the West, the French traders remained disorganized and suffered narrow profit margins. The British Hudson's Bay Company, founded in 1670, siphoned off furs to the north, and in the Great

Lakes region the independent *coureurs de bois* did a reasonably good business with limited capital.

The fall of New France with the surrender of Montreal to Lord Jeffery Amherst in 1760 did not much affect the western trade. By the time of the peace treaty that ended the French and Indian War in 1763 Britain had gained control of all of Canada and Louisiana east of the Mississippi. The part of Louisiana that lay west of the Mississippi went to Spain. Minnesota was thus divided between Britain and Spain, but neither European country exercised any control over the area. The voyageurs continued their annual treks, and the beaver pelts continued to flow to Europe through Montreal.

The only immediate result of the change in ownership was a visit, for the first time, of an English-speaking traveler. Jonathan Carver, born in New England, had participated in the fighting around Lake Champlain during the French and Indian War. He had almost certainly made the acquaintance of Robert Rogers, commander of a Yankee daredevil unit, Rogers' Rangers. At the end of the war Rogers received a commission as a major in the British army and took command of the garrison on Mackinac Island. Carver joined him there and, for eight shillings a day, Rogers hired him to explore the region to the west and north of the straits of Mackinac. Rogers's instructions—deliberately vague because Rogers had no authority to finance explorers—hinted at a further search for the long-sought Northwest Passage to the Pacific. Departing in September 1766, Carver followed the Fox-Wisconsin route to the Mississippi, and by mid-November he reached the Falls of St. Anthony. Returning to the Minnesota River, he paddled for a hundred or more miles into the interior. The prairie Dakota welcomed him, and he spent the winter in their village.

Rogers had promised to forward trading goods and additional scouts to the falls, but when Carver returned there and farther south to the trading post at Prairie du Chien in April 1767, he found neither the goods nor Rogers's men. Carver traveled to the Grand Portage to obtain supplies from traders. He reached Lake Superior by way of the Chippewa and Brule rivers in Wisconsin, but he was again disappointed. Carver returned to Mackinac only to find Rogers under arrest and court martial for spending unauthorized sums on exploration.

Carver returned east, moved to London, and published the journal of his travels in 1778 under the title *Travels through the Interior Parts of North America, in the Years 1766, 1767, and 1768*. Although Carver's exploration added little to European knowledge of Lake Superior and the upper Mississippi valley, his account was far more descriptive of the landscape than any earlier travel journal. It was also the first to appear in English and thus gained Minnesota a new audience.

Although of no immediate consequence in this area, the British conquest of Canada did have a long-term impact on the fur trade and the lives of the voyageurs. Scottish merchants, shrewd businessmen all, quickly realized that the problem of the fur trade was chaotic competition, which kept profits low and confused and alienated the western Indians. A typical "company" was a single trader, backed by a Montreal merchant, with anywhere from three to sixty voyageurs under contract. Alexander Henry, a Scot employed by one of the larger firms, arrived at the Grand Portage in summer 1775 with sixty-two men in sixteen canoes. He "found the traders in a state of extreme reciprocal hostility, each pursuing his interests in such a manner as might most injure his neighbour. The consequences were very hurtful to the morals of the Indians."

By this time a mass meeting of voyageurs and Montreal merchants at the Grand Portage in July had become standard. By Ojibwe tradition, summer get-togethers were family reunions that included marriages, religious observances, music, and dancing. The white traders adopted the same custom. A British officer who visited the Grand Portage in 1778 estimated that forty thousand pounds of furs passed through the settlement annually and the trade involved about five hundred individuals who, "for about a month in the summer season, have a general rendezvous at the Portage, and for the refreshing and comforting [of] those who are employed in the more distant voyages the Traders from hence [Montreal] have built tolerable Houses; and in order to cover them from any insult from the numerous savage Tribes, who resort there during that time, have made stockades around them."

Although a military expedition commanded by George Rogers Clark seized the Illinois country during the American Revolution, that war had no impact on the Great Lakes fur trade. Though the part of

Minnesota that lay east of the Mississippi came under the American flag by the treaty that ended the war in 1783, the Scottish merchants of Montreal continued to dominate the fur trade. They were more determined than ever to bring order and discipline to the exchange. After experimenting with a "gentlemen's agreement" and limited partnerships in the mid-1780s, the merchants of Montreal formed a permanent partnership known as the North West Company. The new company was essentially an alliance of independent mercantile houses, each keeping separate books and dealing in furs in proportion to the number of shares they owned. The winterers (wintering traders), many of whom had a share in the company, became heads of regional "departments" and lived in established outposts.

The fruits of organization were soon evident. The North West Company supplemented the sea-worthy Montreal canoes with a sailing vessel that made four or five trips each summer between Lake Huron and the Grand Portage. On the bay at the mouth of the Pigeon River the company built a stockade with walls of more than one hundred yards in length. Inside this wooden palisade, wrote one visitor, were sixteen buildings "made with cedar and white spruce fir split with whipsaws after being squared" and "painted with Spanish brown." Six of the buildings were storehouses for the company's merchandise and furs. The remainder included a counting house, residences, and a mess hall that could feed one hundred men at a time. Partners of the company and their clerks and traders lived in the fort during the summer, while the pork eaters and winterers camped outside the stockade. A shipyard stood on the waterfront where Indians built up to seventy canoes a year for the interior trade. By 1800 the settlement at Grand Portage had a herd of cattle for milk and a vegetable garden several acres in size.

In addition to the establishment at Grand Portage, the North West Company built forts to house its winterers in Minnesota—at Fond du Lac (Duluth), Sandy Lake, Leech Lake, and Snake River (Pine City). These posts traded primarily with the Ojibwe. Because Indians owned the land, local Indian leaders were consulted before determining the location of each new trading post. (The U.S. government, during the presidency of George Washington, officially recognized the Indians' title to the lands they occupied.) Even though the Ojibwe in the vicinity agreed to a site, traders worried about theft from jealous rivals or attacks by the Dakota; thus each post was surrounded by a wooden palisade. Gates that could be locked at night provided entry. Inside the stockade the winterers built a dwelling for the clerk, who commanded the post, a storehouse, and a bunkhouse for the ten or twenty men who wintered over.

Because nails were too heavy to be transported into the interior, the buildings were held together without them. Upright logs stood at the

A more modern trading post, Carson's,
supplied trappers and settlers near Bemidji in the 1890s.

Photo by George P. Metcalf

corners of the structure with grooves cut along the length of each. To make the walls, horizontal logs with tongues carved at each end were slipped into the grooves; the logs were pinned together with wooden dowels. Roofs were covered with sheets of bark, sod, or shakes, and a stone-and-mud fireplace and chimney stood at each end of a building. Construction of a trading fort took about two months.

Wintering over was a matter of hard work mixed with sheer survival. The clerk employed an Indian as a full-time hunter, and the voyageurs, when not trapping or handling furs, spent their time on the hunt. Venison and fish were the staples of the winter diet. The clerk purchased a winter's supply of wild rice (the voyageurs called it "oats," which was no more inaccurate than calling it "rice") from Indian women. In the spring the women came by the fort with maple sugar to exchange for blankets, utensils, or gunpowder. The larger outposts, such as those at Leech Lake and Sandy Lake, developed gardens to aid in the wintering over. By 1807 the post at Leech Lake had horses, cows, chickens, and gardens that reportedly produced a thousand bushels of potatoes.

The main business of the winter was collecting the pelts of beaver, otter, muskrat, deer, bear, marten, and many other hides. Dakota and Ojibwe men killed and skinned the animals. Women scraped meat fragments from the hides, stretched them, and dried them. The women, who regarded the pelts as their property, negotiated the sale to the clerk of the trading post. The wintering voyageurs sorted the furs into packs and stored them for the July canoe trip to Grand Portage.

The fur trade was thus mutually beneficial. In exchange for furs, which brought a fancy price among the fashion-conscious European gentry, the Indians received the products of early industrialization, everything from firearms to blankets and cooking utensils. By custom, the Dakota and Ojibwe people expected those who had supplies to share with those who had none; the debt would be repaid when possible, and all would survive. At certain times of the year when the Indians were particularly needy (late spring, early summer), they expected the traders to supply them with goods for which they would pay later in the year with a harvest in furs. In the fall, traders advanced supplies, expecting that Indian hunters would return with their catch. Certain "common law" trading practices also existed. One such practice held that a trader passing through the lands of one tribe on the way to another had an obligation to pay for the right of passage. An Ojibwe leader told one trader that if his party passed through the country without giving presents, "he would put us all to death on our return." Consequently, "he expected us to be exceedingly liberal in our presents."

Both clerks and voyageurs often married Indian women. Such unions could provide more than simple companionship and domestic ease. Wives could be interpreters and good-will ambassadors. In addition, marriage brought a trader a new family, with members who supported one another in disputes with outsiders and shared food and possessions. When a Dakota or Ojibwe woman married a trader, he became part of her family and was expected to provide support when it was in need. The traders, in turn, received an education in Indian customs and social relationships and, most important, a relatively safe passage through the lonely woods. The children of these mixed marriages, called *métis*, usually remained in the fur trade, though some became farmers. By the mid-nineteenth century the métis made up a sizable portion of the population of the Red River Valley in western Minnesota.

Under the American Flag

The Continental Congress, which governed the United States for nearly a decade after the Revolution, was too weak to impose its authority on the Lake Superior region. John Jacob Astor and other Americans entered the fur trade in the years after the Revolution, but, unable to compete with the North West Company on the western lakes, they traded mostly with the Iroquois and other Indians of the eastern Great Lakes. Astor even exported his furs through Montreal rather than New York.

Congressional authority over the West was weakened further by British retention, in violation of the peace treaty, of military posts on U.S. soil. The most important of these were Detroit and Mackinac Island, where British soldiers reinforced the commercial domination of the North West Company. After the adoption of the U.S. Constitution and the establishment of the federal government, President George Washington made removal of the British from U.S. soil a diplomatic priority. By the terms of the Jay Treaty of 1794 the British agreed to relinquish the western posts, and they did so two years later. The North West Company remained dominant in the Lake Superior region, but by 1800 the *bourgeois* became concerned for the future of Grand Portage should it happen to lie on American soil once a U.S.–Canadian boundary was established in the area. The treaty that ended the American Revolution had specified the Great Lakes and the Mississippi River as the northern and western boundaries of the United States republic, but it was vague about the gap between Lake Superior and the Mississippi.

In 1798 a Scottish explorer rediscovered an alternative route to Lake of the Woods that had been known to the French. It began at the Kaministikwia River, which flowed into Lake Superior at Thunder Bay some fifty miles north of Grand Portage. A succession of lakes and portages brought the canoeist into Rainy Lake and the old route to Lake of the Woods. The new route was longer, but it clearly lay on the Canadian side of any future international border. The North West Company began constructing Fort William on Thunder Bay in 1802 and soon moved its annual rendezvous to that site.

President Thomas Jefferson's purchase of Louisiana the following year further jeopardized the North West Company's position on the upper Mississippi. Only the present state of Louisiana had a large enough population to warrant becoming a federal territory; Congress placed the remainder of the purchase—from Arkansas to Minnesota and the Dakotas—under military rule, with a headquarters in St. Louis. In 1805 the general commanding the Military District of Louisiana ordered one of his officers, Lieutenant Zebulon Montgomery Pike, to explore the Mississippi as far as its source, befriend the Indian tribes in the region, and "attach them to the United States." Pike was also to confer with the Indians about the possibility of establishing military posts and "trading houses" in the area. (In 1795, to regulate the fur trade and prevent unscrupulous traders from cheating the Indians, Congress specified that trade with Indians could be conducted only through government-controlled trading posts.) Thus the army, in the person of Lieutenant Pike, provided the first challenge to the North West Company's dominion.

Pike left St. Louis in August 1805 with nineteen men in a seventy-foot keelboat (the standard freight craft of the western rivers). At Prairie du Chien he exchanged his keelboat for two flat-bottomed, shallow-draft bateaux. Seventeen days later he camped at the mouth of the Minnesota River, where he raised the Stars and Stripes, probably for the first time in the upper Mississippi region. Summoning the Dakota who lived in the area to a conference, Pike obtained permission to erect two military posts on the Mississippi and managed to purchase tracts of land for the posts. One tract was at the mouth of the St. Croix River. The other, larger tract ran from the mouth of the Minnesota River to the Falls of St. Anthony, stretching to a distance of nine miles on either side of the Mississippi. He distributed $200 in trading goods and sixty gallons of liquor, promising further payment but leaving the amount to the U.S. Senate. Although Pike had no authority to purchase land from the Indians, the government honored his bargain. For land he had valued at $200,000, the Senate approved a payment of $2,000-worth of goods. Some thirty years later, when the Dakota realized the value of the land they had sold and demanded more money, the government paid again.

Pike then resumed his quest for the source of the Mississippi, although winter was beginning to set in. He and his men celebrated Christmas near present-day Brainerd; a few days later the party straggled into the North West Company post on Leech Lake. They were greeted warmly by the company clerk and treated to a dinner of roast beaver tail and boiled moose head. In a mood more churlish than diplomatic, Pike had his men shoot down the Union Jack that flew from the post's flagstaff and raise the American flag. He then wrote the post commander a stiff letter (probably intended more for President Jefferson's eyes than the British) reminding him that he was on American soil and that he had a legal obligation to pay customs duties on the trading goods brought in from Canada. Pike had no more authority to challenge the British than he had to buy Indian lands, and the North West Company paid little attention to his threat. Although the company had started to move its operations from Grand

Portage to Thunder Bay three years earlier, it would maintain its trading posts in Minnesota for ten more years.

Pike's chutzpah was still not exhausted. Before leaving Leech Lake, which he arbitrarily declared to be a "main source" of the Mississippi, he summoned a council of the regional Ojibwe. He advised them that they were now Americans, and he told them to give back any British medals, flags, or insignia that they had received. He also admonished them to cease their warfare with the Dakota. He then spent the winter with his British hosts, whose reaction to his visit has mercifully not survived in the record, and he was back in St. Louis by April 30. Pike's report to his military commander, which he dedicated to President Jefferson, was published in 1810 and earned him more public renown than his later expedition into the southern Rockies where he discovered the Colorado peak that bears his name.

In 1808 John Jacob Astor incorporated his business under the laws of New York as the American Fur Company. Although this gave him more operating capital, he was still not able to break the North West Company's stranglehold on the trade of Lake Superior and the upper Mississippi. The War of 1812 had no more impact on the western fur trade than earlier wars, but it did generate a wave of American nationalism that Astor was able to turn to his advantage. In 1816, upon Astor's urging, Congress passed an act that excluded aliens from engaging in the fur trade on U.S. territory. Two years later the North West Company sold its trading posts in Minnesota and Wisconsin to Astor, and in 1821 it was absorbed by the British Hudson's Bay Company.

In the 1820s the locus of the trade in beaver furs expanded to the Rocky Mountains. Minnesota's trade continued, though, with muskrats and, later, buffalo hides from Winnipeg providing the bulk of the business. But land cessions and competition from independent traders brought decline in the 1840s. Changing fashions also played a part: European demand for American furs collapsed altogether as the tastes of fashion shifted to Russian ermines for cloaks and Chinese silk for hats. The American Fur Company, the grandfather of U.S. corporate giants, went bankrupt in 1842 and continued doing business only in much reduced form after reorganization. The day of the commercial trade was over. In Minnesota the voyageurs became

U.S. citizens, and a few practiced their craft as guides for military and scientific expeditions. Others became village raconteurs of tall tales about a bygone era.

American Explorations

In 1818 Congress, preparing to admit the state of Illinois to the Union, erected the remainder of the Old Northwest, the land between Lake Huron and the Mississippi River, into the Territory of Michigan. The governor of the new territory, Lewis Cass, was intent upon knowing the extent of his jurisdiction as well as its geography. He was particularly interested in finding the source of the Mississippi River, although that had ceased to be an international boundary after Jefferson purchased Louisiana in 1803.

The gap between the unknown source of the Mississippi and Lake of the Woods remained, however, a potential source of international friction. An 1818 treaty between the United States and Great Britain established the 49th parallel as the boundary between the United States and Canada from Lake of the Woods to the Continental Divide. It also granted to Minnesota a slice of Lake of the Woods by angling a line across the lake (the Northwest Angle). From the northwest shore of the lake the treaty makers drew another line due south to the 49th parallel. The agreement left the international boundary between Lake of the Woods and Lake Superior undefined. Finding the source of the Mississippi would help clarify the map of this "no-man's-land."

In 1819 Cass asked secretary of war John C. Calhoun for authority to lead an expedition, supplied and manned by the army, into his western confines. Without mentioning the Mississippi, he stressed the importance of establishing contacts with the Indians and investigating reports of mineral deposits (the lodes of copper on the south shore of Lake Superior had been reported by Radisson and other explorers). Calhoun authorized the expedition, and Cass departed Detroit on May 24, 1820, with a party of thirty-eight, including ten Indians, seven soldiers, and ten voyageurs. The expedition's mineralogist was Henry R. Schoolcraft, later famed as one of the founders of American Indian ethnology.

The expedition proceeded by canoe to the Sault Ste. Marie and then across Lake Superior to Fond du Lac. From there the St. Louis River and a series of portages led to the American Fur Company outpost on Sandy Lake. Stopping there, Cass sent a scouting party up the Mississippi. It reached a sizable body of water that Schoolcraft named Cass Lake. Without exploring further, the party returned to Sandy Lake with assurances to the governor that Cass Lake was the source of the Mississippi (although Schoolcraft noted privately in his journal that several streams entered the lake, presumably from some other body of water). The expedition then descended the Mississippi and reached the Minnesota River around the end of July. Cass found the U.S. Army busily building a fort at the river's junction; he tarried only long enough to be treated to a dinner of fresh vegetables from the soldiers' newly planted gardens. Cass returned east by the Fox-Wisconsin waterway and reached Detroit by the middle of September.

Besides the source of the Mississippi, another mystery was the source of the Minnesota River and what connection, if any, it had to the Red River that flowed north into Lake Winnipeg. The War Department itself took the lead in solving this puzzle, perhaps in part because of complaints from the American Fur Company that a Hudson's Bay Company trading post on the Red River was channeling Minnesota furs northward. Major Stephen Long, who in 1817 had led the first American exploration of the upper Mississippi, commanded the expedition. An assortment of scholars, including a zoologist, a geologist, and a landscape painter, accompanied Long's band of soldiers and voyageurs.

Long reached the army's fort at the Mississippi-Minnesota river junction in early July 1823 and started up the Minnesota River by canoe. He abandoned the canoes because of low water at Traverse des Sioux, a ford where the Dakota crossed the river on their hunting expeditions and the site of a Sisseton Dakota village. From there he proceeded along the riverbank, with civilians and officers on horseback and infantrymen on foot. Learning that the Dakota people residing in the valley were off hunting buffalo on the prairies, he sent most of his soldiers back to the army's fort. The expedition reached the river's headwaters at Big Stone Lake, and Long's geologist noted the low and undramatic headland north of the lake, from whence waters began flowing north into Lake Traverse and beyond, into the Red River.

Still proceeding by land, Long followed the Red River northward until he came upon a settlement called Pembina, populated by some 350 Scots who had been evicted by landlords from their homes in the Scottish Highlands. The Hudson's Bay Company had helped them resettle in the Lake Winnipeg vicinity, where a handful of Swiss immigrants and assorted Indians joined them. Long learned that the British company annually took more than six hundred packs of furs out of the Red River Valley, but, unlike Lieutenant Pike, he did not make an issue of it. He merely reported the intelligence to the government and let the diplomats handle it.

Long's astronomer determined that the 49th parallel lay a short distance to the north of the settlement and that the Scots were therefore

Itasca Lake
The Mississippi headwaters as Schoolcraft may have seen them
Chromolithograph by Seth Eastman, 1860

on U.S. soil. They were quite content with that outcome. (Many of the residents of Pembina later moved to the farmlands at the Mississippi-Minnesota river junction when the fur trade gave out.) Long traded his horses for canoes at Pembina and proceeded home by way of Lake Winnipeg and the voyageurs' route to Lake Superior.

Other exploring parties roamed the forests of Minnesota in the late 1820s without adding much to the pool of knowledge about the region. Henry R. Schoolcraft resolved the final mystery—the location of the headwaters of the Mississippi. In 1822 he became a federal Indian agent at Sault Ste. Marie and married an Ojibwe woman. Throughout this time the Cass expedition of 1820 seemed to haunt him; Schoolcraft was determined to complete the unfinished task of locating the true source of the Mississippi. In 1832 he wrote to his old friend Cass, now secretary of war under President Andrew Jackson, seeking authorization for a new expedition into the Ojibwe country. He did not mention the source of the Mississippi but focused instead on Indian culture and welfare. Cass approved the expedition and assigned a physician to investigate the incidence of smallpox among the Indians and a minister to study their spiritual needs. He also gave Schoolcraft an escort of ten soldiers.

Schoolcraft left Sault Ste. Marie in early June 1832 and paddled along the south shore of Lake Superior. At the mouth of the Brule River he encountered a party of Ojibwe whose leader, OzaWindib (Schoolcraft's spelling), claimed to have come from the headwaters of the Mississippi. Schoolcraft persuaded the Ojibwe leader to return to his homeland while serving as a guide to the expedition. Schoolcraft later wrote that OzaWindib, who also seemed to have a fair knowledge of English, proved "to be a trusty and experienced guide."

With OzaWindib in the lead, the expedition followed the well-trod route to Fond du Lac, Sandy Lake, and Cass Lake. OzaWindib's home was on an island in Cass Lake, and, given advance notice of the whites' coming, the village staged a welcoming reception. OzaWindib warned the explorers of the many rapids north of Cass Lake but indicated that canoeing was possible because the water was still high from winter snows. He enlisted a number of villagers to go along as guides and help with the paddling.

The expedition, now numbering sixteen, followed the stream from Cass Lake, where the river's entrance was obscured by a maze of wild rice, to Lake Bemidji. From that point the watercourse bent oddly to the southwest, and after passing through a small lake the expedition came to a fork in the river. OzaWindib claimed the west fork was the longest and brought down the most water; however, it contained some treacherous rapids. Accordingly, the party went up the east fork, now called the Schoolcraft River, and then portaged over to the main river, reaching it at a point where it emerged from a long, narrow lake surrounded by low hills and fed only by small creeks and bogs.

The Ojibwe called this Elk Lake, but that name seemed too pedestrian as a source for one of the mightiest rivers of the world. Indeed, throughout his journey Schoolcraft had pondered a proper name for his discovery. He asked the expedition's minister for suggestions borrowed from classic Greece and Rome, but all the poor man could think of were the Latin words for "true head"—*veritas* and *caput*. From that Schoolcraft fashioned a name that was both classical in origin and Indianlike in sound. He struck out the first syllable of *veritas* and the last syllable of *caput* and announced that the name of the source, whenever he found it, would be "Lake Itasca."

And so it came about.

VISITING HISTORY

Lakes and rivers, the highways for travelers of earlier times, lend these sites especially beautiful settings.

Fort St. Charles

In the Northwest Angle on Magnuson's Island, Lake of the Woods, accessible by boat from Angle Inlet, maintained by Angle Outpost Resort; 218/223-8101. Reconstruction of the fort built by La Vérendrye in 1732.

Grand Portage National Monument

Grand Portage; 218/475-2202. Reconstructed 1797 palisade and buildings, with costumed interpreters and exhibits on Native Americans and the fur trade.

Itasca State Park

Jacob V. Brower Interpretive Center; 218/266-2100. Exhibits on the search for the source of the Mississippi and the human and natural history of the area.

Jay Cooke State Park

3 miles east of Carlton on MN Hwy. 210; 218/384-4610. Hiking trails include a portage used by voyageurs to avoid the rapids of the St. Louis River.

Lac qui Parle Mission

8 miles northwest of Montevideo on Co. Hwy. 13, off U.S. Hwy. 59; 320/269-7636. In 1826 Joseph Renville established a fur post here and was soon joined by missionaries. A wooden chapel stands on the original site of the mission.

Mille Lacs Indian Museum

U.S. Hwy. 169, 12 miles north of Onamia; 320/532-3632. Extensive exhibits on tribal history, culture, and sovereignty.

Mille Lacs Kathio State Park

Co. Rd. 26 off U.S. Hwy. 169, about 8 miles north of Onamia; 320/532-3523. Includes the site of the great Dakota village Izatys.

North West Company Fur Post

1.5 miles west of Pine City on Co. Hwy. 7; 320/629-6356. Living history of 1804 in a reconstructed post; interpretive center with extensive exhibits.

Old Crow Wing historic marker

Co. Rd. 27 in Crow Wing State Park, about 1 mile west of MN Hwy. 371. Site of a major Dakota-Ojibwe battle, several fur posts, and a stop on one of the Red River oxcart trails.

Sibley House Historic Site

1357 Sibley Memorial Hwy., Mendota; 651/452-1596. The home of the fur trader and governor; the oldest residence in the state (1837).

4

From Wilderness to Statehood

Shortly after Congress set up Michigan Territory in 1818, Governor Lewis Cass organized southwestern Wisconsin into Crawford County and included in its limits what is now Minnesota east of the Mississippi. Prairie du Chien became the seat of the new county and thus provided such civil administration as Minnesota required, which was for the moment nil. Another twenty years passed before the civilian population in the delta between the St. Croix and Mississippi rivers rated a resident justice of the peace. And yet another decade (1847) passed before the territory that was to become Minnesota witnessed its first jury trial. In the meantime the U.S. Army kept law and order and performed any necessary policing.

In 1819 Colonel Henry Leavenworth led a detachment of the Fifth U.S. Infantry out of Detroit to establish a military post near the junction of the Minnesota and Mississippi rivers on the land that Pike had purchased in 1805. A military presence in the region, it was hoped, would keep British fur traders out of the upper Mississippi. While Leavenworth prepared to leave Detroit, the government discovered it had never actually paid the Dakota the two thousand dollars in goods that Pike had promised. Accordingly, a federal Indian agent joined Leavenworth en route. Upon arriving at the Minnesota River, the agent distributed the goods among a half-dozen Dakota leaders along with liberal allotments of whiskey. Leavenworth had about two hundred men with him and had arrived near the end of summer. As a result, he only had time to set up a temporary cantonment on the south side of the Minnesota River. Short of supplies, he suffered through a miserable winter, during which about a fifth of his men died of scurvy. Before Leavenworth could resume work on the fort the following summer, the War Department relieved him and ultimately assigned him to a new command on the Missouri River (a position that would result in his lending his name to the city of Leavenworth, Kansas).

Colonel Josiah Snelling replaced Leavenworth and infused new energy into the operation. The New Englander chose a new, and far better, site for the fort on a bluff above the river junction, and he designed the fort with the aid of Lieutenant Robert McCabe. The edifice they created was a masterpiece by frontier standards. Shaped as an elongated diamond with a large round tower at the northern apex overlooking the Mississippi and about thirty feet high and thirty feet in diameter, this round bastion had gun ports for infantry on the sides and for cannon on the top. At the other apex, overlooking the Minnesota River, a half-moon battery and smaller batteries for infantry guarded the two broad angles. The limestone walls of the fort, ten feet in height, were impregnable to Indian attack. The fort created the impression of a medieval castle towering over the landscape, symbolizing the power of the republic that was fast becoming an empire.

Two interior buildings were made of pine, the other eight structures of limestone. The limestone was easily quarried from the bluff, but because the region around the river junction was oak opening prairie, the soldiers had to venture north to the Rum River to find a suitable forest of white pine. They floated logs down the Mississippi and built a sawmill at the Falls of St. Anthony. Within the stone enclosure they built officers' quarters, barracks, storehouses, a hospital, and even a schoolhouse. Colonel Snelling remained in command of the garrison for seven years, and in 1825 the War Department, recognizing his achievement, named the fort in his honor.

The environs of the fort soon showed the trappings of civilization. The oak trees quickly disappeared, victims of the garrison's need for firewood. Every winter the fort consumed the equivalent of a pile of wood four feet high, four feet wide, and two miles long. Vegetable gardens appeared in the alluvial flatlands along the Minnesota River, along with corn and wheat fields and a pasture for cows and horses.

The army had long recognized the importance of fresh fruit and vegetables in the soldiers' diet, and it made the establishment of gardens a specific responsibility of post commanders in the remote outposts of the frontier. In 1820, the year of his arrival, Colonel Snelling managed to cultivate ninety acres of river bottomland, planting mostly corn and potatoes. For the next few years military duties were virtually forgotten (and, Snelling admitted, discipline suffered), as most of the garrison worked on the fort and the rest were detailed as company gardeners. Guard duty at the fort consisted mostly of protecting the garden from the depredations of Indians, blackbirds, and

Fort Snelling
*This wilderness outpost signaled the impending tide of settlers
that would soon make Minnesota a state.*
Watercolor by John Casper Wild, 1844

deer. By 1823 Snelling had over two hundred acres under cultivation, about half of it in wheat. To grind the wheat into flour, he purchased buhrstones from St. Louis and built a grist mill on army land at the Falls of St. Anthony. (Minneapolis, "Mill City," thus had a flour mill before it had residents or a name.)

In 1822, at the urging of John Jacob Astor, Congress abandoned the idea of government-controlled "factories" and threw open the fur trade to free competition. In that same year the American Fur Company built a permanent trading post called Mendota on the Minnesota River opposite the fort. (*Mdote* is the Dakota word for "meeting of the waters.") In the following year steamboats began arriving with visitors and supplies from Prairie du Chien, Rock Island, and St. Louis. Although the army expected the soldiers to grow their own vegetables, it supplied the post with pork, flour, beans, soap, candles, salt, and vinegar.

Some of the officers brought their wives, children, and even servants to live in the fort. Abigail Snelling, twenty-two years old and nine months pregnant, arrived at the river junction with her husband in 1820. Two weeks later she gave birth to a baby girl who lived only thirteen months. A solid army wife, she gave parties, arranged dances, entertained visitors, and started a school for army children. In 1823 Colonel Snelling was able to hire a Harvard graduate to tend the school for seventy-five dollars a term. After the graduate departed two years later, the ladies of the garrison took up the teaching duties.

The Dakota too felt the onset of "civilization." Five Dakota villages stood within twenty miles of the fort, and the people watched in dismay as the oaks disappeared and the deer and buffalo became scarce. The U.S. government established an Indian agency in the form of a log council house next to the fort. For twenty years the resident agent was a rigidly honest, courtly gentleman from Virginia, Lawrence Taliaferro (pronounced "Tolliver"). He made treaties with the Indians, listened to their grievances, and punished their troublemakers, but he had neither the resources nor the authority to give them assistance in money or goods. As the game animals disappeared, the Dakota often went hungry in the wintertime, while the well-supplied soldiers played card games in their warm barracks. For the first time the Indians learned the meaning of poverty in a world seemingly full of riches. Army doctors vaccinated them against smallpox, but many died of whooping cough, pneumonia, and other pulmonary diseases introduced by whites.

In 1825 the United States sought to end the intermittent fighting between the Dakota and the Ojibwe, which disrupted the fur trade and distracted the Indians from taking up farming as the government hoped they would. Government representatives summoned a huge conference of Indian leaders at Prairie du Chien with the object of drawing a boundary between the two nations. Ojibwe came from as far away as Lake Superior and Dakota from the Iowa prairies, all to be entertained at government expense. Taliaferro accompanied a large delegation of Indians from central Minnesota. The treaty signed at the conference drew a boundary line that ran from roughly Eau Claire, Wisconsin, northwest across Minnesota to the Red River near present-day Moorhead (more or less following Interstate 94 today). Whatever it meant to the Indian leaders, the boundary meant little to their people, who crossed it in hunting parties without sensing its presence and continued to ambush one another. Its principal significance was to provide a demarcation line for Indian land cessions to the government a decade later.

Indian Cessions and White Pioneers

Through the 1820s refugees from the Red River Valley trickled into the Fort Snelling environs. They came not only from Pembina but from Canadian settlements farther down the valley. Some were unemployed voyageurs; others were farmers rousted by long, hard winters, spring floods, or summertime grasshopper plagues. Some brought cattle, and when they pastured the animals on the military clearings along the Minnesota River, Agent Taliaferro persuaded the refugees to move across the river. Some settled around Mendota; others moved to the east bank of the Mississippi, squatting on the army's nine-mile-wide tract.

Following the Black Hawk War (1832) the federal government forced the Indians to cede the entire eastern half of Wisconsin. That created pressure for cessions in the territory that would become Minnesota, which, except for the Fort Snelling Military Reservation and the mouth of the St. Croix, was still entirely in the hands of the Indians. In 1836, when Michigan became a state, the area from Lake Michigan west to the Missouri River became Wisconsin Territory. Wisconsin governor Henry Dodge urged the federal government to remove the Indian title to the Minnesota lands east of the Mississippi, which he assumed would be the western border of the future state of Wisconsin. Because the 1825 Indian boundary passed through the middle of this tract, the U.S. government in 1837 undertook separate negotiations with the two tribes. Agent Taliaferro led a delegation of Dakota leaders to Washington, DC, where they negotiated directly with President Martin Van Buren's secretary of war. Governor Henry Dodge met that same summer with the Ojibwe at Fort Snelling. By the resulting treaties the Ojibwe sold the lands between the St. Croix and the Mississippi rivers north to a point a bit beyond the St. Croix falls. The Dakota sold their lands between the boundary line and the junction of the St. Croix and the Mississippi rivers. The price was to be paid in annuities, that is, annual allotments of merchandise, food, and medicines. The federal government also promised to give the Indians instruction in farming, an offer accepted by members of several of the villages near Fort Snelling. Lumbermen and the squatters on army land were the first to benefit from the cession, and their efforts brought into being Minnesota's first village communities—St. Paul, Stillwater, and St. Anthony.

Major Joseph Plympton arrived to take command at Fort Snelling in the same summer that the cession treaties were negotiated. In assessing the fort's jurisdiction he discovered about 150 squatters—émigrés from the Red River and ex-voyageurs—on army land east of the Mississippi. He asked them to move below the mouth of the Minnesota River onto lands newly ceded by the Dakota. They did so and immediately began organizing themselves to protect their rights when the federal government got around to putting up for sale the lands ceded by the Indians.

Since 1785 it had been U.S. government policy in the territory north and west of the Ohio River to sell land only after it had been surveyed. Beginning at the point where the Ohio River emerged from Pennsylvania, government surveyors drew a grid of latitudinal and longitudinal lines six miles apart across the Old Northwest. Each square of the grid, called a "town" or "township," thus contained thirty-six square miles (or "sections"). The government sold its land by sections or subsections (thus the standard American farm would be a quarter section or 160 acres). Land sales took place at auction with a minimum price, after 1820, of $1.25 an acre.

The problem was that surveying, while providing accuracy of land titles, took time, and pioneers looking for the best land were often well in front of the surveyors. Such people were known as "squatters" because they had no legal title to the land. Because they were years, often decades, in front of the surveyors, the squatters usually made substantial improvements (buildings, cleared fields, fences) by the time the land came on the market. At the moment when Major Plympton evicted his squatters, for instance, the surveyors were still working in the southeastern corner of Wisconsin.

When the surveys were completed and the government opened a land office in the area, the squatters on the east bank of the Mississippi wanted the right to "preempt" the land they held—that is, to buy it without competitive bidding at the government minimum of $1.25 an acre. Other farmers residing on unsurveyed lands in Illinois, Michigan, and Wisconsin joined them in this demand. In 1841 Congress yielded to pressure from the West and passed a Preemption Act that allowed settlers who could present evidence of having resided on the land (a requirement that was satisfied by building a "claim shed" on the property) to buy up to 160 acres at the government minimum price when the land was surveyed.

In the meantime, in 1839 the Catholic bishop of Dubuque, Iowa Territory, whose diocese included the upper Mississippi, learned of the band of settlers in the vicinity of the trading post at Mendota, a community that he referred to as St. Peter's. (Early missionaries had conferred the name St. Peter's River—an incorrect translation of the French *Sans Pierre,* or "river without stones"—on the Minnesota River.) That summer the good bishop journeyed by steamboat to the settlement to conduct a visitation and a mass. He later wrote to his sister that "the Catholics of St. Peters amounted to one hundred and eighty five." Following this visit the bishop sent a priest, Father Lucien Galtier, to care for the flock of recently discovered Christians.

Father Galtier arrived in 1840 and settled in St. Peter's (Mendota).

He soon learned of the settlement of Red River émigrés on the east bank of the Mississippi and decided it offered a better location for a church. That area contained a likely steamboat landing and potential for commercial development. Two of the French settlers offered him a commanding site for a church on the bluff overlooking the settlement with land sufficient for a garden and a graveyard. Others provided materials and labor for the construction of a log chapel. "I had previously to this time," Father Galtier later wrote, "fixed my residence at Saint Peter's and as the name of Paul is generally connected with that of Peter . . . I called it Saint Paul." The community around the mission became known as Saint Paul's Landing and later simply as St. Paul.

Growth of the village was slow because so little of Minnesota was as yet open to settlement. Only about thirty families lived in the community in 1845, and all but three or four families spoke French. The army fort served as the chief source of commercial traffic. Because the army supplied its soldiers with room, board, and clothing, the men were free to spend their pay on civilian luxuries, chiefly, it is sad to say, on whiskey. The pay for enlisted men in the 1840s ranged from sixteen dollars a month for a first sergeant to seven dollars for a private. Their purchases were a major source of cash for the handful of traders in St. Paul.

The village obtained a U.S. post office in 1846, and the following year steamboats began regular service between St. Paul and Prairie du Chien. In that year, 1847, U.S. government surveyors began platting the land between the St. Croix and the Mississippi rivers. Seizing the opportunity, the residents of St. Paul banded together and had some ninety acres along the riverfront, comprising their residences and shops, surveyed and platted into lots. When a land office opened the following year, they attended en masse to make a preemptive bid at $1.25 an acre.

To this point there was little to sustain St. Paul's growth. The local fur trade had virtually died out, and the village had, as yet, no agricultural surroundings. In the mid-1840s, however, the people of the Red River settlements discovered that the road to St. Paul was shorter and quicker than the long canoe routes to Hudson Bay or Montreal. By 1847 there was an annual summertime stream of Red River carts—

two-wheeled, wooden carts drawn by a single ox—down the Red River trails and the Dakota path along the Minnesota River to St. Paul. Each cart carried a half-ton of furs and buffalo hides, and they returned to the Red River with the usual stock of frontier merchandise, kitchen utensils, clothing, and tools. St. Paul thus survived and grew until new Indian cessions in the 1850s opened the western prairies and a vast agricultural hinterland.

Stillwater, which obtained a post office in the same year as St. Paul, also sprang up from the 1837 Indian land cessions. In the summer of that year, as soon as the Ojibwe initialed their treaty, enterprising lumbermen canoed the St. Croix River to the vicinity of its falls and staked out squatters' claims to large tracts of white pine forest. They experimented with a small sawmill just below the falls and then built larger commercial ones at Marine on St. Croix in 1837 and Stillwater

Following assorted trails from the Red River,
métis traders drove laden oxcarts to St. Paul.

Photo by James E. Martin, 1858–59

in 1844. Over the next few years the growth of Stillwater was so rapid that boosters predicted it would become the largest city in the territory. Pine lumber from Stillwater rafted down the Mississippi to the booming river towns of Keokuk, Illinois, and Hannibal and St. Louis, Missouri. Stillwater never lived up to its early promise, however, and in the 1850s it was overshadowed by mills at Winona and the Falls of St. Anthony.

Entrepreneur Franklin Steele also saw opportunity in the Ojibwe cession. He came to the area as post sutler (that is, operator of the fort's general store) and later turned to lumbering and other activities. On learning of the treaty signing, he immediately staked a claim on the east bank of the Mississippi with frontage sufficient to command the waterpower of St. Anthony Falls to midchannel. Over the next decade, using friends and dummy claimants, Steele gained control of all the lands adjacent to the falls on the east side of the river. After the federal government surveyed the lands in 1847, he made a preemptive purchase at the government minimum price. In that same year he built a dam across the east channel (between Nicollet Island and the riverbank) and erected a sawmill. Loggers floated white pine down the Rum River to Steele's mill, and the community of St. Anthony developed around the mill. In the mid-1840s Steele contracted with the army to supply Fort Snelling with hay, oats, beef, and firewood. Assembling these stores seems to have been a principal occupation of the traders of St. Anthony.

By 1849, when Minnesota achieved the status of a territory, St. Paul numbered about 900 inhabitants, Stillwater about 600, and St. Anthony about 250.

Minnesota Territory

On October 28, 1834, Henry Hastings Sibley rode into the cluster of log huts that made up the community of Mendota on the Minnesota River. Only twenty-three years old, he was already a partner in the American Fur Company and had been named its resident agent at the Mendota trading post. Sibley lived until 1891, and he would become the most important single figure in the territorial and early state government of Minnesota.

The son of a Michigan territorial judge, Sibley attended private schools in Detroit and studied law for two years. A love of the outdoors drew him to the frontier, where he first worked as a clerk for a fur trader on Mackinac Island for five years. When John Jacob Astor retired in 1833, the American Fur Company split up, although each group of partners retained the company's name. One group, headquartered in St. Louis, dominated the Rocky Mountain fur trade; the other, headed by Ramsay Crooks, took over the upper Mississippi and Lake Superior trade. Crooks had long been concerned about resident agents who were acquainted with Indian languages and customs but were poor accountants and businessmen. He chose Sibley for the Mendota post because of Sibley's clerical experience, business acumen, and ability to speak French.

Foreseeing the decline of the fur trade in Minnesota, Sibley began investing in real estate, specializing in urban lots, first in Mendota and later in St. Paul. After Crooks's American Fur Company went bankrupt in 1842, Sibley contracted independently with the St. Louis branch of the company. Through contacts with a trader at Pembina he purchased buffalo hides and furs smuggled out of the Hudson's Bay Company preserve and sold them in St. Louis. Sibley married Sarah Jane Steele, a sister of Franklin Steele (proprietor of St. Anthony), and became a leader in the development of St. Paul. When the ninety acres that St. Paul's squatters had privately platted came up for sale at the government land office in summer 1848, Sibley, acting on their behalf, made the single bid for all. In later years Sibley remembered with a chuckle that his fellow squatters were armed with clubs, hoping to intimidate any competitive bidder who might appear.

In that same year Wisconsin became a state, and Congress established its western boundary at the St. Croix and Mississippi rivers. As a territory from 1836 to 1848, Wisconsin had extended from Lake Michigan to the Missouri River. The new, more limited boundary left the Minnesota communities in a governmental limbo. In August 1848 several prominent men, including Sibley and Steele, issued a call for a convention to meet in Stillwater to draft a petition asking Congress to provide a territorial government for the region west of the St. Croix. The resulting convention chose Sibley to carry the petition to Washington and to plead its cause. Hoping to clothe Sibley with sufficient status as a territorial delegate to gain the attention of Congress, the convention adopted the fiction that the Territory of Wisconsin (that is, the land west of the St. Croix and Mississippi rivers) still existed notwithstanding statehood for the region east of the rivers.

Arriving in Washington just as the congressional session opened in December, Sibley presented his credentials as a delegate from Wisconsin Territory to the House Committee on Elections. Dressed in a suit of the latest fashion and exuding an air of Eastern gentility, Sibley tactfully pointed out to the committee that Congress, by admitting as a state only a portion of Wisconsin Territory, had accidentally disfranchised "thousands" of American citizens and placed them beyond the protection of the law. In an atmosphere of political camaraderie and, no doubt, with some bemusement, the House seated Sibley as the delegate from the Territory of Wisconsin. Among those voting in favor of this unusual arrangement was a handful of congressmen who disliked slavery and were happy to see on the political horizon the nucleus of another free state. Their number included young Abraham Lincoln.

A few weeks later, in early 1849, Stephen A. Douglas, chair of the Senate Committee on Territories, brought to the floor a bill to erect Minnesota Territory. For several years Douglas had foreseen a future for the upper Mississippi valley, and he had preserved its geographical integrity from raids by border politicians. In 1846 he prevented the newly formed state of Iowa from extending its northern boundary to include Fort Snelling and the Falls of St. Anthony, prized for its potential economic development. The following year, when Wisconsin was struggling toward statehood, Douglas kept the politicians in Madison from grabbing St. Paul and the waterfall. Had Minnesota been shorn of these centers of population, statehood would have been delayed for decades.

Thus, the boundaries outlined in Douglas's territory bill created an economically viable political unit. The northern boundary would be the Pigeon River, Rainy River, and Lake of the Woods—an international boundary agreed to by the United States and Great Britain in the Webster-Ashburton Treaty of 1842. The Missouri River would form the western boundary and the state of Iowa the southern boundary. The bill proposed Mendota as the territory's capital, but Douglas yielded to Sibley's preference for St. Paul. Sibley, who owned parcels in both communities, likely voted for St. Paul because of its commercial potential as head of steamboat navigation on the Mississippi River.

Beginning with the Northwest Ordinance of 1785 Congress set aside one section of land in every township for the maintenance of schools. Minnesota's Organic Act set aside two sections—not because Congress had become more education-conscious, but because it had doubts about the fertility (and hence value) of Minnesota's soil. To easterners the territory seemed equally divided between pine "barrens" and prairie grassland; neither was considered prime land for farming. (Although the steel plow, the "plow that broke the plains," had been developed in the 1840s, no proof yet existed that it could turn over the tough prairie sod that had resisted wooden plowshares.)

Douglas's bill glided through the Senate without a diversion but then ran afoul of politics in the House of Representatives. The Whig Party controlled the House; its candidate, Zachary Taylor, had wrested the presidency from the Democrats in the election of 1848. Taylor would not take office until March 5, 1849. Because the territorial offices were within the gift of the president, the Whigs wanted to delay recognition of Minnesota as a territory until they controlled the government. It did not help matters that Sibley and most of the other prominent leaders of St. Paul and Stillwater were Democrats, like their brethren in southwestern Wisconsin. (The Whig Party in Wisconsin centered on the Yankee émigrés in the southeastern counties; people of similar background would be the foundation of the Whig Party in Minnesota.)

The parties reached a compromise in which Minnesota was coupled with a new cabinet post, the Department of the Interior (which Democrats had threatened to block). The bill creating Minnesota Territory passed on March 3. Before the news reached St. Paul in early April, President Taylor loaded the territorial offices—governor, secretary, three judges, and U.S. attorney—with Whigs. The governor, Alexander Ramsey, proved to be a man of considerable ability, even though his appointment was nothing more than a political payoff for having helped carry Pennsylvania in the election. A graduate of

Lafayette College, Ramsey had practiced law and been a member of Congress from 1843 to 1847. Legend has it that, seated next to David Wilmot in the House of Representatives, Ramsey had provided the wording for the 1846 "Proviso" that sought to bar slavery from the territory acquired from Mexico in the war and hence ignited the fourteen-year controversy over "free soil" that led to the Civil War.

The differences between Whigs and Democrats, originating in the policies of President Andrew Jackson, had little relevance for Minnesota, and neither Ramsey nor Sibley was an intense partisan. As men who valued refinement (and probably secretly scorned the rough-hewn descendents of the voyageurs), the two became fast friends. That alliance permitted Minnesota to grow for the next few years without the divisive partisanship that tore Wisconsin apart a decade earlier.

As hosts to the territorial legislature scheduled to meet in September 1849, St. Paul's merchants and builders, who had gained legal title to their city lots only a year earlier, sprang into action. "The whole town is on the stir," exulted an editor-booster. "Stores, hotels, houses are projected and built in a few days. California['s gold rush] is forgotten, and the whole town is rife with the exciting spirit of advancement." A visitor from Ohio in midsummer estimated the population at twelve hundred and counted two hotels, numerous stores and saloons, a school, a Catholic church, four Protestant ministers, and three printing shops. Such growth was truly impressive considering that the entire white and mixed-blood population of the territory numbered fewer than four thousand.

In August voters chose members of the territorial legislature and elected Sibley as the territory's congressional delegate. A month later, the legislature held its first session in a St. Paul hotel. The pioneer legislature that met intermittently from 1849 to 1851 reflected St. Paul's hustle. Legislators adopted the civil and criminal code of Wisconsin, established (at least on paper) a state public school system, mapped out nine counties, incorporated the Minnesota Historical Society, and chartered the University of Minnesota (which, unfortunately, did not open its doors to students until almost twenty years later). All of this was little more than paper progress, however, so long as the Indians owned 99 percent of the land in the territory.

Displacing the Native Inhabitants

Addressing the related problems of Indians and land ownership, territorial officials turned first to the Dakota, whose leaders had visited Washington in 1837 and returned quite awed by the power and numbers of the white population. Three of the original seven council fires of the Dakota had moved out to the western plains. The remaining four lived in the Minnesota River valley, two in the upper reaches of the river (the Upper Sioux, to the U.S. commissioners) and two in the lower part (the Lower Sioux). Because the Lower Sioux had already made one cession (1837), for which they had been only partially paid, the clans were extremely reluctant to part with any more. As a result, Governor Ramsey initiated talks with the Upper Sioux. He led a delegation that met with perhaps two hundred Indians at Traverse des Sioux in July 1851. The delegation included Henry Sibley, who represented the interests of fur traders claiming that the Dakota owed them nearly half a million dollars in debts for provisions. Treated to several days of feasting and drinking as well as lavish promises of good farmland and training in mechanical arts, thirty-five leaders signed a treaty selling their lands south of the 1825 boundary. The Dakota retained a reserve extending ten miles on either side of the Minnesota River from Lake Traverse to the mouth of the Yellow Medicine River.

After signing the treaty, the leaders were led to a table (a board sitting on a barrel) where a trader asked them to sign another document. Assuming that it was simply another copy of the treaty, the Indians obediently signed. They later learned that it was a separate contract by which the traders put a lien of $410,000 on the federal government's payment for the land. This meant that the traders would get their money from the government before the Indians did. The Dakota leaders were enraged at the deception, but they couldn't do anything about it because the treaty of cession gave the governor complete power to distribute government monies. The anger among the Dakota, who felt betrayed by Henry Sibley, who was heavily involved in the negotiations, simmered for years, and it was certainly a factor in their bloody uprising of 1862.

With these documents in hand, Ramsey and his delegation returned downriver to Mendota where in August they persuaded the

Lower Sioux to part with their lands south of the Ojibwe boundary. The total Dakota land cession in southern Minnesota and northern Iowa amounted to nearly twenty-four million acres, for which the government paid about $1.6 million (that is, seven cents an acre). The money, minus the sums paid to the traders, went into a trust fund; from it, the Dakota received annual interest payments in the forms of cash and provisions.

Ojibwe lands in the north became Ramsey's next target. However, some of the governor's unwitting chicanery softened Ojibwe resistance. In 1842 the Ojibwe of Wisconsin ceded their lands to the federal government on the promise that they would be allowed to live in their villages indefinitely. In 1850, under pressure from lumbering in-

The Signing of the Treaty of Traverse des Sioux
With these land cessions, the Dakota were confined to reservations along the Minnesota River.
Oil by Francis Davis Millet, 1905

terests, government leaders changed their minds and ordered the Ojibwe to move to Minnesota. Governor Ramsey took charge of the removal. He decided to place the Wisconsin Indians at Leech Lake, which was suitably distant from the white settlements. Unfortunately, he neglected to obtain the consent of the resident Ojibwe, and when they protested, Ramsey hastily sent the Wisconsin bands to Sandy Lake. Again the resident Ojibwe protested. This quagmire of incompetence and callousness went on for three years, while several hundred Indians died of starvation and disease. In the end, Democratic President Franklin Pierce, elected in 1852, replaced Ramsey with a Democrat and allowed the Wisconsin Ojibwe to remain on reservations in that state.

Appalled by the treatment of fellow tribesmen yet relieved at the outcome, the Minnesota Ojibwe readily agreed to new treaties in 1854 and 1855 by which they ceded their lands along Lake Superior and the future Iron Range, as well as the central lake district. They drove a hard bargain, however, and received a rare guarantee of permanent reservations within the lands they ceded. They selected their most cherished locations: Grand Portage, Sandy Lake, Mille Lacs, and Leech Lake. The Ojibwe clung to the lower Red River Valley until 1863 and finally ceded the last of their holdings in the Rainy River–Lake of the Woods region in 1889.

The Indian land cessions, shabby though they were, ensured future economic growth for Minnesota. Of more immediate importance, however, was the multiplier effect of federal expenditures. Between 1849 and 1859 the federal government paid $4.2 million to the Indians to fulfill its treaty obligations, an average of $380,000 a year. The territory's largest private industry, lumbering, did not realize that much in profits until 1855. Indians used the money to buy utensils and clothing and to pay off debts to traders. Traders invested their profits in urban real estate and the construction of buildings. The federal government's annuity payments to Indians, in short, financed much of the growth of Minnesota's cities.

Minnesota's boosters were well aware of the benefits. As early as 1850 St. Paul's *Minnesota Pioneer* complained editorially: "One would suppose by the promises about town, that the Indian payment would square every debt in Minnesota, but the 'debt of Nature.'" A year later Governor

Ramsey told the legislature with rare candor, "The payments of the Indian annuities supply much the larger portion of our current currency, and through the various channels of trade contribute greatly to our prosperity." The governor was correct. By comparison, the federal government spent only $120,000 a year on the territory, building forts, military roads, and lighthouses on Lake Superior.

The Fast-Moving Frontier

Senate amendments to the Dakota treaties, which required Indian approval, delayed ratification until 1852. Thus, President Franklin Pierce did not get around to setting up the Dakota reservation on the Minnesota River until 1853. These delays did not deter land-hungry pioneers, however. Estimates are that some five thousand whites trespassed on Dakota lands by the end of 1852. They marked out desirable lands and established individual claims. Groups of pioneer farmers then formed "claims associations," which kept law and order and protected claims from other trespassers. In 1854 Congress yielded to pressure from squatters in Minnesota, Wisconsin, and Iowa and passed an act allowing squatters to preempt their claims at the government minimum of $1.25 an acre even before they were surveyed.

With land virtually free for the taking, the wealthy had little to gain in amassing large tracts of rural land. Promoters and speculators concentrated instead on new sites for towns. By the end of 1852, Winona, Belle Plaine, and Mankato had been platted and lots were up for sale. A rage of town-site fever arose by the middle of the decade. Wherever a promoter found a site along a riverbank that held the promise of a steamboat landing, he would establish a title by preemption, lay out town lots, and draw up an attractive plat map. One historian has estimated that by 1857 more than seven hundred towns had been platted on paper with enough potential residential lots to house one and a half million people.

In 1854, the year Congress further relaxed the preemption law, a railroad line from Chicago reached Rock Island on the Mississippi. It was now possible to travel by rail and steamboat from the East Coast to St. Paul. A journey from the nation's capital to Minnesota took four days and nights. In New England, New York, and Ohio, restless farmers by the thousands began the journey. When the river opened in April 1855, the first packet vessel from Rock Island docked in St. Paul with 814 passengers. The packet company brought thirty thousand people to Minnesota in that season alone. A census taken in 1857 as the territory prepared for statehood showed a population of a little more than 150,000.

The migrants quickly headed west into the interior, with steamboats carrying the more well-to-do. By 1857 St. Paul counted almost three hundred steamboat arrivals from points on the Minnesota River. However, the majority of people went by wagon. In 1854 a surveyor stood by while a train of "immigrant wagons, filled with Norwegians," passed him on the road to Mankato. He also claimed that as many as two hundred wagons of emigrants could be seen "on the road at one time." Those coming from Wisconsin or another state to the east often drove herds of cattle tended by children.

As settlers arrived in ever-greater numbers,
St. Paul's levee bustled with steamboat traffic.

Many, perhaps a majority, of the emigrants were transplanted Yankees. Some came directly from New England; others had paused to farm in New York, Ohio, or Wisconsin before moving on to Minnesota. The great potato famine in western Europe in the 1840s sent a wave of emigrants to America, and many made their way by Great Lakes steamers and overland wagons to Minnesota. By 1860 foreign-born individuals made up 30 percent of the state's population. Germans were the largest group, followed by Irish, Norwegians, and Swedes.

As St. Paul grew in wealth and population its social elite yearned for artistic refinement. The centerpiece of the city's economy, the garrison at Fort Snelling, took the lead in providing the city with music for concerts and dances. When Congress established the peacetime army after the War of 1812, it created the rank of "musician" with the same pay as a private and authorized two musicians (presumably a fife and a drummer) for each regiment. Later regulations allowed enlisted men to be detailed as musicians. By the 1850s every regiment had a band. The Sixth Regiment band, stationed at Fort Snelling, numbered fifteen musicians and gave frequent concerts in St. Paul. Its repertoire ranged from classical symphonies to the popular operas of Verdi, Bellini, and Rossini. On the occasion of the Minnesota Historical Society's first public program in January 1850 the band gave a concert that prompted one listener to declare that he had "never heard a band anywhere that appeared more complete masters of their profession."

The fort library contained the works of several English playwrights, and for some years the fort's theater troupe gave performances for visiting inspectors and the amusement of the garrison. In 1856 army officers organized the Fort Snelling Dramatic Association and solicited the patronage of St. Paul's social elite. The citizenry responded handsomely, offering both financing and home talent, and the city's theater became a frontier landmark.

While St. Paul evolved from a cluster of pine-board huts to cultured urbanity, town planners busied themselves in the original Fort Snelling Military Reserve on the west bank of the Mississippi. The pioneer in this enterprise, John H. Stevens, settled in Minnesota in 1849 and worked as a clerk in Franklin Steele's St. Anthony Mill Company. Steele pointed out to Stevens that the land on the west side of the falls was a promising site for future mills. Because the land on the west bank of the Mississippi was part of the military reserve, Stevens approached Fort Snelling's commander with an offer. He would provide free ferry service across the river in exchange for a tract of 160 acres at the head of the falls. The army, which had recently built Fort Ripley on the upper Mississippi (near present-day Brainerd), saw that a ferry across the river would become part of the military road connecting the new fort with Fort Snelling. The secretary of war approved the bargain, and Stevens built a house on his claim in 1850.

Other pioneers followed Stevens's example and badgered the officers at Fort Snelling for permits to settle on military lands. The officers, some of whom became partners with real-estate speculators, granted the permits on the basis of friendship and mutual interest. In 1852 when the territorial legislature established Hennepin County on the west bank of the Mississippi, Stevens's community was the logical choice for a county seat. The problem was that it as yet had no name. Some civic boosters suggested "All Saints," implying superiority over St. Paul and St. Anthony, but that was unacceptable popery to the transplanted Yankees who made up most of the population at the falls. As one resident pointed out, "It is a name that is applicable to no more than two persons in the vicinity of the falls, and of doubtful application even to them." With the same ingenuity Henry Schoolcraft had shown in naming the source of the Mississippi, the citizenry concocted a mixture of Indian and Greek. They took the Dakota word for falls, *Minne ha-ha*, or "laughing water," and added the Greek word for city, *polis*. The result was *Minnehapolis*, "Laughing Water City." The *h* was silent and was soon dropped.

In 1854 the army recognized the land titles of the squatters, and Stevens quickly platted the new city. Development occurred more easily here than in St. Paul, where the land rose steeply away from the river and developers imposed a variety of street plans that did not always mesh with one another. In Minneapolis the land sloped gently from the bluff below the falls, a mixture of oak opening prairie and maple-birch hardwoods. Stevens's plan followed the bend of the river at the falls, with a 100-foot-wide Hennepin Avenue as the baseline. The other streets, a generous 80 feet wide, were laid in a grid off Hennepin.

In that same year, 1854, enterprising citizens formed a corporation to build a toll bridge across the river, linking Minneapolis with the village of St. Anthony. Something new in bridge engineering, the span was suspended from steel cables that stretched across the river from a tower on the west bank to a tower on Nicollet Island just above the falls. It met a bridge built earlier that connected the island with the river's east bank. A seventeen-foot-wide roadway crossed the bridge; the company charged a toll of five cents for pedestrians and twenty-five cents for horse-drawn wagons. The bridge was the first of any kind across the Mississippi River.

A suspension bridge linked St. Anthony to Minneapolis in 1855,
seventeen years before the towns united as one city.

Photo by William Henry Illingworth, 1868

Two of the most important builders of Minneapolis were non-residents. Robert Smith, a businessman from Alton, Illinois, and member of Congress, used his political influence to persuade the army to lease him its grist mill and sawmill at the Falls of St. Anthony in 1849. Although Smith told the army he planned to become a resident of Minnesota, he never did and instead subleased the mills to local operators. In 1853 he purchased the army's mills for $750 and began looking for investors to turn Stevens's community on the west bank into a milling center. Cadwallader C. Washburn, a lawyer from Mineral Point, Wisconsin, and member of Congress from 1855 to 1861, was the most important of these investors. Washburn had substantial investments in Minnesota and Wisconsin timberlands, and he recruited trusted relatives—a younger brother, William, and a cousin, Dorilus Morrison (Minneapolis's first mayor)—to manage his investments in Minnesota. By 1855 a partnership of twelve men, including Washburn's brother and cousin, owned Smith's mills and lands.

Establishing a corporation became the next step. The Minneapolis Mill Company received a charter from the legislature in 1856. At the same time, Franklin Steele and his partners across the river obtained a charter for the St. Anthony Falls Water Power Company. The two companies then began building a dam at the head of the falls to divide the water and the logs it bore evenly between them. When completed in 1858, the dam, in the shape of an inverted V, angled out from each shore and met upriver in the middle of the river. It was constructed of rock-filled timber cribs anchored to the river bottom. Twenty feet high at the river banks and only four feet high in the middle, the dam allowed excess water to flow through and channeled the log-laden current into log-retention ponds on each side.

Both Minneapolis and St. Anthony were essentially sawmill towns for the first two decades of their existence. (Minneapolis absorbed St. Anthony in 1872.) Six mills sat on the east side of the river and seven on the west during the 1850s. The pine logs (marked for identification by the mill operators) floated down the Mississippi from the Rum River valley and Mille Lacs. As early as 1856 Minneapolis mills turned out twelve million board feet of lumber a year. Even at that rate its mills were unable to keep up with the upriver pace of lumbering, and the vast majority of logs passed down the river to mills at Winona.

Some rafted all the way to St. Louis, which milled lumber for the thriving Missouri River towns of Kansas City and Omaha and scores of towns and farms in between.

The mill company's investment in new mills and a dam turned Minneapolis into a boom town. By 1857 it had two hotels and three churches, with new structures going up on an average of one a day. The "balloon frame" method of building, developed in Chicago in the 1830s, made such rapid construction possible. Earlier buildings had been "pyramids" of bricks and mortar or notched logs piled on top of one another. They required complicated joinery and skilled hands to achieve artistic style and permanence. The balloon frame house contained an inner frame of standardized boards, such as the basic two-by-four, held together with machine-made nails. It could be erected quickly and without much expertise.

In the 1890s Permelia Atwater published a reminiscence of life in early Minneapolis: "We many times saw a load of lumber deposited on a lot in the evening, and by noon of the next day a balloon frame with board roof would appear in its stead, as if by magic—the familiar stove pipe sending up its wreathes of smoke, telling of the home and family life already established below." The balloon frame method, with some variations, remains today the basic technology of house construction.

By the census of 1860 St. Paul had a population of 10,400; St. Anthony about 3,200; Minneapolis, 2,564; Winona, 2,464; and Stillwater, 2,380. Five years earlier the territory had achieved sufficient population to qualify for statehood, but amid rising sectional tensions in the late 1850s, that proved an elusive goal.

The Thirty-Second State

Minnesota could, with justice, have adopted the state motto of Kansas, *Ad Astra per Aspera* ("To the Stars through Difficulty"). The irony is that Kansas caused the "difficulties" Minnesota encountered in adding its star to the American flag.

The issue of slavery in Kansas arose with the passage of the Kansas-Nebraska Act of 1854. The act created the Territory of Kansas west of the state of Missouri, and it erected the rest of the region between the

Missouri River and the Rocky Mountains into Nebraska Territory. The bill's author, Stephen A. Douglas, wanted to test popular sovereignty as a solution to the issue of slavery in the West by allowing the people of Kansas and Nebraska territories themselves to decide whether they wanted to become "slave states" or "free states." To give voters a genuine choice, Douglas accepted an amendment to his bill that repealed the Missouri Compromise (1820), which had guaranteed that the Louisiana Purchase north of latitude 36° 30' would be free soil. The northern public immediately assumed that Douglas was handing Kansas to the South as another slave state because proslavery emigrants from Missouri were certain to dominate its politics. In the ensuing uproar the disintegrating Whig Party disappeared altogether, and a new antislavery Republican Party was born.

Prior to 1854 Minnesota politics focused on personalities, rather than on parties or ideologies. Territorial delegate Henry Sibley, who considered himself a "Democrat of the Jeffersonian school," got along well with the Whig governor, Alexander Ramsey. When Sibley retired from Congress in 1853, the voters replaced him with another Democrat, Henry M. Rice. Like Sibley, Rice came to Minnesota as a fur trader and settled initially in Mendota. He later moved to St. Paul, purchased a tract of land adjacent to the original ninety-acre plat, and replatted a town of his own, with streets at angles from St. Paul's initial grid. He gave away lots to stimulate settlement and built stores, warehouses, and a large hotel. As a territorial delegate in Congress, Rice worked with leaders of both political parties to promote the interests of Minnesota. His pet project, for which he had the support of Illinois Senator Stephen A. Douglas, was a railroad between St. Paul and Lake Superior, with a branch south of St. Paul linking it to the Illinois Central. That project died amid the furor over the Kansas-Nebraska Act and Douglas's declining political fortunes.

In summer 1854, popular meetings across the North organized a new antislavery political party. Speakers at an anti–Nebraska Act rally in Ripon, Wisconsin, the previous February had suggested the name "Republican," and in June Horace Greeley, editor of the *New York Tribune*, endorsed the name because it linked the new party with the Jeffersonian political tradition and Jefferson's well-known critique of slavery. Conventions that met in the course of the summer to organize state parties generally approved the name. With the exception of the Democratic *Minnesota Pioneer*, Minnesota newspapers were sharply critical of the Kansas-Nebraska Act, but no concerted effort to organize a Republican Party occurred in the territory until spring 1855. Ramsey, the former Whig governor, took the lead in forming the new party. Kentucky-born William R. Marshall, another St. Paul businessman and a future governor of the state, played an important role as well.

As the party organization gradually developed, a succession of conventions worked out a party platform. It denounced the repeal of the Missouri Compromise and the potential expansion of slave territory. It favored river and harbor improvements, as had its predecessor, the Whig Party. It also adopted the Whigs' Yankee morality by demanding prohibition of the manufacture and sale of intoxicating liquors. Not surprisingly, Minnesota's transplanted Yankees were the core of the new party, and Scandinavians generally shared their antipathy to slavery and liquor. Germans and Irish, suspecting anti-immigrant feeling in the new party, generally remained Democratic, as did most of the long-time residents of St. Paul and St. Anthony, such as Henry Sibley.

Until 1856 there seems to have been little sentiment in Minnesota for statehood. As a territory, its economic infrastructure—roads, river improvements, the harbor at Duluth, and Lake Superior lighthouses—were the responsibility of Congress. The population's greatest source of income came from federal largesse (partly through payments to Indians). The prospect of a transcontinental railroad changed the situation. A railroad linking California with the eastern half of the nation had been a hot topic of discussion since California's admission to the union in 1850. And, like most issues of the day, it had become embroiled in sectional rivalries. Senator Douglas had organized Kansas and Nebraska territories primarily to enhance the chances of a northern route with terminus in St. Louis or Chicago. Henry Rice and other Minnesota promoters favored an even more northerly route, linking Oregon to the Mississippi valley by way of St. Paul. In dedicating the new bridge across the Mississippi River in 1855, Territorial Governor Willis A. Gorman urged the people of Minneapolis to inform Congress of their accomplishment because the bridge could serve as a railroad crossing. "Who knows," he predicted, "but this mighty structure may yet bear . . . the commerce of the Pacific, as it mingles with that of the Atlantic!" In 1850 Congress pioneered the idea of federal support for railroad construction by a gift of public lands to the state of Illinois for the construction of the Illinois Central Railroad. To compete for a similar grant Minnesota needed statehood.

When the congressional session opened in December 1856, Henry Rice was ready with two bills—an enabling act that would allow Minnesota to draft a state constitution and a railroad land grant bill. Ever the optimist, Rice envisioned five railroads across Minnesota, serving every interest in the state: one would go from Winona up the Minnesota River valley, the others would radiate north and west from St. Paul. The Winona–Minnesota valley project was shrewdly designed to cripple the demands of farmers in the southern prairies who wanted an east-west state extending to the Missouri River, with a northern boundary somewhere around St. Paul. If the farmers had insisted on this reorientation, they would have delayed statehood and endangered the railroad land grant. Rice's enabling act preserved the north-south orientation of the territory, with a western boundary at the Red River and a longitudinal line south from its headwaters.

Congress passed the enabling act in February 1857 over the noisy opposition of southerners who objected to the further dilution of their voice in national councils. It also passed the railroad land grant act, but Rice's scheme for a state transportation network died in the financial panic that summer. The failure of the Ohio Life Insurance and Trust Company in August 1857 triggered a nationwide depression that dried up eastern investment capital and ended the building boom in St. Paul and Minneapolis. Except for a ten-mile line connecting St. Paul with St. Anthony built in 1862, there would be no railroads in Minnesota until after the Civil War.

The enabling act offered Minnesota a number of financial enticements to become a state. It retained the allocation of two sections in each township for the maintenance of schools and set aside seventy-two sections of public land statewide for the benefit of a state university. The act offered the state legislature five percent of the proceeds from the sale of all public lands for roads, harbors, and other internal improvements. By the terms of the act voters were authorized to elect a convention to meet on July 13 to draft a state constitution.

Bloodshed in Kansas that spring—with the "sack" of Lawrence by Missouri "border ruffians" and John Brown's retaliatory massacre of proslavery settlers at Pottawatomie—poisoned the atmosphere of the Minnesota election. The U.S. Supreme Court added to the tension by denying the petition of an African American slave, Dred Scott, the servant of an army surgeon who claimed his freedom on the basis of a temporary residence on free soil while his master was stationed at Fort Snelling. The court held that Congress lacked the power to limit slavery in the West and thus declared the 36° 30′ line of the Missouri Compromise unconstitutional. Minnesota had never been "free soil," and Scott was still a slave. The North again erupted in a wave of anger. Even those who were indifferent to the moral issue of slavery subscribed to a "slave power conspiracy" by which a handful of

Dred Scott's quest for freedom linked Minnesota to the national debate regarding slavery.

Sketch published in *Frank Leslie's Illustrated Newspaper*, 1857 southerners were thought to be secretly manipulating the Congress, the president, and now the Supreme Court.

Candidates for the Minnesota constitutional convention ignored the legal niceties of constitution-making and divided along party lines on the issues posed by Kansas and *Dred Scott*—the expansion of slavery (Republicans opposed, Democrats waffling) and the status of free blacks residing in Minnesota (should the males be given the vote?). The census of 1860 counted 259 persons of African descent in the state, most of them living in St. Paul.

The arrival in 1857 of the state's first outspoken abolitionist, Jane Grey Swisshelm, added to the din. Swisshelm, like most female reformers of the day, blended a crusade for women's rights with one for the abolition of slavery. She settled in St. Cloud, a village on the upper Mississippi populated by Scandinavians and transplanted Yankees, and published a succession of newspapers, the *St. Cloud Visiter* and the *St. Cloud Democrat*. Unlike most Minnesotans, who were content to leave slavery alone where it already existed and sought only to prevent its expansion into the trans-Mississippi West (a position known as "free soil"), Swisshelm advocated the immediate, uncompensated freeing of slaves everywhere. While rejecting this extreme notion, the press elsewhere adopted a shrill rhetoric of its own. The *St. Paul Pioneer and Democrat* proclaimed that the fundamental issue facing the constitutional convention would be "White Supremacy Against Negro Equality," while other Democrats predicted that Republican control of Minnesota would "inaugurate scenes of violence and bloodshed, as they have in Kansas."

With the electorate polarized, it is scarcely surprising that the convention assembled on July 13 was fairly evenly divided, fifty-nine Republicans to fifty-five Democrats. Because control of the convention machinery—chair, committee heads—was crucial to the direction it would take, each side feared a takeover coup by the other. After a turbulent scene of conflicting chairs on the first day, the two parties met separately, each claiming to be the legitimate convention. Each party debated and drafted its own version of a state constitution, and after they adjourned, each published a volume of *Debates and Proceedings*.

The two constitutions were, in fact, quite similar since the drafters, as was the custom, borrowed heavily from the constitutions of states immediately to the east. After much posturing, the parties agreed to a joint committee to reconcile the two drafts. The main hang-up was a Republican proposal to extend the vote to free black males. Democrats were firmly opposed, and in the end Republicans themselves decided to drop the idea lest it lead to a defeat of the constitution at the hands of the voters (as happened in Wisconsin ten years earlier). After seven weeks, when the committee finally agreed on a document, each party caucus received separate copies. Republicans signed one copy; Democrats signed another. Because many people helped prepare the copies, numerous errors and minor variations occurred. To this day the precise wording of the original Minnesota constitution remains uncertain. Fortunately, over the years the doubt has not produced any legal disputes.

In October 1857 Minnesota held an election for state officials, even though Congress had yet to approve its admission to the union. Henry Sibley defeated Alexander Ramsey for the governorship, and the Democrats also won control of the legislature. Triumphantly they forwarded their version of the state constitution to Washington.

Once again Minnesota's drive for statehood ran afoul of Kansas. That same summer Missouri crossover voters elected a proslavery convention that met at Lecompton, Kansas, and drafted a constitution allowing slavery in the state. When the constitution was submitted to Congress, Republicans were outraged and Democrats split, tabling Minnesota's petition while North and South struggled over Kansas. Republicans feared that if Minnesota were admitted, its Democratic leadership would support slavery in Kansas. Congress eventually rejected the Lecompton constitution, largely due to the opposition of Stephen A. Douglas, who felt that the fraudulent elections in Kansas had not been a legitimate application of popular sovereignty. With the Kansas problem shelved (it was admitted to the Union in 1861 after the South seceded) Congress turned to Minnesota and admitted the "Star of the North" state to the Union on May 11, 1858.

VISITING HISTORY

Much of the activity in these early years took place close to the tiny cities of St. Paul and St. Anthony, later Minneapolis.

Alexander Ramsey House
265 S. Exchange St., St. Paul; 651/296-8760. An 1872 Second Empire mansion built by Minnesota's first governor and filled with family furniture; tours by guides dressed as servants.

Blue Earth County Heritage Center
415 E. Cherry St., Mankato; 507/345-5566. Includes exhibits on the Dakota and the early history of the area.

Camp Coldwater
Off MN Hwy. 55, Minneapolis, .2 mile east on 54th St. E., .5 mile south on access road past government buildings. Summer camp of the Fifth U.S. Infantry, 1820; water source for Fort Snelling; settlement of Selkirk refugees from the Red River Valley until 1840.

Hennepin History Museum
2303 3rd Ave. S., Minneapolis; 612/870-1329. Exhibits on city and county history.

Historic Forestville
Forestville/Mystery Cave State Park, off MN Hwy. 5 west of Preston; 507/765-2785. Costumed guides impersonate the actual residents of the small town of Forestville in the 1890s.

Historic Fort Snelling
MN Hwys. 5 and 55, St. Paul; 612/726-1171. Large living history site with troop drilling, cannon firing, blacksmith, bakeries, and more; military history exhibits.

Joseph R. Brown Minnesota River Center
600 Main St., Henderson; 507/248-3234. Interprets the life and times of the influential fur trader, businessman, and politician.

St. Anthony Falls Heritage Trail
4th and Main St., Minneapolis. A two-mile signed trail through the National Historic District, giving an overview of the history and technology of the businesses at the falls. Includes views of the city from the Stone Arch Bridge, built by James J. Hill's Great Northern Railway; Upper St. Anthony Falls Lock and Dam; and Mill Ruins Park.

St. Peter's Church

1405 Sibley Memorial Hwy., Mendota Heights; 651/452-4550. The oldest church in continuous use in Minnesota (1853).

Sandy Lake historic marker

MN Hwy. 65 about 8 miles north of McGregor at Sandy Lake. The site of the camp in which four thousand Lake Superior Ojibwe people waited for a late treaty payment; about 150 died here in November 1850 of dysentery and measles, and another 150 died as they returned to Wisconsin.

Sibley House Historic Site

1357 Sibley Memorial Hwy., Mendota; 651/452-1596. The home of the fur trader and governor; the oldest residence in the state (1837).

Treaty Site History Center

1851 N. Minnesota Ave., St. Peter; 507/934-2160. Exhibits on the 1851 Treaty of Traverse des Sioux and area history.

Warden's House Museum

602 N. Main St., Stillwater; 651/439-5956. The only building left from the territorial prison. Exhibits on prison life, as well as on lumbering and area history.

5

Minnesota's Two-Front Civil War

Governor Alexander Ramsey was in Washington on April 13, 1861, when Confederate forces began the Civil War by bombarding the U.S. garrison at Fort Sumter in the harbor of Charleston, South Carolina. His election as governor two years earlier launched an era of Republican control of Minnesota that would last until the end of the century.

Ramsey went to Washington after Abraham Lincoln's presidential inauguration hoping to secure patronage appointments for Minnesota Republicans. After hearing of the attack on Fort Sumter, he dashed over to see the new secretary of war, Simon Cameron, an old friend and one-time ally in Pennsylvania politics. Ramsey offered the secretary one thousand Minnesota volunteers. Cameron, who was on the way to see the president, conveyed Ramsey's offer and Lincoln accepted. Thus, Minnesota was the first state to volunteer soldiers for the Union army, two days before the president issued a public call for seventy-five thousand enlistments to serve for three months.

A telegraph line had reached St. Paul the previous summer, and Ramsey used the new device to send a wire to his lieutenant governor, Ignatius Donnelly, advising him of the offer and urging him to put out a call for volunteers. The word quickly spread around the state, and within a few days a thousand men were marching on the parade ground at Fort Snelling. In early May, when Lincoln called for three-year enlistments, the companies at Fort Snelling were formed into the First Regiment of Minnesota Volunteers, the first three-year regiment to join the Union army.

By the end of 1861, Minnesota men in uniform numbered 4,400, or about ten percent of the white males of military age in the state and comparable to the turnout of volunteers in neighboring Wisconsin. For both states the enlistments represented a higher proportion of the population than has ever stepped forward in the first year of any war the United States has fought. Motives for enlisting were mixed, as they are in all human endeavors. Opposition to slavery seemed perhaps least important because Minnesotans had little contact with the "peculiar institution" and were as racially biased as most white Americans, northern or southern. The soldiers themselves most commonly expressed the sentiment of patriotism and a desire to preserve the Union. A typical enlistee wrote his parents in May 1861, "I go feeling that I am right and in a good cause, and if that be the case, I will not fear. Tell all my brothers and sisters to stand firm by the Union and by the glorious liberties which, under God, we enjoy."

Equally important, it seems likely, was an opportunity to escape the drudgery of farm chores and see a bit of the world at government expense. For many rural youths the trip east was their first ride on a train and first glimpse of a bustling city. No one thought the conflict would be lengthy or very bloody. Indeed, many a young man fretted over the need for military exercises, fearing that the war would be over before he could experience the thrill of battle.

From Bull Run to Shiloh

The First Minnesota began marching and drilling at Fort Snelling in May 1861. The ladies of Winona had sewn neat gray uniforms for the company enlisted in that town, but the rest of the regiment wore state-furnished garments of red-flannel shirts, black trousers, and black hats. The regiment was not issued regulation blue army uniforms until August, after its first combat experience. The governor appointed the officers of the regiment, and political favoritism inevitably became a factor. However, Ramsey's choice for commander, with the rank of colonel, was an excellent one. Willis A. Gorman, former governor of the territory, veteran of the Mexican War, and a strict disciplinarian, ignored the grumbling and complaints and forged the unit into one of the army's crack regiments.

In mid-June, after only a month of training, the First Minnesota was ordered to the nation's capital, which was threatened by a buildup of Confederate forces in northern Virginia. The men went by steamboat to Prairie du Chien and from there by rail to Chicago and the East Coast. They camped near Alexandria, Virginia, and resumed their training, now uniformly equipped with army muskets. (They would later receive Springfield rifles.) A scant three weeks later the regiment got its baptism of fire at Bull Run.

On July 16 the regiment was ordered to march toward Manassas, a railroad junction in northern Virginia. A Confederate force commanded by General P. G. T. Beauregard stretched along Bull Run, a creek near the town. The Union army under General Irvin McDowell began the fight early that day. The Minnesota regiment arrived in the midst of the battle with orders to strike at advancing Confederate infantry. After beating back the attack, the regiment paused to regroup. About three o'clock in the afternoon the Confederates counterattacked, and McDowell ordered a retreat that turned into a panicky flight. Ill-trained Union troops dropped their weapons and fled into the nation's capital, carrying with them politicians who had come out in their carriages to see the show. The Minnesota First was one of the few regiments to hold its ground and retreat in good order. Jasper Searles of Hastings, who served as a medical corpsman, described the action in a letter home. We were "placed in the most dangerous position on the field and stood the fire *better than any of the other regts,*" he wrote. "We were commanded to retreat *three times* before we obeyed and then Gen'l McDowell's aid[e] was compelled to drive us off by such expressions as 'Retreat'!! 'God damn you'! 'Retreat'! 'What do you stand there for'!! 'I never saw such men to fight'!!" The regiment lost 20 percent of its men as killed, wounded, or missing.

President Lincoln replaced McDowell with General George B. McClellan, who spent the autumn and winter shaping civilian volunteers into the Army of the Potomac. In spring 1862 McClellan determined to make use of the Union's naval power to ferry his army down the Chesapeake Bay to the York River for an assault on Richmond, the Confederate capital. By the time McClellan completed this move and fought his way through Confederate defenses at Williamsburg it was early June, and the Confederates had a new commander, Robert E. Lee. The two armies fought a series of bloody but inconclusive battles from June 25 to July 1 (the Seven Days Battles). At Savage Station on June 29 the Minnesota First lost forty-eight killed and wounded, and the regiment suffered further losses while providing rear guard protection for McClellan's retreat to the James River landing. Twenty-two-year-old James A. Wright later recalled, "each day of the Seven Days added a full year to our ages, and the whole campaign left us ten years older than we began it."

By early 1862 three more regiments of Minnesota volunteers had formed, and they were sent to reinforce the army in the West in Tennessee along the Cumberland and Tennessee rivers. On January 19 the Second Minnesota received its combat experience in a relatively minor skirmish at Mill Springs, Kentucky. The regiment had the good fortune to arrive at Shiloh—the bloodiest battle of the war in the West—on April 9, two days after the fighting ended, and it was assigned to burial duty. That detail was bad enough. "Most of the Union soldiers had been buried already," wrote Private William Bircher, a drummer boy, "and the pioneers yonder in the mist were busily digging trenches for the poor fellows in gray. As we passed along we stopped to observe how thickly they were lying, here and there, like grass before a scythe in summer time."

The Third Minnesota was less fortunate. After Grant's victory at Shiloh, the Confederates retreated to east Tennessee and fortified the hills around Chattanooga. The Third Minnesota was given occupation duty and assigned to Murfreesboro, a rail center southeast of Nashville. On July 13, 1862, a force of Confederate raiders led by General Nathan Bedford Forrest struck the town, catching the Union troops completely by surprise. The commander of the Minnesota regiment lost his nerve and surrendered the garrison. The regiment was paroled (at this time, neither side in the Civil War had adequate facilities for prisoners of war) and sent home without its arms. The War Department discharged its officers from the army and sent the regiment, with new officers, to guard the Minnesota frontier. Ironically, it found itself in a new kind of war, this one with the Dakota people.

Members of the Third Minnesota Regiment, Company F, in Nashville, Tennessee, 1862. This regiment soon returned home to serve on the frontier.

Roots of the Dakota Conflict

Taoyateduta, whose name translated as His Red Nation (he was known to whites as Little Crow), was born about 1810 in Kaposia, a Mdewakanton Dakota village a few miles below modern St. Paul. After the Dakota land cession of 1837 his family moved across the Mississippi to the west bank. Little Crow received the training of a Dakota youth in the arts of the hunt and responsibilities to the community. He also exhibited an intense curiosity about the white intruders. When missionaries arrived in Minnesota in the 1830s, he attended a mission school and learned a bit of English and mathematics. Missionaries had devised an alphabet representing the sounds of Dakota speech, and he studied reading and writing his own language, a skill that later made him a force in treaty negotiations.

By the 1840s Little Crow rose to a position of leadership among the Mdewakanton. He married a succession of women, and each match secured him political allies, both among the Dakota and among the mixed-blood traders who moved up and down the Minnesota River valley. The clerk of one trader wrote of Little Crow: "He possesses a shrewd judgment, great foresight, and a comprehensive mind, together with the greatest of requisites in a statesman, caution." Little Crow was determined to preserve the Dakota culture and religion, but he was also shrewd enough to see the overwhelming might of the advancing white frontier and thus bargained for the best arrangement for his people.

Little Crow participated in the negotiations between the Mdewakanton and Wahpekute with the U.S. government that led to the Treaty of Mendota in 1851, and his role reflected his political ambiguity. He realized that a land cession was inevitable and that it was even strongly desired by some of the Dakota, including several of his relatives, who had become farmers and thus stood to benefit from government allotments and cash annuities. Instead of resisting the cession, he insisted on the payment of monies owed the Dakota from earlier treaties and concentrated on increasing the size of the proposed reservation to include some of the woodlands in the lower reaches of the Minnesota River where the Dakota could continue to hunt deer and make maple sugar. Government negotiators agreed to these terms, but later Congress reneged on the bargain. The Dakota Reservation was confined to the upper reaches of the river—largely a barren prairie. This betrayal was another in a series of incidents that made Little Crow and many members of his tribe distrust and detest the white people and their government.

The Mdewakanton and Wahpekute resettled at the southern end of the reservation near the government's Lower Sioux, or Redwood, Agency. In the mid-1850s, indicating the growing frustration of the Dakota, a radical element appeared—young men who favored active resistance to the advancing white frontier. When these militants left the reservation to slaughter settlers' cattle and steal their horses, the army treated them as renegades. In spring 1857 Inkpaduta (Scarlet Point), a renegade former leader, with a small band of Wahpekute militants, murdered more than thirty white settlers near Spirit Lake, Iowa. The army gave chase, but Inkpaduta slipped into Dakota Territory and disappeared in the plains.

In desperation, the Indian Department in Washington informed the Dakota of the Minnesota River that they were responsible for capturing and punishing Inkpaduta. Until they did so, they would receive no further annuities for the lands they had sold in 1851. Little Crow, still seeking some sort of compromise between a bull-headed government and his frustrated people, led a hunt for the renegade band that brought in a few captives

The Inkpaduta affair had at least two repercussions. It exposed the weakness of the government and its army on the frontier and reinforced the scorn of many Dakota for whites generally. In traditional Dakota culture young men proved their manhood by a coup that demonstrated courage in battle. Confined to a limited space by the reservation system and forcibly separated from their time-honored enemies, the Ojibwe, Dakota youths formed soldier lodges, a traditional organization for the hunt or in time of war, and dreamed of military glory. Each lodge selected its own leaders and rejected external authority, whether exercised by the U.S. Army or Dakota leaders.

The Inkpaduta affair also opened the eyes of Little Crow and other moderate leaders to what was happening to their society. An ever-larger number of Dakota tried to accommodate the white settlers' ways, learning to plow the tough prairie sod and tend cattle, exchanging blankets for pantaloons, and cutting their hair. Traditionalists, particularly the warriors of the soldier lodges, scorned the accommodators and called them "cut hairs." Thus the sense of community that had bound the Dakota together for centuries began to unravel, making effective leadership difficult, if not impossible.

The following year, under pressure from white pioneers who coveted the Dakota-occupied river bottomland, the federal government made new demands on the beleaguered tribes. In spring 1858 federal representatives invited Little Crow and other leaders to Washington. The Indians went willingly, thinking it a chance to make a plea for land-sale payments already due them that had never reached the tribe. Little Crow, "splendidly dressed" in a "calico hunting shirt" (observers often commented on his sartorial taste at negotiating sessions), pointed out to the commissioner for Indian affairs that the federal government had not lived up to any of its promises under the land-sale treaties, and, as a result, it had beggared his people, who now had neither land nor credit. Making vague promises of payments, the commissioner put off the Indian leader and for the next two months deliberately wore down the Indian delegation with half-promises and counter-allegations. He then revealed the true purpose of the talks and demanded that the Dakota cede the half of their reservation that lay on the north side of the river.

The Indians resisted. Little Crow pointed out that they had little incentive to sell additional lands when they had not been paid for

1858 Dakota Indian treaty delegation in Washington, DC.
Standing: Big Eagle, Traveling Hail, Red Legs. Seated: Medicine Bottle,
Thief, unidentified man. Broken promises and late annuity payments
led to the U.S.–Dakota War of 1862.

Photo by Charles DeForest Fredericks

past sales. The commissioner never made a serious attempt to negotiate and instead tried to intimidate the Indians by claiming that, under the principle of national supremacy, the United States was the actual owner of their lands and could remove the Indian people at will. Realizing that they had no alternative but to sign a treaty, Little Crow and the others sought the best price possible. In this they were supported by several traders who had accompanied the delegation to Washington. The Indians expected a fair price, which for bottom-lands could reach five dollars an acre. The wording of the signed treaty, however, left the price up to the U.S. Senate, which would have to ratify the agreement. The Senate delayed its consent for three years and then inserted a price of thirty cents an acre.

After signing the treaty, the commissioner gave the Dakota leaders some extra travel money (warning them, to Little Crow's disgust, not to spend it on whiskey), and the delegation returned to Minnesota. Upon his arrival at the Lower Sioux Agency, Little Crow tried to sell the treaty to his people by telling them of the handsome price they would get for their lands. The farmers were quite content, since the government cash would enable them to buy plows and oxen. The warriors were angry, and the soldier lodges were outraged. Congress delayed until March 1861 before appropriating funds for the sale. When the money finally arrived in the Minnesota River valley all of it went to the traders to pay for food, clothing, and utensils sold to the Indians on credit.

Discredited among his own people and superseded by other leaders, Little Crow virtually disappeared from the historical record until the Dakota War broke out in summer 1862.

The Dakota War

The winter of 1861–62 was unusually severe, and by spring the Dakota suffered an acute food shortage. The agencies at Yellow Medicine (Upper Sioux) and Redwood (Lower Sioux) had food in their warehouses, but U.S. government agents were holding it in reserve until the annuity money arrived. The government's annuities were due to be delivered in mid-summer, but Congress delayed the appropriation, in part over a debate on whether to make the payment in paper currency or gold coin.

By mid-summer Indian agents had given out some supplies at the Redwood Agency, but the Sisseton and Wahpeton at Yellow Medicine were still going hungry. On August 4 a mob of angry Indians broke into the Yellow Medicine Agency warehouse and carried off several sacks of flour. Learning of the incident, Little Crow hurried north to consult with the Yellow Medicine agent. Reminding the agent that the government annuities were due any day, Little Crow suggested that he persuade private traders to loan food to the Indians until the government funds arrived. The agent summoned a meeting of traders and conveyed the request. One of the most important traders, Andrew Myrick, who had stores at both agencies (and with whom Little Crow had an account), arose and said, his voice full of scorn, "So far as I am concerned, if they are hungry, let them eat grass." This was a deliberate insult thrown in the face of Little Crow and the Dakota leaders.

In the meantime, a troop of soldiers had arrived from Fort Ridgely, and the army persuaded the government agent to release barrels of pork and flour to the Indians. Placated, many of the Sisseton and Wahpeton departed on August 9 to hunt buffalo in Dakota Territory. Little Crow returned to the Redwood Agency, giving the agent there the impression that he was satisfied with the outcome. Ominously, Myrick's stinging insult spread from one mouth to another throughout the reservation.

As so often happens, the powder keg was set afire by youthful hotheads. On August 17 a party for four young men were hunting near the farming community of Acton, some thirty miles from the reservation. They quarreled with a settler and shot the settler, his wife, and a family of neighbors—five whites in all. Taking the settlers' horses, they raced home to their village of Rice Creek near the Redwood Agency. In the past, the village leaders would have turned the culprits over to the army for punishment. The four youths, arriving late in the evening, reported their deed, not to village elders, but to members of the soldier lodge.

The lodge summoned members for a meeting and debated throughout the night. More than the fate of the young culprits was at stake, for the federal government was certain to hold the entire village liable for recompense to the settlers. Because that was a new reminder of the Indians' growing subjection, militants came to dominate the discussion. Toward dawn the lodge concluded that war was preferable to continued subservience and that a united Dakota nation had a good chance of driving all the white farmers out of their river valley permanently. Militants dismissed the U.S. Army as preoccupied with the Civil War and reminded their lodge soldiers that the Spirit Lake and Acton massacres had shown that whites were easy to kill.

By dawn the lodge had decided on war, but they had to bring into the cause soldiers from other lodges in the villages grouped around the Redwood Agency. To recruit openly was not possible because village councils would be dominated by moderates and farmers. They needed a charismatic leader who could attract an instant following throughout the Dakota nation. There was only one such leader.

As the sky turned light in the east, members of the Rice Creek lodge along with leaders from other villages appeared at Little Crow's door. Although Little Crow had spurned farming, he lived in a wood-frame house built by agency carpenters and possessed a cow in a shed at the rear. He listened to the militants' litany of complaints against the agency thieves employed by the U.S. government and the "Dutchmen" (a term they applied to both the Germans in the neighborhood and the Indian farmers) who were defacing the land.

Little Crow was reluctant to join the cause, knowing full well that it meant disaster for his people. He pointed out that the young men standing at his door knew nothing of the power of the U.S. government and the number of soldiers it commanded. "We are only little herds of buffaloes," he said, but "the white men are like the locusts when they fly so thick that the whole sky is a snowstorm. You may kill one—two—ten; yes as many as the leaves in the forest yonder, and their brothers will not miss them. . . . Count your fingers all day long and white men with guns in their hands will come faster than you can count." But the militants would not be put off by logic. They began to taunt him for cowardice, an unbearable slander. In the end, Little Crow relented, declaring, "You will die like the rabbits when the hungry wolves hunt them in the Hard Moon [January]. Taoyateduta is not a coward; he will die with you." His decision, though fateful, was quite understandable. Little Crow clearly felt the need to recover the leadership prestige that he had lost, and he had been repeatedly stung by a government that failed to appreciate his efforts at compromise.

Runners carried word to the villages around the Redwood Agency. Most of the village leaders declared that it was folly to make war on the whites, but they were ignored. The Dakota were deeply divided on the issue of war. Many full bloods were traditionalists and favored war to preserve the old ways. Other full bloods had accommodated the white man's ways and favored peace. Both groups had relatives who were mixed bloods, some who were willing to fight but many more who were peaceful. The war, like the one being fought to the east, split families. Regardless of family ties, the young men made the decisions, and the village leaders went along in order to hold on to their putative positions of leadership. Like Little Crow, they had become visible commanders without real authority.

The Redwood Agency became the first target. Traders and Indian agents were sitting down to breakfast in the early morning of August 18 when a long file of painted men entered the compound, broke into small groups, and, at a prearranged signal, began firing into the shops and houses. Many people died in the initial attack, and more lost their lives while trying to flee. Among these was Andrew Myrick, who leaped out of a second-story window and was shot before he could reach the woods. When his body was found days later, his mouth was stuffed full of grass. Forty-seven people escaped, in part because the undisciplined soldiers paused to loot the stores and in part because a courageous ferryman made several trips across the river before succumbing to an Indian bullet.

Fort Ridgely, on the edge of the Dakota reservation and some thirteen miles to the east of the Redwood Agency, was the nearest army post. The first refugees reached the fort about ten o'clock in the morning. In command was Captain John S. Marsh, who had been at Bull Run with a Wisconsin regiment but knew little of fighting Indians. Leaving thirty men to hold the fort, Marsh started for the Redwood Agency with forty-six men. Marsh rode a mule; most of the others were in horse-drawn wagons. He appeared at the Redwood ferry about noon and found the flat-bottomed boat conveniently moored as if ready for the crossing. The men left the wagons and proceeded single-file toward the ferry. Indians hiding in the underbrush opened fire, and a dozen soldiers fell. Marsh rallied the remainder of his troops, but his losses mounted as the afternoon wore on. Marsh tried to swim the river and drowned in the attempt. That night twenty-three infantrymen straggled back to Fort Ridgely.

By the afternoon of August 18 word of the conflict had spread to the villages around the Upper Agency at Yellow Medicine. Soldier lodges prepared to attack the agency, but a Christian Indian, John Other Day, who had a white wife and a mixed-blood child, warned the traders and led them across the river and on to prairie farm communities. The Dakota attacked the next morning, looting and burning the stores, but only one trader was killed.

After the ambush at the Redwood ferry Fort Ridgely was virtually defenseless. Because many men were sick or wounded in the fighting, the lieutenant in command could count on only twenty-two effectives. More than 250 refugees milled about the compound, but they were more hindrance than help. The majority were women and children, and the wounded filled the fort's hospital.

Little Crow's strategy was to gain control of the entire Minnesota River valley and force the federal government, distracted by war in the South, to the bargaining table. But before his forces could sweep down the valley, he first had to capture Fort Ridgely. On the morning of August 19 Little Crow summoned a council to plan an attack on the fort. Unfortunately, he discovered that his army had largely evaporated. With no leadership except their own instinctual frustration and anger, his young soldiers had dispersed into the countryside, indiscriminately attacking farm families and launching an attack on New Ulm. Within days the entire south and west portion of Minnesota was a battleground, from Fort Abercrombie north of Breckenridge to Stearns and Wright counties along the Mississippi to the state boundary with Iowa.

Little Crow was unable to collect a force sufficient to mount an attack on Fort Ridgely until the morning of August 20. The group numbered about four hundred. In the interim word of the fighting had spread, and U.S. Army units that had been sent elsewhere raced back to Fort Ridgely. By the time the Indians attacked, the fort's defenders, including some armed settlers, numbered about 180. Like most frontier outposts of the time, Fort Ridgely was a collection of buildings gathered around a parade ground with no outer stockade. The Indians attacked from three sides, capturing and burning some outer buildings, but the defenders held firm. Little Crow withdrew to await reinforcements. On August 22, with a force numbering about eight hundred, he attacked again. The defenders had placed a couple of the army's artillery pieces at strategic locations, and again the attackers were driven back.

The Dakota warriors abandoned the assault on Fort Ridgely and, on August 23, turned toward New Ulm, a predominantly German community of about nine hundred people some ten miles downriver from the fort. Little Crow had been wounded in the attack on the fort, and it is not clear whether he participated in, or even favored, the attack on New Ulm, which turned out to be the fiercest battle of the war. Youthful Dakota soldiers took an uncoordinated swipe at the town during the wild afternoon of August 19, and they may have insisted on a return. The town was rich in booty, and most of its young men had gone off to fight the Confederates. Unfortunately for the Dakota, the communities farther downriver sent detachments of armed men to New Ulm when they learned of the conflict, and by August 23 the village had about three hundred defenders.

The houses of the village were widely scattered on a narrow plateau between a wooded bluff to the rear and a wooded descent to the river below. The 650-man Dakota force, using the woods for cover, quickly captured and burned the outer houses, squeezing the populace into a four-block-square center of the town. There the attack faltered as twilight fell upon the scene. The next day the Indians maintained a semblance of siege with some long-range gunshots while the noncombatants in the village, who had been huddling for five days "in cellars and close rooms like sheep in a cattle car," ran short of food, medicine, and ammunition.

On the evening of August 25 Little Crow participated in a council that decided on a gradual withdrawal to the west. Little Crow reached the Yellow Medicine Agency three days later and found the Dakota people more badly divided than ever. Some of the Sisseton and Wahpeton had fled onto the plains to join their brethren living along the Missouri River. Others organized a soldier lodge to make peace with the federal government. The remnants of Little Crow's army, primarily made up of Mdewakanton and Wahpekute, wanted to continue the fight. The two factions squabbled over possession of the approximately 150 whites and mixed bloods they held captive, each aware that the captives would be an important bargaining chip when the U.S. Army arrived.

On the day after the conflict broke out, Governor Alexander Ramsey had given Henry H. Sibley a colonel's commission and asked him to lead an expedition against the Dakota. Sibley had no military experience, but he knew the landscape and the Dakota language and customs. He put together a force of fourteen hundred, including the newly recruited Sixth Minnesota. He set out from Mendota on August 20 and reached Fort Ridgely eight days later. After sending the refugees to St. Paul, Sibley dispatched a detachment of 170 men into the countryside to discover the whereabouts of the Indians and to bury the bodies of murdered settlers. On September 2 the men were

Attack on New Ulm during the Sioux Outbreak
The determined townsfolk held off a disorganized siege by the Dakota.
Oil by Anton Gag, 1904

camped in a wooded site called Birch Coulee, some sixteen miles from Fort Ridgely. A force of 350 Indians led by Little Crow's lieutenants, Gray Bird and Mankato, attacked the group at dawn. Thirty men from the detachment were wounded and most of the party's horses killed in the first few minutes. Sounds of the fighting were heard at Fort Ridgely, and Sibley sent out a relief force. By the time it arrived the Indians had departed and thirteen soldiers lay dead on the field, four more were dying, and nearly fifty were seriously wounded. These were, for the U.S. Army, the heaviest casualties of the Dakota conflict.

Sibley decided to use the occasion to establish direct contact with Little Crow. He left a message attached to a stake on the Birch Coulee battlefield asking why Little Crow had started the war. Indian scouts carried the paper to Little Crow, who was camped near Hazelwood, a community of Indian farmers, some of whom were his relatives. Little Crow replied that the federal government had repeatedly broken its promises and betrayed the Indians and mentioned a "great many prisoners women & children." These captives were both white and mixed blood. In a second communication of September 12 Little Crow referred again to the "one hundred and fifty-five prisoners," implying that the captives might be exchanged for government concessions. Sibley, having been informed by mixed-blood scouts that the Indians were hopelessly divided, did not reply. Instead he asked the governor for reinforcements. General John Pope (after being humiliated by Lee and Jackson at the Second Battle of Bull Run) now commanded the army units involved in the Dakota conflict. He sent Sibley the Third Minnesota, recently paroled from Kentucky.

Sibley resumed his march and by September 21 camped near Wood Lake, a few miles from the Yellow Medicine Agency. Little Crow's army had dwindled and was rife with internal squabbling. On the morning of September 23 the men of the Third Minnesota wandered a half-mile from the army camp to dig potatoes in a field. They stumbled upon Indians who were creeping through the grass to mount a surprise attack on the army camp. A general melee ensued, and this time the Indians got the worst of it. They withdrew after two hours, leaving fourteen dead on the field, among them Mankato, Little Crow's most valuable lieutenant.

Vengeance

While the Battle of Wood Lake was in progress, the farmer Indians recovered most of the captives remaining in Little Crow's camp. The farmers took the captives to their own camp and dug trenches to fortify the camp against an expected attack by the militants. When the defeated Indian militants straggled back from the battlefield and realized what had happened, some were outraged and demanded an assault on the fortified village. Little Crow, however, could not bear the thought of a fratricidal war among the Dakota, especially because a number of the peace-minded people were his relatives. He realized, moreover, that the war was over, and he told his wives and children to pack for a flight to the West. As his final act before departing, he addressed the remnants of his army and persuaded them not to attack the village holding the captives. Many militants decided to join him on his trek to the western plains and Canada. The fortified village and its 269 white and mixed-blood captives soon became known to the army as Camp Release.

During his march west from Fort Ridgely, Sibley let it be known through his mixed-blood emissaries that he intended to punish only those Indians who had killed white civilians. When Sibley arrived at Camp Release on September 26, he did not attack. Instead he set up his own camp nearby and staged an impressive ceremony for accepting the released captives. Persuaded by Sibley's apparent altruism, Indians who had been involved in the fighting, many of them from Little Crow's tribe, drifted into Camp Release. The settlement numbered more than two thousand by mid-October.

Then Sibley struck. On October 11 his troops surrounded Camp Release as well as another village at Yellow Medicine. The Indians were disarmed, and the men were brought before a military tribunal, a procedure never before used with Indians. Acting as prosecutor, judge, and jury, the military commission "tried" up to forty Dakota men each day. The Indians were not formally charged with crimes; they were simply asked to tell their stories. Many readily admitted that they carried a gun and participated in a battle, though most insisted that they had not harmed anyone. The commissioners decided that being at a battle and firing a gun was sufficient evidence of guilt warranting capital punishment. By November 5 the commission had "tried" 392 Indians, sentenced 307 to death, and sent 16 to prison. Sibley commuted one death sentence, approved the remainder, and forwarded the court records to General Pope.

While the Minnesota press, mindful that more than four hundred settlers had been killed, screamed for blood and vengeance, President Lincoln requested the records and calmly reviewed them. He concluded that capital punishment was warranted only where there was concrete evidence of murder or rape of civilians. He accordingly approved death sentences for only thirty-nine of the convicted men. Although disappointed by the president's charity, white Minnesotans were determined to make the most of the public execution. The condemned men were taken to Mankato, where a gallows, designed to accommodate all of them at once, was built. One Indian received a last-minute reprieve; the remaining thirty-eight were hanged in a single stroke on December 26, 1862, while a crowd of thousands cheered. It was the largest mass execution in U.S. history.

Lincoln had only commuted the death sentences to prison terms, so the federal government sent 326 Dakota men to a prison in Davenport, Iowa. Government representatives seized what remained of the Dakota reservation in Minnesota and marched seventeen hundred Indians, mostly women and children, to temporary confinement at Fort Snelling. Many of these people died during the winter from bad food, disease, and exposure. In the spring they were moved to a reservation on the Missouri River. The rest of the Minnesota Dakota people fled to the plains to join the tribes that had moved there a century earlier. Of the once-great Dakota nation only about 250 Dakotas and mixed bloods remained in Minnesota.

What of Little Crow? He found himself unwelcome both in Canada and among the Indians of the plains. The tribes living along the Missouri River feared that his presence might bring the U.S. Army down on them, and they urged him to move on.

In June 1863 Little Crow, with some of his family and a few friends—the party totaled nineteen—returned to Minnesota and camped near Yellow Medicine. Realizing that his days were numbered, he apparently wanted nothing more than to return to the forests of his youth. On July 3 he was picking wild raspberries with his son Wowinape when two settlers came upon them. Without bothering to identify the Indians or determine their intentions, the men opened fire. Little Crow fired a shot in return and fell, mortally wounded. His son put new moccasins on his feet for his trip to the next world, gave him a drink of water, and memorized his last words. His body was taken into the town of Hutchinson where the townspeople desecrated it. Although some thought it might be Little Crow, the body was not positively identified until a few days later.

Thus ended the life of a man who, had he been born of another race and perhaps in another time, might have been a Bismarck, a Churchill, or a Woodrow Wilson—gunned down while picking berries.

Captured Dakota in enclosure along the Minnesota River
below Fort Snelling, 1862. During their confinement
and after their removal from Minnesota, many died of hunger and disease.

Photo by Benjamin Franklin Upton.

From Antietam to Appomattox

When General George McClellan abandoned his bloody but inconclusive Peninsula Campaign in July 1862, President Lincoln replaced him as commander of the Army of the Potomac with General John Pope. While the navy shuttled the army, including the First Minnesota Volunteers, back up the Potomac River to Washington, generals Robert E. Lee and Stonewall Jackson dispatched Pope at the Second Battle of Bull Run. Lee then led his army across the Potomac to mount his first invasion of the North. Lincoln restored McClellan to command, and the two armies met at Antietam Creek, in Maryland, on September 17, 1862, the bloodiest single day of the war. The First Minnesota was involved in one of McClellan's ill-coordinated attacks that day and lost 147 men, killed and wounded.

Private Samuel Bloomer, a Swiss immigrant who had enlisted two weeks after Fort Sumter fell, was wounded in the leg that day and left a diary of his experiences. The Union army began sending nurses onto the battlefield after the hideous experience of First Bull Run where wounded men lay untended for days, but in 1862 it was only beginning to develop field hospitals and an ambulance corps. Wounded in the leg while in a cornfield where some of the fiercest fighting occurred, Bloomer lay there amid a sea of corpses the rest of the day and all night. In the morning he was awakened by a "secesh" (short for secessionist, a common pejorative term for Confederate soldiers) who wanted nothing more than a drink from Bloomer's canteen. Late in the afternoon "4 secesh came with a stretcher & took me up to a barn where there were about a 100 more of our men. & there took our names intending to perrol us in the morning."

The mixture of terror, hate, and human kindness that emerges from the pages of Bloomer's diary is a microcosm of this terrible war. During the predawn hours of September 19, "the secesh skedaddaled of[f] for pards unknown" (Lee's army had retired back across the Potomac), and members of the First Minnesota came around looking for their dead and wounded comrades. The diary entry for September 20 reads: "This day will long be remembered by me, for about 8 o'clock AM the doctors put me on the table & amputated my right leg above my knee. And from then the suffering commenced in earnest." Private Bloomer returned to Stillwater, married, raised a family, and lived until 1917.

The First Minnesota, its ranks severely depleted, took part in some skirmishes in the Battle of Fredericksburg in December, but after that did not see combat again until the following summer at Gettysburg. The stream of volunteers that had sustained the regiment through the first year of the war dried up by the end of 1862. Volunteers stepped forward early in the war on the quaint notion that the war would be relatively brief and bloodless. That idea evaporated in the ferocious fights of 1862—the Seven Days, Shiloh, and Antietam. In March 1863 Congress instituted a draft. Every man between the ages of twenty and forty-five had to register, and a lottery determined which men would be conscripted. Once drafted, a man was entitled to hire a substitute if he could find one, or he could pay the federal government a commutation fee of three hundred dollars. Small wonder that critics would label it a rich man's war and a poor man's fight.

While draft resisters rioted in some of the eastern cities, the men of Minnesota, for the most part, accepted the need for military conscription. Wealthier men naturally looked for substitutes, and sharp entrepreneurs responded to the demand by opening business offices that guaranteed to furnish substitutes. The extent of their reach can be measured by the admission of the *St. Paul Pioneer* a year later: "Most of the substitutes enlisted have been Indians and half-breeds of the Chippewa persuasion."

The practice throughout the Union army was to use volunteers and draftees to form new regiments, rather than reinforce old ones. As a result, the First Minnesota stood at only half-strength when General Lee crossed the Potomac in late June 1863 to undertake his second invasion of the North. President Lincoln, still searching for a general who could win a battle, placed George G. Meade in command of the Army of the Potomac three days before the two armies stumbled into one another on July 1 near the Pennsylvania hamlet of Gettysburg.

By the end of a day of ragged fighting Meade had concentrated his forces in a defensive posture on a range of low hills. The Union line was in the shape of a fishhook with the left flank (the eye of the fishhook) anchored on two steep hills, Round Top and Little Round Top. In front of Little Round Top lay an array of huge boulders with crevices between them up to ten feet high. Beyond this moonscape, called "The Devil's Den," lay an open field planted in wheat and beyond that, a peach orchard. The Confederate army lay farther beyond, on another low ridge. In the center of the Union force the Second Corps stretched along Cemetery Ridge, and to its left the Third Corps occupied the gap between Cemetery Ridge and Little Round Top. A New York politician, General Daniel E. Sickles, commanded the Third Corps. The First Minnesota arrived on the battlefield at dawn on July 2 and was placed on Cemetery Ridge with other regiments of the Second Corps.

Lee's strategy on that morning was to send one of his corps, commanded by General James Longstreet, on a flanking move against the Union left on the Round Tops. Longstreet started slowly, and his men did not reach the peach orchard until mid-afternoon. In the meantime, Sickles foolishly abandoned his defensive position on the ridge and advanced his corps into the wheat field and the peach orchard. There, in mid-afternoon, he encountered Longstreet's advancing men. A ferocious fight ensued with staggering losses on both sides. Toward sundown, Sickles's line broke and retreated in disorder across Cemetery Ridge, passing the men from Minnesota. A. P. Hill, commanding the Confederate center, sent two brigades into the gap, and it looked as if the Union line would be broken.

General Winfield S. Hancock, commanding the Second Corps, had several regiments in reserve, but he needed time—five or ten minutes at least—to bring them up. He spotted the Minnesota troops and galloped over to their commander, Colonel William Colvill, shouting "What regiment is this?"

"The First Minnesota."

"Colonel, do you see those colors?" said Hancock, pointing to the regimental flags of the advancing Confederates. "Take Them!"

The Minnesotans poured off the hill amid a storm of shot. "Bullets whistled past us," wrote Sergeant Alfred Carpenter, "shells screeched over us; . . . comrade after comrade dropped from the ranks; but on the line went." The First Minnesota slammed into the first Confederate line and drove it back. The regiment then took cover under the bank of a dry brook and poured a withering fire into the attackers. Its action bought the time Hancock needed to bring up his reserves, and the Union line was stabilized. Concluded Civil War historian Bruce

Catton, "The whole war had suddenly come to a focus in this smoky hollow, with a few score westerners trading their lives for the time the army needed.... They had not captured the flag that Hancock had asked them to capture, but they still had their own flag and a great name."

Because three of its companies were on skirmishing duty July 2, the regiment that went on the attack at Hancock's command numbered only 262 men. All but forty-seven were killed or wounded, including Colonel Colvill and all his field officers. The companies that had been

Battle of Gettysburg
Minnesota's troops fought bravely and well in this pivotal battle.
Oil by Rufus Fairchild Zogbaum

employed as pickets returned to the regiment that evening. The next day, July 3, the First Minnesota stayed in the center of the Union line on Cemetery Ridge. General Lee had but one option. In desperation, he ordered a suicidal charge up the ridge by General George Pickett's division. Standing there, the First Minnesota bore the brunt of Pickett's charge, losing another seventeen men. But this day they achieved the triumph denied them the previous day—the capture of the enemy's flag. Marshall Sherman of Company C had seized the flag of the 28th Virginia. The battle was won; the tide of war had changed.

But there was no relief for the battered First Minnesota. Within six weeks it was facing, not Confederates, but angry Irishmen in New York.

On July 13, ten days after the Battle of Gettysburg, Irish workers in New York City attacked and burned the draft office. As Democrats, they had opposed the war, and as unskilled laborers, they had no desire to free the slaves of the South, who were certain to come north seeking jobs. What started out as a draft riot quickly turned political and racial. The mob of mostly Irish sacked and burned the homes of prominent Republicans and then turned against the city's black community. It lynched six blacks and burned the Colored Orphan Asylum. On the fourth day of rioting regiments detached from the Army of the Potomac rushed into the city. Treating the rioters as enemies, they fired indiscriminately into the mob and killed more than one hundred.

At that point the army ordered the First Minnesota to the city, expecting the westerners to have cooler heads. By the time the regiment arrived on August 23 calm was restored, and the regiment's only job was to keep order while the federal government completed its draft lottery. On September 5, the ladies of the Carlton Avenue Methodist Episcopal Church treated the regiment to a sumptuous dinner, and the next day the men boarded a steamship to return south. The regiment fought two more battles in central Virginia that autumn before returning home in February 1864. Their enlistments having expired, these brave men mustered out of the army at Fort Snelling.

The other regiments recruited in Minnesota at the beginning of the war fought with generals Grant and Sherman in the West. The Third Minnesota, having proved its mettle in the Dakota conflict, rejoined Grant's army and participated in the siege of Vicksburg, as did the Fourth and Fifth Minnesota. The fall of Vicksburg on July 4, 1863 (a day after the Battle of Gettysburg) split the Confederacy and opened the Mississippi River to Union gunboats and supply vessels. Thereafter the Third Minnesota marched west to capture the Arkansas capital of Little Rock, while the Second and Fourth moved east to join in the assault on Lookout Mountain and Missionary Ridge, the heights overlooking Chattanooga (November 1863). In spring 1864 President Lincoln ordered Grant east to take command of the Army of the Potomac, and Sherman became commander of the armies in Tennessee.

In summer 1864, with an army now numbering almost one hundred thousand men, including six Minnesota regiments, Sherman moved south from Chattanooga toward Atlanta, capturing the city on September 2. The southern commander, General John B. Hood, slipped around the Union army and dashed for Tennessee, hoping to cut off Sherman's line of supplies. Instead of giving pursuit, Sherman detached a corps, including the Fifth, Seventh, Ninth, and Tenth Minnesota, to keep an eye on Hood. This detachment defeated Hood in the Battle of Nashville in December.

Meanwhile, Sherman decided to forget about supplies, live off the land, and cut a swath of destruction across Georgia from Atlanta to the sea. He started out on November 15 with sixty-two thousand men, including the Second and Fourth Minnesota. Unencumbered by a baggage train, the army moved rapidly, but the soldiers themselves became pack mules. Each man carried an eleven-pound rifle, one hundred rounds of ammunition, clothing, cooking utensils (each had a one-or-two-quart pot, every sixth carried a frying pan), blanket, and a piece of a tent. The total load, even without food, was about forty pounds.

The army marched on parallel routes, pillaging the orchards and vegetable gardens of Georgia farmers, slaughtering their cows and pigs. "Bummers" roamed the countryside without command or discipline on the flanks of the army, gathering food and livestock and looting plantation houses. Although the forefront of each column fared rather well, the center and rear came upon nothing but smoke and ashes and often went hungry. On December 15, as the army approached Savannah, William Bircher, a Second Minnesota drummer boy, complained that the only food yielded by the countryside was rice, and when threshed it was so full of sand that they dared not chew it. "By doing so we did not feel the grit until we got through, then, after rinsing the mouth, we soon forgot that we had been filling up on sand mixed with a little rice."

Sherman's army rested for six weeks in Savannah, recovering its strength with supplies brought in by the navy. On February 5, 1865, it crossed the Savannah River into South Carolina, "the hell-hole of secession," in the opinion of a Union cavalry commander. "Our army did not lack enthusiasm," William Bircher recorded in his diary, "and the prospect of a march through South Carolina was one that was exceedingly relished." Three days later he recorded the day as "Warm and very windy. We marched eleven miles. The whole army was burning with the insatiable desire to wreak vengeance on South Carolina." On February 9 he reported: "Warm and pleasant. Marched twenty miles and destroyed all the houses, barns, and fences on our route." Then the spring rains set in, and the mood of joyful exuberance faded. Streams swelled and roads turned to mud. On March 1 Bircher recorded a march of twelve miles that lasted well into the night before they found high ground for their camp. "If we never knew before," he wrote, "what South Carolina mud was like, we knew it then. It was not only knee-deep, but so sticky that, when we set one foot down we could scarcely pull the other out."

As he had in Georgia and Mississippi, General Sherman ordered his army to tear up every railroad they encountered. Both sides depended heavily on railroads throughout the war for the movement of troops and supplies, and, unsure of the location of the Confederate armies he bypassed, Sherman did not want to risk a surprise attack on his rear. Detail parties of soldiers lifted entire sections of track, detached the rails from the ties, and built bonfires with the ties. They heated the iron rails over the fires and wrapped them around trees ("Sherman's neckties") to ensure that the rails could never be used again. Sometimes the rails were bent into a "U.S." and left standing against a tree as a reminder of Union patriotism.

The march continued into North Carolina, a state that seceded only reluctantly after the war began, and the vandalism ceased. A

Confederate army commanded by General Joseph E. Johnston appeared on Sherman's front but declined to give battle. On April 9 news spread through the ranks of Lee's surrender to Grant at Appomattox. Colonel Lucius Hubbard, commander of the Fifth Minnesota, then stationed in Alabama, wrote to his wife: "The heat, dust and fatigue were forgotten; the weary became rested and the footsore suddenly cured. Officers and soldiers abandoned themselves to the most extravagant demonstrations of joy. Everybody cheered and shouted until they were hoarse." Five days later came news of the assassination of President Lincoln, and the joy turned to mourning. "There is a feeling of regret among the troops," wrote Colonel Hubbard, "that the war is likely soon to cease. They feel that the Presidents assassination calls for a terrible vengeance, and they regard themselves the proper instruments for its execution. Woe be to the people of the south, if hostilities again commence. In President Lincoln [the southerners] lost their best friend."

The war, nevertheless, did not resume. A week later Sherman accepted the surrender of General Johnston, and in May other Confederate generals surrendered their forces in Tennessee and Texas. The war was over. The Minnesotans went home. The hale and hearty found new opportunities in the government's offer of free land under the Homestead Act. The maimed and shell-shocked were less fortunate since the government had no facilities for the long-term care of veterans. Within a few years, however, the Grand Army of the Republic, a veterans' organization that functioned as a fund-raising arm of the Republican Party, persuaded Congress to grant generous pensions to Civil War veterans, as well as to their widows and orphans.

VISITING HISTORY

The state's few Civil War sites are outnumbered by places associated with the Dakota War, a traumatic event for both Dakotas and whites.

Birch Coulee Battlefield

3 miles north of Morton at the junction of Co. Hwys. 2 and 18, 1 mile east of U.S. Hwy. 71; 507/697-6321. A trail with interpretive signs provides a moving account of the battle.

Brown County Historical Society

2 N. Broadway St., New Ulm; 507/233-2616. The third-floor gallery focuses entirely on the Dakota Conflict and the Civil War.

Camp Release State Monument

U.S. Hwy. 212, 1.5 miles southwest of Montevideo. The site of Sibley's camp at the time of the surrender of the Dakotas and the release of whites who had been protected and held captive.

Civil War Recruiting Station

Wasioja. A small stone building constructed in 1855 and used in 1861 to sign up troops. The state's only remaining recruiting station, operated by the Dodge County Historical Society (507/635-5508).

Dakota Internment Camp historical marker

MN Hwy. 5 in Fort Snelling State Park. Some sixteen hundred Dakota people were held here in the winter of 1862–63. About 130 died during the captivity, and the rest were sent to South Dakota and then Nebraska.

Fort Ridgely

Fort Ridgely State Park, off MN Hwy. 4, 7 miles south of Fairfax; 507/426-7888. The restored commissary building houses historical exhibits on both fronts of the Civil War.

Grand Army of the Republic Hall

308 Marshall Ave., Litchfield; 320/693-8911. The last remaining GAR hall in the state, built to look like a fort, with an exhibit of Civil War artifacts.

Historic Fort Snelling

MN Hwys. 5 and 55, Minneapolis; 612/726-1171. Interpretive center with military history exhibits; special Civil War weekend in August.

Upper Sioux Agency State Park

About 8 miles west of Granite Falls on MN Hwy. 67; 320/564-4777. Signs mark the foundations of the agency buildings; an employee duplex still stands.

6

Empires in Green

Like most people in Minnesota, Cadwallader Washburn had not expected a lengthy war, nor a very deadly one. Even so, he was in a position to respond handsomely to any wartime summons—to provide lumber, for instance, for the Union military bases built in Missouri, Illinois, and Kentucky. In 1856 Washburn and his brother William purchased stock in Robert Smith's newly chartered corporation, the Minneapolis Mill Company. And Washburn was actually able to expand his Minneapolis investments during the panic that flattened other businessmen in 1857. The small investors who had helped Smith form the corporation were forced to sell their stock in the hard times, and the Washburn brothers, who had made a fortune in Wisconsin's pineries, bought them out. By the time the Civil War broke out in 1861 the Minneapolis Mill Company was in the hands of only four men—Smith, the two Washburns, and Dorilus Morrison. Morrison, a cousin of the Washburns, moved with them from Maine to Mineral Point, Wisconsin, and managed their Wisconsin-Minnesota lumbering interests.

A native New Englander, Cadwallader Washburn took Lowell, Massachusetts, as his model in developing Minneapolis. There, early in the century, Boston investors built a canal around the falls of the Merrimack River and channeled a stream of rushing water through a succession of water-powered textile mills. In 1857 the Minneapolis

Mill Company undertook construction of a dam at the head of the Falls of St. Anthony. Completed the following year, the structure channeled the waters of the Mississippi into a millpond for logs and thence into a canal fifty feet wide and 215 feet long below the bluffs on the west side of the river. Lengthened in later years, the canal thus opened a large area for future mills. Minneapolis Mill leased sites along the canal and built a maze of underground tunnels and mill-races to drive the mills' water wheels. Each lease agreement contained strict regulations concerning the use of water. Minneapolis Mill thus maintained tight control over the whole west-side manufacturing district.

The war stimulated the demand for lumber, and by the end of the fighting Minneapolis Mill Company owned or leased eight west-side sawmills, and the population of the young city had tripled to about ten thousand. By contrast the St. Anthony settlement on the east side of the river had languished. Franklin Steele, pioneer of St. Anthony, had obtained a corporate charter for the St. Anthony Falls Water Power Company in 1856 and had joined Minneapolis Mill in constructing the dam above the falls. Unfortunately, in forming his corporation Steele had turned to New York investors, and after the panic of 1857 this source of capital dried up. The shareholders held on to their stock but refused to invest in more. The company management was thus internally divided throughout the war and chronically short of money. In desperation it leased water rights and mill sites on an annual basis for whatever rent it could get, and without coordination the company fell steadily behind the west-side manufacturers in lumber output.

By the end of the war Cadwallader Washburn, who made his residence in La Crosse, Wisconsin, and never moved to Minneapolis, bought out Smith's interest in Minneapolis Mill Company and diversified into flour milling. Grist mills, small operations that ground the corn or wheat of neighboring farmers in return for a share of the crop, had been part of the Minnesota landscape since the first farmers appeared in the 1830s. The first merchant mill—where the mill owner purchased the grain and marketed the flour—was established on Hennepin Island in 1854 and leased water power from Franklin Steele. However, so little wheat was grown in the region at the time that the millers had to buy their product in Iowa and Wisconsin. When Minnesota farmers took up wheat growing in the 1860s, flour mills appeared among the lessees of Minneapolis Mill Company. Ever in the forefront of industrial progress, Washburn completed a mill of his own in 1866. An imposing structure of limestone six stories high, it was thought to be the largest flour mill west of Buffalo, New York (the milling center of the country up to that time).

By the end of the Civil War, Minneapolis— "Sawdust City"—was the lumbering capital of Minnesota and second only to St. Louis in lumber output in the Mississippi valley. Thanks to the organizational acumen of Cadwallader Washburn and his associates, it was also poised to become the flour milling center of the nation. Making possible these twin industrial developments—which together comprised Minnesota's "industrial revolution"—was the opening of Minnesota's two wilderness empires, the prairies of the southwest and the pine forests of the north.

From Prairie to Wheat Belt

In 1858, the year Minnesota became a state, it imported from its neighbors, Wisconsin and Iowa, more food than it exported. Its farms were small, with only a few acres under cultivation, and farm families consumed nearly everything they grew. Not surprisingly, the primary crop was corn, which fed not only the family but also its horses, cows, pigs, and chickens.

Even after the Dakota land cessions of 1851 farmers moving to the west clung to the valleys of the Minnesota River and its tributaries, where they continued to till small plots of land while letting their animals roam in the woods. The river bottomlands contained stands of oak, hickory, elm, and cottonwood that provided pioneer farm families with the wood they needed for shelter, fences, heating, and cooking. The soil below these trees was easily stirred, and among the tree stumps the pioneer farmers could plant corn and a garden of vegetables. In the uplands away from the river bottoms, the prairie soil, though actually richer in nutrients than woodland soils (a fact known to university agronomists but not to untutored farmers), was a tangled mass of roots that resisted the plow. The roots of big bluestem, the standard grass of the prairies, penetrated more than six feet into the earth.

In 1860, two years after Minnesota attained statehood, wheat passed corn as the state's ranking crop, and Minnesota became a food exporter as the first shipments of flour made their way to Chicago. The river bottoms had filled up, and new emigrants were moving onto the prairies. In 1862 Congress gave new stimulus to this movement of people by adopting the Homestead Act, the culmination of a sixty-year trend of making public lands more easily and cheaply available to western pioneers. The act offered 160 acres of public land to any "citizen or intending citizen" who was the head of a family or over twenty-one years of age, provided the recipient lived on the property for at least five years. Although it took five years before a homesteader could "prove up" a title to the land, he or she was entitled to farm it in the meantime. Of note also was that the statute did not distinguish gender. As a result, many women, especially those who had been widowed, deserted, or divorced and had children to rear, took up homestead farms.

The open grasslands presented a novel set of farming conditions, and they proved more hospitable to wheat than to corn. The pioneer's first need was a special kind of plow that could break the prairie sod. Even the steel plow developed by John Deere and others in the 1840s, though sharp enough to cut the sod and slick enough to turn a furrow, could not do the job when drawn by a single horse and steered by a single farmer.

Mechanics on the Illinois prairies developed the breaking plow around 1820. This ungainly instrument consisted of a wooden beam ten or twelve feet long, resting on small, sturdy wheels in front and holding a massive steel share and mould board in the rear. Drawn by a yoke of six oxen or four draft horses, the prairie breaker could turn a furrow thirty inches deep. It required two men to manage, one to drive the team and the other to guide the plow. They could turn about three acres in a day, with frequent stops to sharpen the cutting edge of the share. The prairie breaker was thus a specialized service, and the breaking crew normally charged a farmer two or three dollars an acre. Once the prairie was broken, the farmer had to plow a cross-furrow with his own horse and plow in order to break the sod further before he could plant seeds. Even so, the farmer found that corn had difficulty competing with the grasses that sought to reclaim the land and that wheat fared better on the prairie. Because it could be sold at the flour mills of Minneapolis and other river towns, wheat also provided the farmer with a modest cash income. On the Minnesota prairies, agriculture moved from mere subsistence into the capitalist economy. (The struggle between Minnesota's farmers and the urban capitalists who controlled the grain market and railroad rates will be recounted in the next chapter.)

Next to breaking the prairie, the main problem of pioneer farmers was to find materials for housing their family and sheltering their an-

The western prairies were well suited to growing wheat,
harvested here by a horse-drawn reaper in 1900.
Photo by Brooks

imals. Many of the early entrants to the prairie purchased woodlots in the river bottoms, often ten to twenty miles away, and carted logs to their farms for constructing shelter and fencing. They built log houses, as they had in the eastern woodlands, and split rails for fencing. Cattle and horses roamed the open prairie for pasture; only the wheat field and vegetable garden had to be fenced. Housing, for those without access to woodlots, required more imaginative solutions.

The first house for many a grassland family was the covered wagon which they drove from their prior residence or, in the case of European immigrants, purchased in a lake port such as Chicago or Milwaukee. Even after building a house, the old wagon often served as a spare bedroom for children or a bachelor uncle, and for years it functioned as a storehouse for food, clothing, and tools. In the absence of wood, the first house was usually made of prairie sod. With a sharp steel plow the farmer cut strips of sod a foot deep and two and a half feet in length. He then laid the pieces into a wall, something like setting concrete blocks today, and added a roof of thatched prairie grass. The sod house was thus quick and inexpensive to build, warm in the winter, and comfortably cool in the summer. In time, a sod house might sport a lean-to kitchen in the rear, a board floor, a root cellar, and gaily decorated paper on the walls. In Minnesota, however, most sod houses were replaced by wooden edifices before they achieved such refinements. The lumber for new housing came onto the prairie by rail in the late 1860s.

Railroad construction, much planned in Minnesota during the 1850s, had been held up by the war, except for a ten-mile section of track linking St. Paul with St. Anthony. In 1862 Congress pioneered a new method of subsidizing railroad construction by granting promoters of a Pacific railroad (the Union Pacific/Central Pacific) alternate sections of public land to a distance of ten miles on each side of the right-of-way. Because the land would increase greatly in value once the tracks were laid, the proceeds from land sales were more than enough to finance the cost of construction. In 1865 the Minnesota legislature, taking its cue from Congress, granted promoters ten sections of state-owned land per mile of track to build a line across the prairie from St. Paul to Sioux City, Iowa. The line reached Mankato by 1868 and Sioux City in 1872. During these same years

Winona sawyers formed a corporation to extend a line across southern Minnesota to Rochester and Waseca, from whence it bent northwest into South Dakota. Each railroad had spur lines reaching to nearly every village on the prairie.

The railroads carried sawn lumber to the prairie and brought back wheat to the mill cities on the Mississippi. Prairie villages, such as St. Charles, Dodge Center, and Marshall, sprouted alongside the railroad tracks to provide branch yards and marketing centers for the exchange of lumber and wheat. By 1870 the Winona and St. Peter Railroad sent almost thirteen million board feet of lumber annually to the western grasslands. Minneapolis millers, not to be outdone, formed their own railroad corporation, the Milwaukee and Minneapolis, with a link to Wisconsin, a main line southwest to Mankato, and a branch to Albert Lea. (It later became the Chicago, Milwaukee, and St. Paul Railroad or "Milwaukee Road.") By the early 1870s, Minneapolis shipped fifty to seventy-five carloads of lumber daily to the prairie farmlands, easily surpassing Winona.

Because mill operators were some of the most important stockholders of the Minnesota railroads and the lines carried freight profitably both ways, freight charges were low, and the price of lumber in the prairie towns was well within the range of pioneer farmers. By 1870 land companies advised farmers that, at the nearest railroad station, they could purchase enough pine boards and nails to build a two-room cabin for about seventy-five dollars. A Chicago company advertised precut lumber for homes that could be erected within two or three weeks that it would ship to Minnesota on the Chicago and Northwestern Railroad. Prices for these "prefab" houses ranged from two hundred dollars for a ten-by-twelve cabin to three thousand dollars for a multistory house.

The price of wheat soared during the war but in the late 1860s settled back to around a dollar a bushel. Production averaged twenty to twenty-five bushels per acre, so if a farmer could improve twenty acres for planting, he or she had sufficient credit for a house, a barn, and ample fencing within the first two or three years. Significantly, eastern capitalists regarded investment in midwestern farm mortgages as, in the words of an enthusiastic agent, "gilt-edged, copper fastened, and hot-rivetted." Despite interest rates of 10 to 25 percent, farmers were apparently able to sustain their credit, at least until the disasters of the mid-1870s—nationwide depression and grasshopper plagues.

Spring Wheat and Barbed Wire

There was a one-darned-thing-after-another quality to pioneer farming on the prairie. Having broken the prairie sod and found shelter for the family, farmers looked to the future only to experience the loss of a good part of their first wheat crop to winter kill. In Wisconsin and other Great Lakes states (where many Minnesota pioneers emigrated from), farmers usually sowed winter wheat, a strain that came to the United States from Europe. Farmers scattered seeds in late summer, and the young plants spent the winter under a bed of snow. The plants matured in the spring, like other grasses, and the grain was harvested in June or July. This method worked in the East, but the Minnesota prairie received less rainfall than the eastern states, and the snow was often insufficient to cover the budding stalks of grain. The lumpy prairie sod, moreover, permitted a hard frost to reach deep into the ground, killing the young plants. Spring wheat, sown in the spring and harvested in the autumn, was a likely alternative, but it presented problems to the flour millers and consequently fetched a lower price.

The wheat kernel consists of a soft, glutinous center and an outer shell of bran. Soft and flexible, winter wheat bran remained whole through the grinding process and could be sifted out of the flour. Spring wheat, however, had a more brittle, reddish bran husk that shattered into fine particles in the grinding process and discolored the flour. The bran particles also contained oil that caused the flour to turn rancid after a short time. The problem was to find a way to remove the bran particles from the "middlings," that is, the gluten and endosperm that formed the nutritious part of the flour.

Not surprisingly, the industrial statesman Cadwallader Washburn solved the problem. Learning that French inventors had experimented with a "middlings purifier" in the early 1860s, Washburn hired a pair of French-trained engineers who installed a purifier in one of his mills in 1871. The idea was to set the millstones far enough apart so as to merely crack the bran. The meal then passed through a sieve where blasts of air removed the light bran, other heavier impurities remained on the screen, and the middlings passed through to be reground into a fine white flour. In the next few years Washburn introduced other improvements, including steel rollers that replaced the easily worn sandstones used in grinding. In 1878, after an explosion in one of his mills killed eighteen workers, Washburn responded to the flammability of flour dust by introducing new ventilation systems in his mills.

Innovations in the Minneapolis mill district would make the millstone, shown here with Francis and Ichabod Hill of the Minnesota Flouring Mill in 1858, obsolete.

Nutritionists then discovered that spring wheat contained more nutrients than winter wheat, and bakers discovered that given amounts of its flour produced more bread. The price for spring wheat began to rise, and prairie farmers abandoned their efforts with winter wheat, enthusiastically adopting the new strain. By 1878, 70 percent of all the improved land in Minnesota was planted in wheat, and Minneapolis surpassed St. Louis as the nation's leading flour producer. In that same year, new process flour from the Washburn-Crosby Company won a gold medal at the Millers' International Exhibition in Cincinnati. (John Crosby, another émigré from Maine, became Washburn's partner.) Years later the company began marketing its flour under the Gold Medal brand, and the trademark (continued after Washburn-Crosby Company merged with other companies to form General Mills in 1928) has been internationally recognized ever since.

As the Minnesota prairies turned into wheat fields and the grassland for pasturing animals diminished, an acute need arose for cheap, mass-produced fencing. Because cattle pushed through ordinary wire, inventors for years tinkered with ways of installing pointed barbs on wire. In 1873 Joseph F. Glidden of DeKalb, Illinois, patented a system for mechanically entwining two strands of wire with barbs enmeshed in the strands at regular intervals. It was cheap, effective, and instantly popular with prairie farmers. Those with herds of cattle also approved of the fencing because it enabled them to breed selectively and introduce new strains developed in Europe, notably the German-Dutch Holstein for dairying and the English shorthorn for beef. And in 1874 the legislature passed a herd law that required the confinement of free-roaming animals.

A steel plow, spring wheat, and barbed wire: the technical problems of farming the prairie seemed resolved, and prosperity lay on the horizon. Well, not quite. Not on the prairie. In July 1874 the horizon filled instead with millions of flying insects—Rocky Mountain locusts emerging from years of gestation underground. When they landed and began hopping around—pioneer farmers mistakenly referred to them as grasshoppers—the insects ate every fibrous thing in sight. They especially adored the young shoots of spring wheat. Their taste also went to clothing hanging out to dry.

The Grasshopper Plagues

The locusts first emerged from their underground burrows in the mountain foothills in summer 1873, doing considerable damage in Nebraska, the Dakotas, and a dozen counties in the southwest corner of Minnesota. Toward the end of summer the females deposited their eggs in the ground, usually in cultivated fields. The eggs hatched the following spring about the time the wheat began to sprout. Wingless for six to eight weeks, the larvae crept about the fields devouring all the vegetation. In July they took flight and filled the sky throughout western Minnesota. Unlike most insects, the appetites of winged adults were as voracious as that of the larvae. The state commissioner of statistics estimated a loss of 11 percent of the state's wheat crop and 16 percent of its oats.

A late frost in spring 1875 killed many of the larvae, and the damage that summer was considerably less. But the swarms returned in 1876, and the damage spread to the Mississippi River counties in central Minnesota. Prairie farmers, accustomed to disasters, did their best to meet the storm with humor. One farmer counted 150 eggs to the square inch on his farm in spring 1876. "At this rate," he wrote, "there will be 940,896,000 eggs to the acre, or the nice little pile of 6,586,272,000 on seven acres of my farm." He figured that was enough to supply the whole state if anyone wanted to take some off his hands.

Farmers fought the menace in various ways. Setting prairie fires in the spring killed the larvae, but did nothing to protect the wheat fields. Amateur inventors devised various killing machines called "hopperdozers." The most practical of these was simply a sheet of metal covered with coal tar or molasses, which a person on a horse dragged through a field. The movement forced the insects to hop and get caught in the tar. At the end of each row they were scraped into a fire. The dragging went on for days, with each member of the family sharing in the labor. The effect on the insect population was minimal, but the activity gave the farmers a feeling that they were at least fighting back.

Government relief was not expected in the mid-nineteenth century. In 1849 the territorial legislature adopted a poor-relief law. Modeled on earlier laws that dated back to Elizabethan England, it defined those eligible for public aid as people "unable to earn a livelihood in consequence of bodily infirmity, idiocy, lunacy or other cause." This definition simply did not contemplate healthy and hardworking individuals who found themselves impoverished by a natural disaster. Political thought at the time assumed that churches and other charities would meet temporary distress due to quirks of nature. Unfortunately, private charities in Minneapolis and St. Paul focused on urban problems, such as orphans and "fallen women," and had little money to give to the stricken farmers. When rural county solicitors appealed to charities in Milwaukee and Chicago, they found that devastated farmers in Kansas and Nebraska had already "plowed and scooped to the *bed rock*" the available funds.

The ideological climate of the 1870s was one of governmental "hands off," or laissez-faire (except, of course, when businessmen asked for subsidies in the form of land grants or protective tariffs). Individuals were held responsible for their own success in life, including, if it came to that, their own poverty. Governor Horace Austin, whose term ended in 1874, took note of the insect plague in his final message to the legislature, but he could recommend nothing more than state assistance in providing farmers with seed grain for the following year. "Among a people so well off as ours," he intoned, "this is all that the State as such should be called upon to do."

In 1874-75 the legislature appropriated money to purchase seed grain for afflicted farmers, and it extended the time for the payment of property taxes for those who could prove their inability to pay to the satisfaction of the county treasurers. Even these limited relief measures came to a halt with the election of John S. Pillsbury as governor in 1875. The self-made businessman who had owned a hardware store in Minneapolis (his nephew, Charles A. Pillsbury, started the Pillsbury flour mill) promised "a businessman's administration of the state government." Preoccupied in his inaugural address with the depression that had begun three years earlier, he promised to save money with biennial, rather than annual, legislative sessions and fewer state officeholders. He did not once mention grasshoppers or stricken farmers.

After another disastrous year of swarming insects, Pillsbury was finally forced to address the problem in 1877. He submitted to the legislature a long list of proposals that included a revision of the game laws to protect natural predators of the grasshoppers (presumably pheasants) and a reward for the best hopperdozer design. But he did not mention direct relief. Financial assistance, he reasoned, would demoralize the farmers, cause a loss of self-esteem, and render them evermore dependent on government aid. Pillsbury was, however, amenable to divine help. From the beginning religious-minded individuals—the great majority of the population of the state—had likened the grasshopper hoards to the locust plagues of Egypt described in the Old Testament. Church groups asked the governor to call a day of prayer, and he responded by assigning April 26 as "a day of fasting, humiliation, and prayer."

By chance, the locusts, responding to their own biological clock, took to the air that summer and disappeared, never to return. In November Pillsbury issued a timely proclamation asking citizens to join in a Thanksgiving Day of "fervent manifestations of gratitude to Almighty God for the numberless blessings vouchsafed to us." As insurance, however, he asked the 1878 legislature to provide money for loans to farmers to buy seed and to assume the costs of all hopperdozers built in the previous summer. This latter expense, he believed, would reward the farmers' "commendable efforts" at "self protection" without expectation of reward other than the government's "enlightened policy."

Empire in Pine

The boundary between prairie and woodlands ran roughly along the Minnesota River valley. A traveler journeying north and east of the river would first encounter scattered oak trees amid the grasslands (pioneers would call these "oak openings"). The bur oak, in particular, had a fire-resistant bark, enabling it to survive the periodic blazes—whether set by lightning or Indian hunting parties—that swept and maintained the prairies. Proceeding farther to the north or east the traveler would encounter thick stands of hardwoods—maple, elm, and ash. These trees had little commercial value (except, perhaps, to make wagons and furniture), for the hard, easily fractured wood resisted carpentering. East of the Mississippi the empire of the white pine, with an admixture of balsam firs and hardwoods, stretched north to the Canadian boundary (where it became mixed with spruce) and east into the St. Croix valley.

The white pine and its less abundant cousin, the red pine (sometimes mislabeled Norway pine), were the dream of lumbermen because they grew tall and straight, and carpenters could easily work the light, soft lumber. Because it was light in weight, pine floated buoyantly and thus could be carried out of the woods by water. Green hardwoods, such as maple or birch, dragged sullenly on the gravelly bottoms of rivers or sank altogether. The vast pinery between the Mississippi and St. Croix rivers was laced with the tributaries of each, and when the ice broke in the spring, logs filled the rivers, destined for the mills at the downriver falls.

The U.S. Army, while building Fort Snelling, began harvesting white pine in the Rum River valley in the 1820s. After the Indian cessions of 1837, mill operators began purchasing pine lands from the government at the preemption price of $1.25 an acre in the St. Croix–Mississippi triangle. During the Civil War the Republican U.S. Congress passed two laws making it easier for loggers to acquire timberlands and contributing to the postwar logging boom. The Morrill Act and the Homestead Act passed within weeks of one another in 1862. Both laws were intended to benefit farmers and workingmen, reflecting the Republican Party's early perception of itself as a farmer-labor party.

In practice, highly capitalized businesses, such as lumber and mining companies, warped both acts and the use of military scrip to their advantage. The Morrill Act gave to each state thirty thousand acres of public lands for each of its members in Congress, the proceeds from sales of this land to be used to fund colleges that specialized in agriculture and mechanics. The idea was to provide the country with a trained and educated farmer-labor working force. Because the largest number of land grants went to the populous states of the eastern seaboard that no longer had public lands, Congress provided that such states would be given their allotment in scrip, which could be used to buy public land in the western states. Since the scrip was transferable, most of the eastern states sold it at a discount to have ready cash. By purchasing the scrip of eastern states, Minnesota lumbermen gained title to tens of thousands of acres of pine land in the St. Croix and Mississippi valleys. When that source dwindled in the 1870s, the lumbermen employed "homesteaders" to claim 160-acre tracts that were often cleared of pine before the claim could be "proved up." They used the same technique after purchasing military bounty land scrip from veterans who did not want to move west.

The State of Minnesota was less reckless in disposing of its share of the public lands, but it still managed to further the lumbermen's interests. In 1877 the legislature enacted a law providing for the sale of the timber owned by the state but not the land. The state thus retained the option of holding onto the land or selling it after the timber had been harvested. Timber sales were by auction in St. Paul, which required the lumbermen to send surveyors into the north

The burgeoning city of Minneapolis rises in the background along St. Anthony Falls and the east side mill district, 1898.

woods to estimate the value of timber on the state-owned parcels. Lands the state retained for a second growth of timber became the basis of the state forest lands in the twentieth century. Although the execution of the act had some flaws, the state earned about five million dollars in "stumpage fees" in the last quarter of the nineteenth century.

With public timberlands available at little cost, the logging frontier pushed rapidly northward. It reached the Grand Rapids area in the mid-1870s and then tapped two pine-rich tributaries of the Mississippi—the Willow and Prairie rivers—in the last years of the decade. Each river averaged twenty million feet of logs a year between 1878 and 1880. In 1880 alone the Mississippi and its tributaries yielded 247 million feet of pine logs.

Once a lumber company obtained title to a parcel of woodland, the company set up camps for its timber cutters. Before about 1870, these were known as "State-of-Maine" camps, usually employing twenty-five to thirty men and as many horses or oxen. A foreman took charge of the camp along with a cook, and the cook's helper, or "cookee." The manager was often a veteran of the New England or Michigan timberlands—indeed, saying "I'm from Maine" was a blue-chip credential for employment in Minnesota. The cook was a vital feature of the camp because camp morale depended on an abundant supply of food reasonably well prepared. Bread, salt pork, and beans made up the basic fare. The camp was usually located on a river, its perimeter (and hence life expectancy) determined by the distances crew and horses could haul logs by sled. This distance was greatly increased in the 1890s when short, narrow-gauge railroads used steam engines to bring the logs from remote locations to the riverbank. By that time, too, camps had become larger, with sixty to eighty lumberjacks, greater regimentation, and better food.

Logging was a winter occupation because the giant trees could be moved only by horse-drawn sled, usually running on grooves formed of ice. The work of the lumberjack was perhaps the hardest and most dangerous in the country; by 1900 the pay equaled that of urban factory workers. Lumber companies, themselves operating on credit, paid their workers only when the season was over. Logging was thus a wintertime occupation for all but the crews who steered the logs downstream in the spring. In the summer the lumberjacks became itinerant workers in the cities or returned to their farms in southern Minnesota. In the 1870s the grasshopper plagues forced many a farmer to supplement his income with wintertime logging.

The work involved certain specialties, if not skills. Scalers marked the trees to be felled and determined the number of logs to be cut from each. Fellers dropped the tree where it could be most easily worked. By the 1870s the two-man crosscut saw had replaced the ax, doubling the production of a felling crew. A bucking crew limbed the tree and cut it into sixteen-foot logs. Teamsters dragged the logs on the snow to a loading area, where they were piled onto sleds. A crude horse-drawn block and tackle lifted the top logs in place; the piles extended anywhere from ten to twenty feet high. Horses, oxen, or—by the end of the century—steam engines pulled the laden sleds to the riverbank, where the logs were piled to await the spring thaw. An inspector armed with a stamp hammer pounded the company's log-mark on the butt of each log so the mass of wood could be sorted out and each company could claim its own timber when it reached the millponds at the falls.

The log drive began when the snow melted, the river rose, and the current freshened. The log drive crews, whose job it was to keep the unruly logs moving and gather up those that had fallen into back-waters and eddies, have often been portrayed in romantic fashion as courageous souls, riding the bobbing logs with a rhythmic sway, deftly stepping from one to another with only a long pike for balance. A contemporary described them as "hard-living, hard-drinking, blasphemous pioneers" chosen from the camp crews for their agility and strength. French Canadians allegedly were best at riding a log through a rapids.

The most dangerous part of a log drive was breaking up a jam. A narrow bend in the river, a rocky stretch, or an unexpected shoal could cause the logs to go aground and pile up. Because all the logging companies throughout the watershed put their winter's crop in the river about the same time—April and May—a jam, once started, quickly piled up into a mountain of timber. An infamous jam just above the St. Croix falls in 1886 tied up 150 million feet of logs and took two hundred men six weeks to break.

This 1865 logjam on the St. Croix River at Taylors Falls,
smaller than the infamous jam two decades later, is impressive nonetheless.

New mills and new technology kept up with the avalanche of timber streaming down from the north woods. By 1870 Minnesota had
207 sawmills in operation using equipment powered by steam, which
was more powerful and more reliable than waterpower. Sawdust,
shavings, and scrap lumber provided fuel for the steam engines. The
circular saw had replaced the up-and-down reciprocating saw, and
steam-driven carriages took the logs through the milling process.
Most mills had two to four circular saws operating at the same time.
After the boards were edged and trimmed to precise lengths, they
were stacked for drying. The most advanced mills had sawdust-fired
heaters to hasten the drying process. Drying was essential because
green lumber tended to warp and, being heavier, incurred prohibi-
tive freight charges.

Frederick Weyerhaeuser and the Passing of the Logging Frontier

At the beginning of 1869 Duluth was a hamlet of fourteen houses and two small sawmills on the shore of Lake Superior overlooking the estuary through which the St. Louis River entered the western tip of the lake. The lumber from its mills, as well as those of Cloquet farther up the river, was shipped east by steamboat in the summer months when the lake was open. In 1870, Jay Cooke, a Philadelphia banker who had made a fortune marketing government bonds during the war, completed a railroad linking Duluth with St. Paul.

In that same year Cooke acquired a controlling interest in the Northern Pacific, the second of the Pacific railroads Congress chartered during the war. Where the Union Pacific and Central Pacific followed the central route from the Missouri valley to San Francisco, the Northern Pacific took the northern route from Lake Superior to Puget Sound. Because of the curvature of the earth, Seattle is much closer to Japan and China than is San Francisco, and Cooke had visions of his railroad becoming a vital link in the vast and largely untapped "China market." He also had an eye on the railroad's lands, for Congress had endowed the Northern Pacific with the same grant as the Union Pacific, a checkerboard of alternate sections of land extending twenty miles on each side of the right-of-way. While on its way to the Pacific, the railroad would tap the growing wheatfields of the Red River Valley and earn its way, as other Minnesota railroads had, by freighting lumber and wheat. With more optimism than sense (construction of the railroad had not even begun), Cooke in 1869 built a grain elevator in Duluth to store Red River wheat for transshipment to the flour mills of Cleveland and Buffalo. Duluth, of course, was delighted; its population boomed to thirty-five hundred by the end of the year.

Construction of the Northern Pacific began in 1870, and within a year it reached Moorhead on the Red River. By far the best customer for Duluth's sawmills, the railroad consumed huge amounts of lumber in laying track, building stations, and establishing freight yards (such as at Brainerd). West of the Red River, construction continued at a furious pace, and the railroad reached Bismarck, Dakota Territory, in 1873. Cooke poured huge amounts of money into the construction, not waiting for the railroad to pay for itself through the wheat and lumber trade. He also spent lavish sums on advertising, seeking to attract immigrants from Germany, Poland, and Scandinavia to populate the railroad's lands in Minnesota and (North) Dakota. So luxuriant was his description of the soil and climate of Minnesota in the brochures posted in the European farming communities that cynics referred to the counties through which the Northern Pacific passed as "Jay Cooke's Banana Belt."

Unfortunately, Cooke was the only one who could see near-term profit in the Northern Pacific or its lands. Both American and European investors shied away from the project, and before long Cooke's own immense resources were exhausted. On September 18, 1873, Jay Cooke and Company closed its doors, and that action precipitated the worst financial panic of the century to that time. Among the victims

Railroad companies encouraged settlement on the western prairies by offering plush accommodations along their lines, like this Northern Pacific Railroad reception house at Glyndon.

Photo by Haynes, Inc., 1876

was the Northern Pacific, which declared bankruptcy and halted construction. Over the next decade promoters in Portland and Seattle began building railroads eastward, linking up with the Northern Pacific in Montana in the mid-1880s. The railroad, however, failed to prosper, and when another panic struck in 1893, it again went into receivership. In the meantime, in 1890, Frederick Weyerhaeuser bought up all the Northern Pacific's lands in Minnesota, and that act initiated a new—and final—phase in the logging of Minnesota's pineries.

Weyerhaeuser was a German immigrant who arrived in the United States in the 1850s. By the end of the decade, through customary German thrift and industry, he owned a sawmill at Rock Island, Illinois. During and after the Civil War he invested in both sawmills and timberlands in Wisconsin's Chippewa River valley. With the purchase of the Northern Pacific lands in 1890, Weyerhaeuser moved the center of his operations to Minnesota and settled his family in St. Paul, building a mansion on Summit Avenue next door to railroad magnate James J. Hill. By 1892 Weyerhaeuser and his fellow investors had either purchased or paid stumpage fees for most of the remaining pine lands in northeastern Minnesota.

Although much of the timber Weyerhaeuser cut floated down the Mississippi to his mills in Minneapolis, a large amount also went to Duluth, which became a major milling center in the 1890s. The city had fourteen sawmills and another nine stood in the valley extending inland to Cloquet. In the depression, which began with the panic of 1893, Duluth was actually able to grow at the expense of Minneapolis. It was closer to its logging hinterland, and shipped the lumber east by lake steamer, which was cheaper than the rail transportation that Minneapolis relied on. Much of Duluth's lumber was marketed in the Lake Erie ports of Cleveland and Buffalo, and the steam-driven barges brought back coal from the anthracite fields of Pennsylvania. By the end of the decade Duluth's lumber output approached that of Minneapolis, with each city turning out half a billion board feet of lumber a year.

By then, however, the pine woods were virtually exhausted. Lumber production peaked in Minneapolis in 1899; Duluth peaked only three years later. In 1900 Frederick Weyerhaeuser shifted his timber investments to the fir forests of the Pacific Northwest, although he continued to reside in St. Paul. He died in 1914, and five years later his Minneapolis mill—at one time the grandest in the country—cut up its last log. The last sawmill in Duluth shut down in 1932.

James J. Hill and the Great Northern Railway

The Northern Pacific Railroad, poorly managed and hastily built, never adequately served the transportation needs of northern and western Minnesota. It was James J. Hill who opened the north woods and the Red River Valley to world commerce during the nineteenth century. Unlike Jay Cooke, a speculator using other people's money, Hill was an empire builder, an industrial statesman like Cadwallader Washburn who nurtured American economic development and in the process gained personal wealth.

Canadian-born (he did not bother with U.S. citizenship until he was forty-two), Hill landed in St. Paul in 1856 at age seventeen. He received a business apprenticeship working as a clerk for a local mercantile firm that dealt in foodstuffs and coal. Seeing that the future lay in railroads, in 1866 Hill went into business for himself as a shipping agent who arranged freight for rail companies that were laying track into the western prairies and northern pineries. While St. Paul's early railroad builders steered themselves toward the southwestern prairies, Hill looked to the northwest. In 1870 he formed a partnership to operate a steamboat line on the Red River. While Minnesota's railroad builders were constructing east-west lines, Hill's vision was to build a north-south connection between St. Paul and northwestern Minnesota and the Red River Valley. His first step was to acquire the St. Paul and Pacific, a branch of the Northern Pacific rendered an impoverished orphan by Cooke's 1873 bankruptcy.

The grandly named St. Paul and Pacific Railroad inherited a land grant from one of the 1850s railroads that was never built, and it laid Minnesota's first ten miles of track between St. Paul and St. Anthony in 1862. When the first train, carrying a load of sightseers, made a trial run to St. Anthony on June 28, 1862, the *St. Paul Daily Press* exulted, "A passenger train departed from St. Paul in the direction of Puget Sound today." The railroad reached only as far as St. Cloud when the Northern Pacific acquired it in 1870. Had the Northern Pacific's managers built a branch connecting St. Cloud with their own main line at Brainerd, the Northern Pacific would have had two major terminals, Duluth and St. Paul, and would have been a much more solid enterprise. Instead, the company was more interested in developing the St. Paul and Pacific's lands at the headwaters of the Red River. The line extended to Breckenridge when the company collapsed in bankruptcy in 1873. In receivership for the next five years, the St. Paul and Pacific crept northward along the Red River toward connection with the main line of the Northern Pacific at Glyndon. Then, in 1878, James J. Hill and a consortium of investors purchased, in the phrase of Hill's biographer Albro Martin, this "shattered but still valuable piece of railroad crockery."

Within a year Hill extended the railroad down the Red River Valley to the town of St. Vincent on the Canadian border. There he linked up with a spur that the Canadian Pacific had obligingly constructed south from Winnipeg. The Canadians were building a line across the continent from Montreal to Vancouver on Puget Sound. Hill thus linked St. Paul to the Pacific Coast without governmental subsidies and at little cost to himself. Even in its local market the St. Paul, Minneapolis & Manitoba Railway (its new, more modest name) was a profitable operation because Hill sent feeder lines into every community in the northwestern quarter of the state. German and Scandinavian immigrants filled its westbound trains, along with lumber hewn in Minneapolis; on the return trip the cars were laden with spring wheat for the Minneapolis mills. By the mid-1880s the stock of the St. Paul, Minneapolis & Manitoba was the bluest of blue chips on the New York Stock Exchange.

It was also the most solidly constructed of all American railroads. The Englishman Henry Bessemer had devised a method of mass-producing steel, and Andrew Carnegie, who had obtained sole rights to the process in America, built a Bessemer plant in Pittsburgh in 1874. Steel (twelve times harder than iron) was ideal for rails, and Carnegie concentrated on that product. Iron rails wore down on heavily used sections of track and had to be taken up, reforged, and replaced every year or two. Hill replaced his iron rails with Carnegie's steel and used steel on all new construction. Hill's was one of the first all-steel railroads in the country. He also put steel wheels on his locomotives and had their steam boilers made of steel, enabling the switch to coal-fired locomotives, a huge saving in the wood-shy Red River Valley.

By informal "protocol" with the Northern Pacific, Hill's railroad retained its north-south orientation and did not extend westward beyond Devils Lake, (North) Dakota, eighty miles from the Red River. Nevertheless, Hill and his partners could not forget the lure of a transcontinental line of their own with potential for a connection to China. Fellow Canadian George Stephen, president of the Bank of Montreal and an important financial backer of Hill, wrote him on Christmas Day 1885, "I hope the time is coming when we shall be able to give the Manitoba road a through line from St. Paul to the Pacific Ocean and on to Japan and China."

With characteristic caution, Hill sent geologists to investigate Montana's mineral deposits because the profitability of a new transcontinental road depended, in large part, on freightage along its route. The report came back noting large quantities of coal in the territory, close to the surface, of a quality equal to the coal mined in Illinois. Next, Hill sought from Congress the grant of a right-of-way through the public lands and Indian reservations of the Northwest. He obtained this grant in 1887, and construction of the nine-hundred-mile railroad—rechristened the Great Northern—began the following year. Hill's route hugged the Canadian border, some two hundred to three hundred miles north of the Northern Pacific's route, crossed the Continental Divide in the far northwestern corner of Montana, and, in 1893, in the mountains of Washington, met an eastbound section extending from Seattle. Everyone agreed it was the best-designed, best-constructed railroad in the West.

By 1893 Hill had a new financial partner, J. Pierpont Morgan, an investment banker specializing in business mergers. The previous year Morgan had consolidated Thomas A. Edison's motley holdings into the mammoth General Electric Company. When the Northern Pacific went into receivership again during the panic of 1893, Hill and Morgan bought a controlling interest in the railroad for a mere four million dollars. Hill estimated that he could save a million dollars a year by eliminating the expenses of competition and by encouraging cooperation between the two northwestern railroads.

Even so, he felt that to complete his railroad empire he needed an outlet to Chicago. Laying new track was out of the question because either the Milwaukee Road or the Chicago and Northwestern already served every community in Wisconsin. In 1901 Hill and Morgan acquired the Burlington Railroad, which ran from Chicago to Denver (with a spur line from Burlington, Iowa) to St. Paul. The acquisition gave Hill the entry he needed to Chicago, and it complemented nicely his Great Northern–Northern Pacific holdings.

Unfortunately, at this juncture Hill's ambition collided with the imperial schemes of another railroad titan, Edward H. Harriman. A financier like Morgan, Harriman knew little about managing railroads, but he loved to own them. He controlled the Illinois Central as well as the Union Pacific and the Southern Pacific and wove the systems together into a near-monopoly of the traffic between Chicago and California. He could not abide the thought of Hill having a monopoly on the traffic between Chicago and the Pacific Northwest. He also had a grudge against J. P. Morgan as a result of earlier battles. In early 1901 Harriman quietly began buying up shares of the Northern Pacific held by small stockholders. Hill and Morgan owned 25 percent of the stock, which normally would be a controlling interest, but they were in trouble if Harriman acquired a similar amount. Learning of Harriman's activities, Hill, using Morgan's money, began adding to his holdings of Northern Pacific. The stock, originally trading at $80 a share, skyrocketed to $180 by May 8. Only three shares were left when trading closed on that day, and Hill bought them for $1,000 each. Hill and Morgan owned 53 percent of the Northern Pacific and Harriman had 46 percent. One percent could not be located. The market for Northern Pacific stock had been "cornered"—the greatest corner in stock market history.

The scandal arose from the fact that many market speculators, realizing that the Northern Pacific was grossly overpriced, had sold short in anticipation of a fall. They expected to buy the stock in the future at a much lower price and make good on their delivery contracts at a tidy profit. However, the delivery dates were approaching, and not a share was to be had due to the Hill-Harriman corner. Hundreds of "bears" faced ruin, and the market itself was likely to collapse. Neither Morgan nor Harriman could afford to see a market collapse, and they quickly compromised. Together they released 78,000 shares onto the market at $150 a share. That same year, Morgan and Hill put together a new stock holding company, the Northern Securities Company, giving it a controlling interest in the Great Northern, the Northern Pacific, and the Burlington. Morgan and Hill appeased Harriman by giving him a seat on the board of directors.

It was James J. Hill's last venture at empire building. In 1904 the U.S. Supreme Court ordered the Northern Securities Company dissolved on grounds that a monopoly on all the rail traffic of the Pacific Northwest was a violation of the Sherman Antitrust Act. Hill has been much criticized for his corner on the stock market in 1901, but he was hardly a major player in that catfight. It began, after all, with his well-conceived desire for a link between the Northwest and Chicago via St. Paul. He might well be likened to the legendary soul who started out to drain the swamp and found himself up to his hips in alligators. Nor was he a money machine like his contemporaries J. P. Morgan and John D. Rockefeller. When he died in 1916 his estate was worth more than sixty-three million dollars, a tidy sum but no more than Rockefeller was clearing in a single year. Nor did Hill ever have a lust for money for money's sake: he seemed most to love building and acquiring things and making them work efficiently. In 1897, at a cost of four million dollars, he purchased several thousand acres of logged-off timberland on the Mesabi Range, where iron ore had recently been discovered. He sold the land for the same amount to a trust fund set up for shareholders of the Great Northern Railway to ensure that they would never take a loss on their stock. The trust was eventually worth $425 million.

Empire in Rouge

Since the days of French control, rich veins of copper were known to exist on the south shore of Lake Superior and in the St. Croix River valley. After Minnesota became a state its governors commissioned state geologists to survey the hill country west of Lake Superior and to hunt for more veins of copper and perhaps gold and silver. The only mineral they reported finding was iron. This aroused little interest because ample supplies of iron were already being mined in

Michigan. A decade later, however, the introduction of the Besse~~mer~~ ~~process for making steel, together with rising demand due to a f~~r ~~of railroad construction, aroused new interest in iron ore.~~ A Duluth businessman, George C. Stone, having read a geologist's report of a huge deposit of iron ore in the vicinity of Lake Vermilion, sought financing for further exploration in the Vermilion Range.

He found the financial angel he needed in Charlemagne Tower, a New York lawyer, friend of Jay Cooke, and major stockholder in the Northern Pacific Railroad. Stone and Tower and others formed the

Fayal underground mine, Eveleth, 1915. Many workers on the Iron Range were Finnish immigrants who brought their skills from the Old Country.

Photo by William F. Roleff

Minnesota Iron Company and purchased twenty thousand acres of logged-out land in the Vermilion Range. Stone, a member of the state legislature, used his political influence to obtain a grant of 500,000 acres of state-owned land to aid in the construction of a railroad from the mountain range to Two Harbors on Lake Superior. The first load of iron ore reached Two Harbors in August 1884. Within two years the Minnesota Iron Company annually shipped a half-million tons of ore. Because the veins of iron had to be blasted out of rock, it was mined in the same way as Pennsylvania coal. Tunnels were dug into the mountain, and the miners worked in "rooms" held up by stone pillars. When the deepest of the mines in the Vermilion Range closed in 1962, its shafts went down tewnty-four hundred feet.

Tower never set foot in Minnesota and never saw an iron mine. He was seventy-eight years old and no doubt ready for retirement in 1887 when John D. Rockefeller offered to buy his controlling interest in the Minnesota Iron Company as well as the railroad to Two Harbors. Rockefeller was eager to diversify the assets of his Standard Oil Company and had already purchased large parts of the Gogebic Range in Michigan. Tower sold his mines, lands, and the railroad for more than six million dollars.

The Vermilion Range was explored and mined for nearly a decade before anyone wondered if there might be iron in the neighboring Mesabi Range, a few miles to the southwest. Lewis H. Merritt, a Duluth timber surveyor who had explored the range for logging companies, was convinced that there was iron in the hills, but he died before his intuition could be confirmed. His sons inherited his passion and became known in Minnesota lore as the "Seven Iron Men." By 1890 the Merritts had spent all the money they had searching in vain for an ore vein worth mining. They assumed that the ore was in the form of rock, as it had been in all earlier finds, when in fact it lay in the loose soil at their feet. The Merritts discovered this when one of their wagons became stuck in the brick-red dust. They decided to have the dust analyzed—it turned out to be hematite, 64 percent pure iron. And it could be mined with a steamshovel, sparing them the cost of sinking shafts and shoring up tunnels.

The Merritts' discovery failed to arouse much interest in the mining community because it was generally assumed—and geologists firmly but falsely asserted—that it was economically feasible to mine only ores imbedded in hard rock. Thus, although the Merritts had the Mesabi Range pretty much to themselves, they still lacked money. Much of the range was school land belonging to the state of Minnesota, and, though logged over, it still commanded five to ten dollars an acre in the 1890s. Leonidas ("Lon") Merritt, the leader of the clan, conceived the idea of approaching the legislature with the idea of leasing the land, much on the same principle that it had sold the timber for a "stumpage fee." The legislature agreed, and the Merritts were able to lease nearly tewnty-three thousand acres of the Mesabi Range for a mere sixty-two cents an acre.

Their next problem was transportation. They asked the Northern Pacific Railroad to build a spur line into the Mesabi Range, but they were turned down by the shortsighted managers of that soon-to-be-bankrupt line. They were, however, able to convince some Duluth businessmen of the ore prospects in their leased holdings (and no doubt appealed to the rivalry between Duluth and Two Harbors): in 1892 built their own railroad, the Duluth, Missabe and Northern.

The Merritts were suddenly rich and famous. John D. Rockefeller offered them eight million dollars for their leased lands and railroad; they turned him down. Henry Clay Frick, the president of Carnegie Steel, told Andrew Carnegie, now retired and spending most of his time in Scotland, that the Merritts "can fill an entire railroad boxcar of the richest iron ore you've ever seen with just five scoops from a steamshovel." Carnegie, aware of the Rockefeller offer, contented himself with buying out one of the Merritts' mining neighbors. For a little more than a year the Merritts exulted in high living, splashing money all over Duluth, but they proved to be backwoodsmen when they ran up against the fiscal genie employed by John D. Rockefeller.

It began with an innocent loan of $400,000 that enabled the Merritts to extend their railroad (previously connected with another road at Stoney Brook on the St. Louis River) into Duluth and build ore-loading docks of their own. Rockefeller's agents took bonds on the Duluth, Missabe and Northern as collateral. The loans, which thereafter came from an ore-barge company that Rockefeller owned, ultimately amounted to $1.6 million. Then, in May 1893, panic struck on Wall Street and the nation plunged into the worst depression of the century. The Merritts were unable to obtain funds to pay back the debts to Rockefeller, and, after some complicated financial dealings—far too complex for the Merritts to fathom—Rockefeller ended up with their mining properties, railroad, and ore docks. Rockefeller was richer by an estimated $330 million, and the Merritts were penniless.

In 1901, when J. P. Morgan organized the U.S. Steel Company, enveloping Andrew Carnegie's steel-making empire, Rockefeller sold his Minnesota mining interests to the new billion-dollar corporation. The wealth of Minnesota's iron ranges thus passed almost entirely into the hands of eastern financiers.

VISITING HISTORY

Use of the new state's resources brought rapid economic development, waves of settlers, and fresh challenges.

FARMING

Gibbs Museum of Pioneer and Dakotah Life
2097 W. Larpenteur Ave., St. Paul; 651/646-8629. Costumed interpretation of an 1867 farmhouse and farm buildings with animals.

Minnesota's Machinery Museum
Hanley Falls; 507/768-3522. Dedicated to Minnesota agriculture; contains a large collection of farm machinery.

Oliver H. Kelley Farm
2.5 miles southeast of downtown Elk River on U.S. Hwy. 10; 763/441-6896. Costumed guides labor on an 1860s farm, with heirloom plants and animal stock; visitors can help. Interpretive center with exhibits.

Olof Swensson Farm Museum
6 miles east of Montevideo on Highway 7, then 5 miles south on Co. Rd. 6. Farmstead of Norwegian immigrants who arrived in 1873, operated by the Chippewa County Historical Society (320/269-7636).

Phelps Mill
I-94 exit 67 north on Co. Hwy. 35, west on Co. Hwy. 1, north on Co. Hwy. 45. Flour mill active from 1889 to 1946, operated by the Otter Tail County Historical Society, Fergus Falls (218/736-6038).

LOGGING

Folsom House

272 W. Government St., Taylors Falls; 651/465-3125. A large Greek Revival frame home in the Angels Hill District overlooking the St. Croix River, built in 1854 by W. H. C. Folsom, a lumber baron.

Forest History Center

Grand Rapids; 218/327-4482. Recreation of a 1900 logging camp, with living history interpreters, museum exhibits, a wanigan, and a lookout tower.

Hinckley Fire Museum

Hinckley; 320/384-7338. Exhibits on the deadly fire of 1894, Native Americans, logging, and railroads.

Lake of the Woods County Museum

119 8th Ave. E., Baudette; 218/634-1200. Includes exhibits on logging and on a 1910 fire.

Mill City Museum

704 S. 2nd St., Minneapolis; 612/341-7555. Exhibits on lumber and flour milling, water power, farming, and transportation, and a fine view of the Falls of St. Anthony.

Virginia Heritage Museum

800 9th Ave. N., Virginia; 218/741-1136. Includes exhibits on logging in the area and two major forest fires.

RAILROADS

End-O-Line Railroad Park

Currie; 507/763-3708. Includes a functioning manually operated turntable as well as historic buildings moved to the site.

Jackson Street Roundhouse

Minnesota Transportation Museum, 193 E. Pennsylvania Ave., St. Paul; 651/228-0263. A collection of rail cars and artifacts housed in a structure built by the Great Northern Railway in 1907. Children can ride a miniature train.

James J. Hill House

240 Summit Ave., St. Paul; 651/297-2555. Massive mansion constructed with all the latest technology in 1891 by the builder of the Great Northern Railway, with living history interpretation.

Lake Superior Railroad Museum

506 W. Michigan St., Duluth; 218/733-7590. Featuring steam, electric, and diesel engines, freight and passenger cars, dining car china, and other railway equipment. Excursion trains offer 90-minute or 6-hour rides along Lake Superior.

MINING

Hibbing Historical Society

400 East 23rd St., Hibbing; 218/263-8522. Exhibits on the town, its diverse residents, and how mining made it move.

Ironworld Discovery Center

801 SW Hwy. 169, Chisholm; 800/372-6437 or 218/254-7959. Exhibits on the state's geology and history and the Iron Range's mining history and ethnic heritage. Tours of the world's largest operational open pit mine, the Hull-Rust-Mahoning in Hibbing, are available in season; the mine's overlook area is open to visitors year-round.

Lake Superior Maritime Museum

Canal Park, Duluth; 218/727-2497. Exhibits on lake shipping history and technology. Situated on the canal, affording a view of ore boats and other ships passing under the aerial lift bridge.

Soudan Underground Mine State Park

1379 Stuntz Bay Rd., Soudan; 218/753-2245. Visitors descend 2,341 feet below the surface for tours of a mine that operated from 1884 to 1963.

Split Rock Lighthouse

Split Rock State Park, 20 miles northeast of Two Harbors on MN Hwy. 61; 218/226-6372. A Minnesota icon: the spectacularly beautiful facility completed in 1910 to aid Great Lakes navigation. Living history interpretation; visitor center with exhibits.

Stearns History Museum

235 33rd Ave. S., St. Cloud; 320/253-8424. Includes exhibits on granite quarrying, which started in the area in 1863.

Paul Bunyan

Like the fur traders, the Mountain Men, and the riverboatmen of the Mississippi who came before them, lumberjacks enjoyed tall tales. Stories of strange creatures in the woods enlivened many a chilly evening in the lumber camps. The Hugag, a monster with jointless legs and corrugated ears, slept by leaning against a tree. One might also encounter the hardheaded Splinter Cat that smashed into trees and splintered them with its head while searching for honey and raccoons. Most feared of all was the awesome Agropelter (*Anthrocephalus craniofractens*), ape-faced, with arms like whiplashes, who with deadly aim pelted unsuspecting lumberjacks with tree branches. The one figure never mentioned in Minnesota lumber camp tales was Paul Bunyan. Agnes M. Larson, who in the 1940s wrote a history of the logging of white pine, interviewed dozens of individuals who had worked in the state's lumber camps, and not one had ever heard of Paul.

Paul Bunyan was popularized by a Detroit, Michigan, journalist, James McGillivray, who wrote a story for the Detroit *News-Tribune* on July 24, 1910, about a heroic lumberjack of immense size and strength. As a folk hero Paul Bunyan appealed to Americans' love of bigness—this was, after all, the age of powerful steam locomotives and city skyscrapers. Someone read the story and added a tale of Babe, Paul's blue ox, who took on her strange color during the winter of the blue snow. She was so big that she measured forty-two ax handles between the eyes, and her hoofprints created Minnesota's lakes. In 1914 a Minnesota lumber company sponsored a pamphlet embellishing the tales of Paul Bunyan with cartoon drawings of his escapades. It then used the figure of Paul as its trademark. By the 1920s the legendary Paul Bunyan was the subject of books, articles, and short stories. A purported biography claimed that, when he tossed in his crib as an infant, he "knocked down four square miles of standing timber."

More than any other state, Minnesota has claimed Paul Bunyan as its own. Familiar to every schoolchild, he is a natural tourist attraction. In 1937 promoters of Bemidji erected a massive statue of him. Not to be outdone, the Brainerd Lakes area is home to a huge concrete Paul capable of conversing with children. Legend is sometimes more real than life. And it is almost always more fun.

VISITING HISTORY

Paul Bunyan and Babe the Blue Ox

Waterfront, Bemidji. An 18-foot-tall Paul built in 1937 for a winter carnival.

Paul Bunyan statue

This Old Farm, 7 miles east of Brainerd on MN Hwy. 18; 218/764-2915. The 26-foot-tall talking statue and a collection of over twenty thousand farm-related antiques and collectibles.

Paul Bunyan rises larger than life at Bemidji.
Photo by Niels Larson Hakkerup, 1938

7

The Age of Reform

Boston-born Oliver H. Kelley was one of many Yankees who sought their fortune in Minnesota Territory. Arriving in St. Paul in spring 1849, he soon became caught up in the town-planning mania and purchased land next to the newly founded village of Itasca on the banks of the Mississippi River about thirty-five miles above the Falls of St. Anthony. Itasca never developed beyond a post office and Indian trading post, and Kelley turned his wistful vista into a farm. The son of a tailor, he had never plowed a furrow or planted a seed in his life, but inexperience rendered him receptive to new ideas. He learned farming by reading agricultural journals and talking to his neighbors. Within a year he formed a county agricultural society, the first in Minnesota, and experimented with various crops and newly invented farm implements. Through the 1850s he published a steady stream of newspaper articles on new farming techniques and the growth of Minnesota agriculture.

In 1864, through the influence of Senator Alexander Ramsey, Kelley obtained a clerkship in the U.S. Department of Agriculture, the most recent addition to the president's cabinet. For the next two years he divided his time between Washington and Minnesota, writing articles for the department's reports during the winter and tending crops during the summer. In 1867, after a visit to the war-torn South, where he became convinced of the need for cooperative farm associations, Kelley and several other agriculture department clerks founded the National Grange of the Patrons of Husbandry. Returning to Minnesota the following year, he formed local Granges in his home of Elk River and in St. Paul. Through his newspaper articles in the 1850s he formed friendships with the editors of the *Sauk Rapids Sentinel,* the *St. Paul Minnesota Democrat,* and the *Pioneer Press,* and these papers became major promotional vehicles for the spread of the Grange. By the end of 1869 Minnesota had forty local Granges and a state organization, and Granges were being formed in Illinois, Iowa, and Wisconsin.

Modern-day costumed interpreter working at the Oliver Kelley Farm historic site, where visitors can experience a day in the life of an 1860s farm

Photo by Bob Stanton

Patterned on the Masonic Order, the Grange adopted secret rituals, code words and handshakes, and status ranks for both men and women. The Washington clerks who founded the society wanted to encourage farmers to educate themselves on new methods while giving them an opportunity—through picnics and barn dances—to develop a sense of camaraderie. From the outset Kelley wanted more than a rural social fraternity (formation of the Grange, incidentally, coincided with the founding of Greek fraternities in American colleges) and demanded a program of collective economic action. He claimed that Minnesota farmers wanted "an association that will aid and protect the farmers as a class." His newspaper articles throughout 1869 and 1870 argued that merchants and manufacturers had formed monopolistic associations that rigged prices, and the farmers needed to organize to protect themselves. Kelley pointed out, for instance, that the pork packers of St. Paul offered farmers a price for their pigs that was below the cost of raising them, while the packers themselves showed a 33 percent annual profit.

Railroads were a prime target for Granger agitation. Freight rates varied wildly as railroad managers were inclined to charge "what the traffic would bear." The problem was that local railroads were a natural monopoly in the communities they served; hence, farmers had to pay the rate charged by the local stationmaster or take their grain home. Freight rates between local communities were thus far higher than rates between large cities where railroads competed with one another. It cost, for example, 35 percent more to ship wheat from Winona to Chicago than from Chicago to New York, a distance almost four times greater. As wheat culture spread in the 1860s, grain storage elevators, sometimes owned by the railroads, appeared at every whistle-stop to hold the crop pending shipment. That presented farmers with yet another monopoly, forcing them to accept the price the local elevator operator offered or feed their crops to their pigs.

Such was the rural anger by 1871, a state election year, that both Republicans and Democrats included in their platforms promises of state control of railroad rates. In his annual message Governor Horace Austin, a Republican, declared that the freight and elevator charges as "practiced by some of our roads are unjustifiable, extortionate, and oppressive to the last degree." The legislature accordingly established an office of railroad commissioner and prescribed maximum fares that railroads could charge. Two things happened as a result. Railroads that were not in compliance with the prescribed rates ignored them because the commissioner had no enforcement powers. Railroads whose rates were below the prescribed maximum (because, for instance, they competed with river transport) simply raised them to the official level.

In the face of such high-handed abuse of power and money, the thinking of farmers in Minnesota and elsewhere in the Middle West underwent a gradual, but quite dramatic, change. They lost faith in the axioms of American individualism and competitive opportunity. Where the journalistic masthead of Jacksonian Democracy before the Civil War had been "The World is Governed Too Much," farmers began to see that the enemy was not government, but the railroads, flour millers, and meat packers. Government became a potential ally in regulating such businesses, but to mobilize the authority of government required concerted political action. For Oliver Kelley and other midwestern Grangers that meant another radical step away from the fraternal organization envisioned by the Washington clerks who had founded, and still claimed to control, the movement.

The Grange grew exponentially over the next few years. By the end of 1873 there were 379 locals in Minnesota and about 9,000 nationwide with a total membership of almost 700,000. In Illinois, Iowa, and Missouri the rural bloc in the legislatures became a political force, and the resulting acts regulating railroad rates and practices became collectively known as "Granger Laws." In Minnesota, former Republican Ignatius Donnelly became one of Oliver Kelley's most important recruits to the cause.

Ignatius Donnelly and the Politics of Reform

A Philadelphia-bred lawyer, Donnelly landed in Minnesota in 1856 at the age of twenty-four. Like Oliver Kelley, he became swept up in the town-site fever, and, in partnership with fellow-Philadelphian John Nininger, platted the city of Nininger on the Mississippi, seventeen miles south of St. Paul. The town failed to develop (Hastings won the county seat and the post office), but Donnelly made it his home

for the rest of his life. He went broke along with other town-site speculators in the panic of 1857 and returned to the practice of law.

Like most urban Irishmen, Donnelly had been raised as a Democrat, but in Minnesota he was attracted to the Republican Party because it favored such reforms as antislavery, temperance, and free
land for farmers. Still in the birthing, the party was eager to find local organizers, and Donnelly, a gifted orator and articulate writer, saw
an opportunity for political office. (For all of his life Donnelly's politics would be a mixture of idealism and self-promotion.) After at-
tending a party convention in St. Paul and being elected secretary, he
set up a county organization in Hastings. He ran for a seat in the state
senate in fall 1857 and lost by only a few hundred votes in a county
that was heavily Democratic. Over the next two years Donnelly wrote
a string of editorials expounding the Republican philosophy, stress-
ing its opposition to slavery and advocacy of free land, while down-
playing divisive issues like temperance and the status of immigrants.
In 1859 the Ramsey forces placed him on the Republican ticket as
lieutenant governor, and he gained his first political office.

In 1862 Donnelly was elected to Congress and later twice reelected. At the end of the Civil War he joined Thaddeus Stevens and
other radical Republicans in promoting the rights of the freedmen—
including the right to vote—and in punishing the South with military
rule. In 1868 Donnelly, now thirty-seven years old, felt himself ready
for the U.S. Senate. Alexander Ramsey was up for reelection that year
and, unfortunately for Donnelly, had a strong following in the state
legislature, which, according to the U.S. Constitution, elected senators. An acrimonious fight ensued, as a result of which Donnelly lost
his House seat to a Democrat and was forced to withdraw from the
Senate race. After the election Ramsey tendered an olive branch, but
Donnelly preferred the role of outcast. He became the political maverick that he was to remain for the rest of his life.

With a characteristic blend of cynicism and social conscience, in
1870 Donnelly became a lobbyist for Jay Cooke's railroad interests
and simultaneously the Washington correspondent for the *St. Paul
Dispatch.* His weekly articles for the newspaper were a scathing in-
dictment of the superficiality of Washington society and the corruption of the Grant regime. Like the liberal Republicans who would

bolt the party in the 1872 election, Donnelly seized upon the protective tariff as the source of business monopoly and political corruption. "The Republican party of the nation must choose between the people and the capitalists," he wrote, arguing that the party must develop a reform agenda as powerful as antislavery: "A party cannot live upon the memory of the past."

When he returned to his Nininger farm in 1872 (Donnelly periodically tried his hand at farming, almost always with disastrous results), he saw the mushrooming Grange as a potential vehicle for reform. He organized a local in Hastings and wrote to Kelley offering his services as a professional organizer. Kelley, who had tracked Don-

Oliver H. Kelley's grange movement gained momentum among Minnesota farmers, some of whom attended the 1875 state meeting in Northfield.

Photo by Edward Newell James

nelly's liberal drift, hired him to give lectures to farmers at forty dollars an appearance. Donnelly toured the state enlarging on the program that Kelley had wished for five years earlier: state laws to regulate railroad rates, subsidies to water transportation to break the railroads' monopolies, farm organizations to negotiate with marketers and suppliers, and elimination of the tariff that raised the price of manufactured goods the farmers had to buy. In its political thought the Granger movement never went beyond this rather limited set of reforms.

And, in the short term, it was immensely popular. A powerful orator who could incite a rural audience into a frenzy of indignation, Donnelly was largely responsible for the spectacular growth of the Minnesota Grange in 1873 and 1874. In the 1873 state election Republicans tried to blunt the rising power of the Granger movement by choosing Cushman K. Davis, an outspoken opponent of monopolies, as its candidate for governor. Unfazed, a number of Grange locals under Donnelly's influence sent delegates to a convention in Owatonna that formed a new Anti-Monopoly Party. The party cooperated with Democrats on a fusion ticket for the state's executive offices, with the Democrats supplying most of the nominees and a joint platform that reiterated Donnelly's program. Although the Republicans retained the governorship in a close vote, many Anti-Monopoly candidates, including Donnelly, won seats in the legislature.

In 1874 the Democrat–Anti-Monopoly coalition in the legislature enacted a law modeled on an Illinois Granger Law that created a railroad commission (rather than a single, powerless commissioner) to regulate rates and gave the commission power to place railroads in receivership if they did not comply with the commission's orders. The statute had more symbolic than real importance, for, in the hard times of the mid-1870s, the commission decided that the railroads had to be allowed to set their own rates or face bankruptcy. In 1875 the legislature stripped the commission of its rate-making authority and rendered it a mere information-gathering agency. The principle of regulation remained viable, however, for in the following year the United States Supreme Court upheld the validity of an Illinois Granger Law in the case of *Munn v. Illinois*. (The companion Minnesota case decided at the same time was *Winona and St. Peter Railroad*

Company v. Blake.) In a landmark decision that provided the philosophical foundation for all modern government regulation of business, the court ruled that a business, though privately owned, was "clothed with public interest" if its primary function was to serve the public and therefore was a proper subject of public regulation.

Unfortunately neither Kelley nor Donnelly could savor that victory, for by 1876 the Minnesota Grange was in shambles. Donnelly's formation of the Anti-Monopoly Party had split the state Grange and aroused the ire of conservative national officers in Washington. The National Grange issued a declaration forbidding members to form political parties or even discuss political or religious questions in Grange meetings. The Grange, they clearly felt, was purely a social and educational organization. Kelley, who had sympathized with Donnelly's third-party experiment, ceased active participation in the movement and moved to Florida.

Disenchanted by the internal bickering and preoccupied with grasshopper plagues and falling farm prices in the mid-1870s, farmers in Minnesota and elsewhere quit the Grange by the thousands. Granges continued (and remain today) as social organizations but never again exerted any political influence. Ignatius Donnelly sought to preserve his personal role as spokesman for rural discontent by founding a newspaper, the *Anti-Monopolist*, with his own money. Full of fight and fun, bristling with invective, the paper sought to keep alive the spirit of rural radicalism. But for the next decade Donnelly's was a lonely voice.

The Farmers' Alliance

The trend toward business consolidation and marketing cartels accelerated in the 1880s. In 1876 Minneapolis flour millers formed a buying pool, the Minneapolis Millers Association, which purchased wheat from farmers at a set price and distributed it to the mill owners in proportion to their flour-making capacities. In 1881 the Minneapolis Chamber of Commerce, which included interstate grain traders in addition to the mill owners, took over from the Millers Association the monopoly on purchasing grain throughout the state. Farmers understandably objected to the lack of bidding in wheat prices. They also suspected that the scales used by elevator operators were artificially low (wheat was priced by weight and grade), thus doubly cheating them of a fair price.

A concentration of mill ownership paralleled the development of marketing cartels. In the primitive mills of the 1860s a small operation was just as efficient as a large one, but as milling technology became more elaborate and expensive and the market for flour expanded to New York and even London, size became important. Only the largest mills could afford the elaborate machinery, skilled management, research and experimentation, and sales force necessary to compete in an international market. In 1876 Minneapolis had eighteen flour milling firms; by 1890 four giants, led by Pillsbury and Washburn-Crosby, controlled 87 percent of the city's milling capacity. The trend toward consolidation had been the product of natural forces—what economists call "economies of scale"—but independent farmers understandably felt that they were being victimized by gigantic trusts. (The term "trust," pioneered by John D. Rockefeller with the formation of the Standard Oil Company in 1882, had become a catchword for overweening size and power.)

In the early 1880s the return of prosperity and relatively high wheat prices muted farmer discontent. But another financial panic in 1883 sent the economy spinning once again into depression, and farmers renewed the search for a political organization that would give voice to their distress. At hand was the Farmers' Alliance, a militant brood formed by politically minded Grangers in New York. (Poor white cotton farmers had formed a separate organization called the Southern Alliance.) Minnesota farmers were slow to join until wheat prices collapsed in the winter of 1884-85; within a year thereafter Minnesota had more than four hundred local units. Needing effective leadership and a coherent program, the state alliance turned naturally to Ignatius Donnelly.

Donnelly ran unsuccessfully for Congress in 1878 and campaigned for the Democratic presidential candidate in 1880 in the hope of earning political office if the candidate was elected. (Republican James A. Garfield won.) Momentarily disenchanted with politics, Donnelly turned to his ever-facile pen. In his first book, *Atlantis: The Antediluvian World* (1882), he attempted to demonstrate that the ancient mid-Atlantic continent of Atlantis, described by Plato as a utopia, actually existed and that it was the fount of western civilization. He followed that with *Ragnarok: The Age of Fire and Gravel* (1883), in which he argued that the earth's deposits of sand and gravel, described by geologists as glacial in origin, were in fact the debris of a comet that passed close to, or perhaps struck, the earth.

Such theories would be dismissed as scientific drivel today, but in that more innocent age Donnelly found believers, and the books actually sold quite well.* "One thing is certain," Donnelly wrote, "my books have lifted me out of the dirty cess-pool of politics, nasty enough at all times, but absolutely foul to the man who does not win." They also kept him before the public eye, and that made him attractive to the alliance men of Minnesota, who did not regard their aims as dirty at all.

"Farmers in this state need your abilities," an alliance member wrote, asking Donnelly to attend the organization's annual convention in 1884. Donnelly joined the alliance and delivered the keynote speech at the 1885 annual convention. He denounced the "Millers' Ring" that rigged wheat prices and proposed that the legislature outlaw conspiracies in restraint of trade. (Congress would accept this concept when it passed the Sherman Antitrust Act in 1890.) When it convened later in 1885, the legislature responded to alliance pressure by creating a railroad and warehouse commission with power to inspect the scales at the terminal elevators in the major milling cities. Legislators did not dare confront the millers' pricing cartel, however.

Far from content with such legislative palliatives, alliance members came to see themselves as part of a larger class conflict. Their 1886 convention platform claimed "that there are really but two parties in this State today—the people and their plunderers. The only issue is: Shall the people keep the fruits of their own industry, or shall the thieves carry them away." In such a conflict the exploited workers of the cities seemed to be natural allies of the farmers. The only labor organization of importance in the Twin Cities was the Knights of Labor, a national fraternal organization (complete with secret

---

* Scientists now agree that a comet struck about 65 million years ago, leaving a large crater off the Yucatan Peninsula and perhaps causing the extinction of dinosaurs— but not bringing sand and gravel.

passwords and handshakes). Based on the philosophy of the universal brotherhood of labor, the knights were open to all workingmen, unskilled as well as skilled. (The skilled workers generally preferred their own trade unions and generally ignored the knights.) In the early 1880s under the leadership of Terence V. Powderly the knights won a major strike against railroads owned by the bogey-capitalist Jay Gould and by 1886 had some 700,000 members nationally.

Farmers gather to discuss grain prices—and probably the weather— at the Pacific Elevator Company in Echo, 1903.

The knights had attracted some support among the semiskilled millworkers of the Twin Cities, and the alliance invited them to send delegates to its 1886 convention. Although the interests of the two organizations did not actually coincide—farmers wanted higher food prices (which would have been to the disadvantage of workingmen), and the knights were interested in social issues, such as a state bureau of labor statistics and prohibition of child labor (which were meaningless to farmers)—there was some talk of forming a farmer-labor third party. The discussion subsided, however, when the Republican Party accepted all the legislative proposals of the alliance convention and wrote them into its own party platform. To the dismay of the alliance and its labor allies the proposals died there. Except for establishing a bureau of labor statistics, the legislature did nothing for the next three years. Ignatius Donnelly had been elected as an alliance candidate to the state House of Representatives in 1886 but went down to defeat in 1888 and once again took up his pen. This time he produced a piece of literature that would have an enormous impact on the third-party movement.

The Rise and Fall of the People's Party

Caesar's Column (1889) was a portrait of American society a century hence, in 1988—Donnelly no doubt borrowed the literary device from Edward Bellamy's highly successful novel *Looking Backward, 2000–1887*, which had been published only two years earlier. But where Bellamy forecast a socialist utopia at the end of the twentieth century in which divisions of class and wealth had been eliminated and everyone was happy, Donnelly prophesied that America would continue to degenerate from its current state of monopoly and corruption into a degraded society of violence and mob rule. Playing upon the anxieties and prejudices of farmers, workers, and even the middle class in the 1880s, Donnelly pictured a nation in which the workers lived in semibarbaric poverty and where a ruling class, living in luxury, was composed mainly of Jews. Crime lords governed society. One of them, Caesar Lomellini, decapitated his enemies and stacked their heads in a column topped with cement—hence the title of the book. The hero of the novel, a visitor from Africa, profits from the exposure to decadence and returns to his homeland to establish a socialist utopia, but that Bellamyesque ending was lost among most readers who saw nothing but the shortcomings of their own age—cynically corrupt politicians and backstabbing capitalists. A literary hit, the book sold four thousand copies in the first four months and a quarter of a million over the next decade.

In this atmosphere of popular anxiety and frustration that Donnelly captured and amplified, the Minnesota Alliance steadily increased its political influence. In 1889 it elected thirty-three members to the state House of Representatives, and the following year the farmer-labor coalition ran its own candidate for governor. Although the Republican candidate won, the legislature that year fell under the control of a Democrat-Alliance coalition. It was the first break in the Republican stranglehold on Minnesota since the Civil War. Unfortunately the programmatic results were, as usual, minimal. The legislature passed a bill prohibiting Minnesota corporations from breaking up labor strikes with armed hirelings, such as those provided by the Pinkerton Detective Agency. But other reforms, such as a bill legislating an eight-hour working day, withered under opposition from Republicans and conservative Democrats. The lesson for the Minnesota Alliance was that fusion with the Democrats was not working—the people needed a party of their own. At that very moment the Farmers' Alliances in the Great Plains and the South were learning a similar lesson.

In 1890 the Southern Alliance demanded that Democratic candidates for office in the southern states commit themselves to the alliance's political program as a condition of farmer support. Many candidates had done so, won election, and then betrayed their promises. Among the poor white cotton farmers of the South and the wheat-growing farmers of the Great Plains—where by 1890 prices for the two crops were below the cost of production—there was growing sentiment for a national third party devoted to the interests of "the people." Ignatius Donnelly, elected president of the Minnesota Alliance in December 1890, watched this development with interest.

The following February Donnelly led a Minnesota delegation to a convention of Farmers' Alliances in Cincinnati where discussion centered on establishment of a People's Party. Although a formal launching was postponed until the presidential election year of 1892, the convention created a permanent national committee at Donnelly's suggestion. The movement reached a climax with a People's Party convention at Omaha's Coliseum on July 2, 1892. Donnelly, who had organized the Minnesota People's Party and was recognized as the national party's most distinguished orator, was called upon to give the keynote address. In this convention, he roared with pride, "There is not a single president of a railroad company; there is not a single representative of any of the rings which are robbing or sucking the life blood out of the American people." Borrowing the rhetoric of Tom Paine and the American Revolution, he declared that "this battle in which we are employed is the battle of mankind. This continent is the last great camping ground of the human race. If liberty fails here, it fails forever." Echoing the jeremiad of *Caesar's Column,* he warned that if the People's Party failed, Americans would descend into a poverty as drab as that of the starving Chinese.

The platform the Omaha Convention adopted was, in many ways, a blueprint for the twentieth century. It demanded government ownership and operation of the railroads and interstate telegraph and telephone systems (the one plank that was never enacted into law). To break the power of banks, the platform demanded that the government issue the nation's currency, including the coinage of silver, and that it ensure a money supply of at least fifty dollars per person. The platform proposed a graduated income tax to spread the wealth and postal savings banks to encourage saving among the poor. Proclaiming an identity of interests between rural and city labor, the platform recommended restrictions on immigration, an eight-hour working day, and laws against the use of Pinkerton-style labor spies. To enhance the power of the people it suggested that laws be submitted to popular referendum, and it proposed the popular election of U.S. senators.

Brimming with ideas, the Populists were unfortunately bereft of leadership. The powerful and popular leader of the Southern Alliance had died the previous year; Kansas had produced a lot of noise but no candidates; Minnesotans preferred to have Donnelly run for governor. As a result, the party nominated for president James B. Weaver, an aged veteran of lost causes. In the election, which Democrat

Grover Cleveland won, Weaver polled more than a million votes (about nine percent of the total) and picked up twenty-two electoral votes, all of them from the Great Plains or the silver mining states of the Rocky Mountains.

As expected the Minnesota People's Party nominated Donnelly for governor. Republicans responded by choosing Knute Nelson, the first Scandinavian to run for governor in the state. With sympathetic clucks and gestures toward reform, the Republican convention adopted a platform favoring a lowering of the tariff, a state railroad commission, and state inspection of factories. The Republican strategy paid off, as Nelson attracted Scandinavian votes in the Red River Valley, the popular base for the alliance movement, while Donnelly ran a poor third behind both the Democratic candidate and the victorious Nelson. Whatever promises his party had made, Nelson was no reformer.

The problem was that Populism, basically an agrarian movement, was strongest among the farmers of the wheat-growing Plains and the cotton-growing South—two crops whose prices were set by the world market, far beyond the ability of an American farmer to control or even understand. This in itself explains much of the Populist conspiracy rhetoric. In states where agriculture was more diversified, such as the corn-hog-beef complex in Iowa and the dairy-cheese complex in Wisconsin, Populism had little appeal. In southern Minnesota most farmers abandoned wheat in the 1880s and turned to corn and hogs, like their neighbors in Iowa, or to dairying, like their neighbors in Wisconsin. Wheat growing in Minnesota was largely confined to the Red River Valley—the only part of the state that voted for Donnelly and the People's Party.

The Populists' notion of class conflict was also far too simplistic for America's—and Minnesota's—increasingly complex society, where ethnic and religious differences were often more important than social class. Minnesota Democrats, for instance, nominated a Roman Catholic for governor in 1892, and he cut heavily into Donnelly's potential support among Irish and Italian millworkers in the Twin Cities.

As a third-party movement, Populism fared best in one-party states where it could present itself as an alternative—the Democratic South, for instance, and Republican Kansas. In states where keen two-party competition existed, one or both bent to the Populist wind and adopted all or part of the Omaha platform. In Iowa, for example, the Republican-dominated legislature set up a strong commission to regulate railroad freight rates and made it work. Thus, support for the People's Party in Iowa was negligible.

In 1892 the Minnesota Republicans put in their platform some of the reforms demanded by the Populists, and Governor Nelson (like many, a reformer in his youth and a conservative in advanced years) felt the party must redeem at least some of its promises. In its 1893 session the legislature passed, and Nelson signed, a law bringing all grain elevators under state inspection. Legislators also authorized construction of a state-operated elevator in Duluth (the act was later declared unconstitutional). They also approved a law modeled, no doubt, on the federal Sherman Antitrust Act, prohibiting business combinations (cartels, pools, and trusts) that hampered trade and commerce. This sort of law was as important to small businessmen as it was to farmers, and, in that sense, it heralded a new middle-class, urban-based reform current, the Progressive Movement. Also important was state Senator Ignatius Donnelly's investigation of the disposal of Minnesota's pine lands—a legislative committee investigation approved by Governor Nelson—that unearthed a good deal of fraud and corruption in the executive offices charged with control of these lands. Governmental corruption was another middle-class, urban concern and a major item on the Progressives' agenda.

It is a sad irony that much of the popular support for Populism in 1892 came not from farmers but from silver interests in the Rocky Mountain West. The Populist demand for silver coinage, which was only a footnote to their general demand for an increase in the money supply, was greeted with joy by silver miners because it meant a better market for their product. (Congress had demonetized silver in 1873, placing the United States on a single gold standard.) In 1896, with the nation in a severe depression, Democrats embraced the coinage of silver as a stimulant to the economy and nominated William Jennings Bryan for president. Populists also made Bryan their nominee, even though "free silver" was the only part of the Omaha platform that he adopted.

Fusion with the Democrats finished what was left of the People's Party in Minnesota. Most of Minnesota's Populists were former Republicans (Scandinavians from the Red River Valley) who could not abide the thought of voting for a Democrat. Even when the Democrats shrewdly nominated John Lind, a "Silver Republican," for governor in 1896, the state's voters were unimpressed. They gave William McKinley a 60,000-vote majority over Bryan, and Republicans swept the governorship and both houses of the legislature. The election of 1896 signaled the death rattle of Populism.

Even so, Donnelly and his fellow reformers had not labored in vain. Theirs had been a voice for change, the vanguard of a growing concern for the future of American society, and their call for reform challenged the cynical, "standpat" conservatism that had characterized American politics since the end of Reconstruction. After 1896 leadership of the reform impulse passed from farmers and workingmen to urban shopkeepers, to small-town professionals, to shippers and tradesmen, and, most interestingly, to women. Though lacking the vote in all but a handful of states, women, through social clubs and consumer organizations, became a political force by 1900. By that date leaders of the new reform movement had begun to refer to themselves as Progressives, and the movement commanded support among both Republicans and Democrats.

Dawn of Progressivism

Historians (or, at least, history teachers) commonly date the beginning of Progressivism to Theodore Roosevelt's ascension to the presidency upon the assassination of William McKinley in September 1901. In Minnesota and neighboring Wisconsin, however, the dawn of the movement can be dated two years earlier, to the emergence of two reform-minded state governors, Robert M. ("Fighting Bob") La Follette in Wisconsin and "Honest John" Lind in Minnesota.

A Swedish immigrant who had served the New Ulm district for three terms in Congress, Lind was a political maverick who drifted away from the Republican Party on the "free silver" issue and became, in his own words, a "political orphan." In 1896 he ran for governor with the support of Democrats and Populists. He tried again in 1898, this time gaining the added support of maverick Republicans unhappy with the Old Guard's cozy alliance with big business—the railroads, lumber companies, and flour mills (the same sort of conscience-driven rebels who supported La Follette in Wisconsin)—and he won. In his inaugural address on January 2, 1899, Lind offered the citizenry a path-breaking "inventory of Minnesota life and problems at the turn of the century."

He called for the establishment of a state commission to reform the state's tax system, in particular to lighten the onerous burden on property owners, and asked specifically for an increase of taxes on railroads. He suggested improvement in state support for education and in the care of the mentally ill. Adopting the Populist idea of involving the people directly in the democratic process, he proposed adoption of a direct primary (that is, a popular vote on party nominees), popular initiative in proposing laws, a popular referendum on certain laws, and the popular recall of certain officials.

Like La Follette in Wisconsin, Lind ran headlong into a solid phalanx of Republican "stalwarts" in the legislature and failed to accomplish any of his major goals. But, unlike La Follette, who would win reelection and go on to spearhead state-level Progressivism, Lind was defeated in 1900. Thus, his was a lonely voice in the wilderness, but it was a powerful one that popularized the reform movement and gave it respectability. His seeming indifference to party loyalty also helped establish a unique feature of Minnesota Progressivism—the idea of voter independence, the concept of voting for the most capable individual rather than for a political party.

Another measure of Lind's impact was the passage of several of his legislative proposals during the four-year administration of his Republican successor, Samuel R. Van Sant. In 1901 the legislature adopted the direct primary in elections for county offices, seats in the state legislature, and congressional races (significantly leaving the nomination of governor and other state officials under the convention system). Also in that session legislators raised taxes on railroad earnings, and the following year they approved an amendment eliminating many of the state constitution's 1850s-born restrictions on the legislature's powers over taxation and revenue.

Van Sant's tentative concessions to the rising demand for reform served only to widen the breach in the Republican Party between Progressives and the Old Guard. In 1904 John A. Johnson slipped into the governorship, the first Democrat to hold the office since the Civil War. A popular and effective politician, Johnson was twice reelected. His administration ended with his untimely death in September 1909. In those four years the spirit of Progressivism swept across Minnesota.

Johnson's first target was the insurance industry, a venerable business that had grown in importance with the maturing of the national economy but which had escaped the attention of both state and na-

Men in front of the C. H. Casey hardware store in Jordan engage in heated political debate, 1895.

tional governments. Life insurance companies, in particular, experienced phenomenal growth in the 1890s by tailoring policies for factory workers with premiums paid out of payroll deductions. After paying premiums for years, many a worker's family discovered that the death benefits amounted to little more than the price of a funeral. In Boston, Democratic Progressive Louis D. Brandeis, who would later become a key adviser to President Woodrow Wilson, earned a national reputation in a crusade for insurance regulation. Governor Johnson became active in the Boston-based organization that Brandeis helped found, and that helped earn the Minnesota governor national recognition. Shortly after Johnson took office, an investigation by the Minnesota legislature turned up extensive corruption and mismanagement in insurance companies and led to a strengthening of the state insurance code.

In 1906 public approval of the constitutional amendment that expanded the legislature's powers over taxation led to the formation of an expert-driven tax commission and the imposition of a state inheritance tax. The following year the legislature tightened railroad regulation with laws that prohibited free passes to politicians and set both passenger fares and freight rates. The 1907 legislature also increased the power of the Bureau of Labor to inspect factory conditions, and it gave Minnesota's cities the power to own and operate such public utilities as streetcar companies, telephone systems, and gas and electric works.

Johnson's political achievements were largely personal ones. He did not revitalize the intellectually dormant Democratic Party nor break the Republican stranglehold on the legislature. In fact, in the two elections in which the public returned him to office, the voters chose Republican Adolph Olson Eberhart as lieutenant governor, who then became governor upon Johnson's death in 1909. A Swedish-born lawyer from Mankato, Eberhart was a man of modest ability and no discernible ideology. When faced with a controversial issue, he simply dumped it in the lap of the legislature. This practice led former Governor John Lind to complain, "The people do not pay a governor $7,000 a year for his autograph."

To complicate matters further, by 1909 a new issue—itself a product of the reform impulse—divided both parties along ethnic and religious lines. The formation of the Woman's Christian Temperance Union in 1874 and the growth of women's clubs in the 1890s pushed temperance, a reform that dated back to the early nineteenth century, to the forefront of the national conscience. Throughout the nineteenth century temperance had been a steppingstone that allowed women to escape the confines of domestic duties and take the public stage because, at least ostensibly, it was a movement to protect the home and family from the wasteful evils of liquor. After 1900 middle-class Progressives took up the cause of temperance—or, alternatively, the outright prohibition of liquor—as a result of their twin concerns over crime and corruption in the cities and the arrival of a flood of hard-drinking immigrants from Southern and Eastern Europe.

Since the mid-nineteenth century people of Scandinavian or New England origin—the two groups that made up the core of the Republican Party in Minnesota—had favored temperance and restrictions on immigration. People of Irish descent (many of whom lived in St. Paul) and German Americans (who farmed southern and central Minnesota) usually voted for the Democratic Party. Both Irish and Germans opposed legislative restrictions on the use of alcohol (though German Americans were also concerned with maintaining parental control over education, that is, the use of German in the public schools). Given this ethnic clash, there was little chance of the legislature's approving statewide prohibition, and by 1908 Minnesota Progressives had settled on local option as a compromise. They drafted a law that would allow voters in each county to determine whether they wanted to ban liquor sales in their locality. Though seemingly a compromise, both sides perceived county option to be a likely precursor to statewide prohibition. Legislators accordingly rejected it.

Eberhart was elected to a term of his own in 1910, but under his feckless leadership the state continued to drift. The political cauldron bubbled with issues, as women demanded the right to vote and Progressives pushed for extension of the direct primary to state offices, a tonnage tax on iron ore, county option, and regulation of political campaign practices. But the governor and the Minneapolis-based Republican machine kept a tight lid on it.

Eberhart could not long ignore the national current of Progressivism, however. In 1909 Minnesota's Republican congressmen broke with President William Howard Taft on the issues of tariff reform and woodland conservation, and the following year several of them, including the influential Charles A. Lindbergh, Sr., joined an insurgency that sharply curtailed the powers of the Republican Speaker of the House of Representatives. In 1910 Theodore Roosevelt, newly returned from a hunting safari in Africa, publicly split with Taft and announced his candidacy for the Republican nomination for president in 1912. Because Roosevelt had easily carried Minnesota in the presidential election of 1904, he was certain to attract support in 1912, whether he ran as a Republican or as a third-party Progressive. Anxious about his own chances for reelection in 1912, Eberhart decided to swim with the tide.

In the summer of that year he convened a special session of the legislature to consider the Progressives' shopping list of reforms. With Eberhart at last exerting some leadership, the legislature promptly approved amendments to the U.S. Constitution allowing Congress to impose an income tax (the Sixteenth Amendment) and providing for the popular election of U.S. senators (the Seventeenth Amendment). It also extended the direct primary to candidates for state offices and enacted a law that sharply limited the use of money in political campaigns. Eberhart's tactical conversion proved timely. The fall presidential election revealed that Minnesota voters were overwhelmingly Progressive—Roosevelt, running as the candidate of the newly formed Progressive (Bull Moose) Party, garnered 125,856 votes, Progressive Democrat Woodrow Wilson received 106,426 votes, and President Taft, renominated by Republican stalwarts, trailed with a mere 64,334 votes. At the same time the voters returned Adolph O. Eberhart to the governorship.

Although Republican Progressives dominated the legislature in 1913, Eberhart reverted to type, and the political system was again deadlocked. Both governor and legislature, for instance, publicly endorsed regulation of utilities, but when Eberhart proposed a regulatory commission based on La Follette's Wisconsin model, legislative Progressives balked, fearing the governor would load the commission with conservatives. When the legislature passed a bill placing telephone companies under the regulatory authority of the railroad commission, Eberhart vetoed the measure. Only two pieces of social legislation filtered through the impasse of 1913—a law establishing workers' compensation insurance (that is, insurance against industrial accidents regardless of fault) and a law establishing minimum wages for women and children.

It is a grand irony that the one piece of legislation for which the 1913 legislative session is best known was approved without any forethought and with precious little debate: a statute forbidding candidates for local offices, as well as for the state legislature, from claiming party affiliation. Progressives had long felt that political parties were detrimental because they fostered urban machines and boss rule, and some Progressives may have voted for nonpartisan government as an interesting experiment. But, in the end, it was apparently the liquor interests who guided the statute through the legislative process. Seeing increasing numbers of Republicans committing themselves to county option, liquor lobbyists concluded that obscuring party lines would help in their battle against prohibition. By spreading the rumor that they were opposed to the measure, lobbyists induced the "drys" to vote for it, and the bill passed. The Minnesota legislature would remain officially nonpartisan for the next sixty years, although the political affiliation and ideology of candidates was usually well known to both politicians and voters. The experiment did, however, further Minnesota's reputation as a political maverick.

On the national level Progressivism reached its zenith in 1913–14 with the enactment of President Woodrow Wilson's New Freedom package: lowering the tariff, banking and currency reform through establishment of the Federal Reserve System, strengthening antitrust laws with the Clayton Act, and establishing a watchdog agency, the Federal Trade Commission, to ensure fair business practices. By the end of 1914 Wilson seemed to feel that his mission as a Progressive was accomplished, and with the outbreak of World War I in Europe, he became increasingly preoccupied with foreign affairs and American neutrality. In Minnesota, too, the reform impulse waned after 1914, or, rather, it became focused on two remnant issues, neither of which had been deemed important when Progressivism began—prohibition and women's suffrage. While the Progressive impulse in general faded with American entry into the war in 1917, each of these single-minded crusades, by contrast, actually benefited from the war.

Women's Suffrage and Prohibition

The suffrage movement was more than fifty years old in 1900, but prior to that date male resistance and internal schisms had impaired its growth. Although by 1900 women had gained the right to vote in four thinly populated Rocky Mountain states, Minnesota had made only minor concessions to feminist demands. In 1875 the legislature amended the state constitution to allow women to vote on local school issues and serve on school boards, and in 1898 another amendment pushed by the state Federation of Women's Clubs allowed them to vote and serve on library boards.

By 1900, because of the strides women had made in breaking free of the bonds of domesticity, educating themselves, and entering the professions, the suffrage movement could no longer be ignored. College education had long been available to females in Minnesota. Hamline University accepted both men and women from the moment it was founded in 1854, and the University of Minnesota was coeducational when it opened its doors to students in 1869. By 1900 more than seven thousand women doctors practiced nationwide, and in Minnesota 20 percent of women over age fourteen worked outside the home.

These advances demonstrated women's capabilities and led to a general public acceptance of a social and intellectual equality between the sexes. That in turn changed the philosophical basis of the suffrage argument. In the nineteenth century women had demanded the vote as a natural right of all people. A corollary to this argument was that women needed the vote to protect themselves. They pointed to the scandalously light punishments meted out to rapists by male-dominated courts and the ridiculously low "age of consent" established by male-dominated state legislatures. After 1900 the argument shifted from what the vote would do for women to what women would do with the vote. Women with the vote would benefit society by applying to the public arena the skills and moral sense developed in household management. With an eye to the Progressives' concern for crime and corruption in the cities, women argued that, with the suffrage and their club organizations, they would clean up the cities and improve municipal services. It was not enough, argued one Minnesota suffragette, "to prepare the children for the world"; women also had to "have a hand in preparing the world for the children."

Even without the vote women's clubs and consumers' leagues were able to induce state and local governments in Minnesota to adopt, in the name of Progressivism, a number of reforms relating to children and the family. One early crusade, dating from the 1890s, was to provide preschool or kindergarten training for children on grounds that they needed to be taught socialization and learning habits prior to the normal school age of six. By 1905 kindergartens were an integral part of the Minneapolis school system. During Governor John A. Johnson's tenure the legislature expanded the right of married women to own property and to sue and be sued. It also enacted a compulsory education law and a law limiting women to a nine-hour working day.

However, the legislature refused even to consider giving women the vote until late in the Progressive period. Legislative committees routinely buried suffrage bills. In 1911 a suffrage amendment to the state constitution finally reached the senate floor where it was defeated by two votes. In 1913 the House of Representatives approved a suffrage amendment, but it again went down to defeat in the Senate. Following that vote Clara Ueland, wife of a Norwegian-born Minneapolis lawyer and a moving spirit in the drive for city-financed kindergartens, decided it was time "to do a little something" for the suffrage movement. On September 17, 1913, she invited about forty Minneapolis women to her home to organize a new and different kind of suffrage organization. Prior to that time the Minnesota Woman Suffrage Association, like the National Woman Suffrage Association, hobbled along with an aged and largely ineffective leadership. Ueland proposed an organization with broader goals that would attract younger and more active members. Women, she announced, would demand the vote in order to do battle against "the three evils of the day—liquor, prostitution, and war." From this meeting was born the Equal Suffrage Association of Minneapolis with Clara Ueland as president. One of its first acts was to establish a state central committee, which would coordinate local clubs in each legislative district.

About the same time a new national organization arose to challenge the staid National Woman Suffrage Association (NWSA). Calling itself the Congressional Union, the new organization was led by Alice Paul, a New Jersey Quaker who while studying abroad became impressed with the confrontational tactics of English suffragettes. Where NWSA had for thirty years focused its energies on state legislatures, Paul hoped to pressure Congress into adopting an amendment to the U.S. Constitution, and she would do it by parades and picketing. Paul's activism appealed to Ueland, who organized a grand suffrage parade in Minneapolis on May 2, 1914. To those women who thought it "unladylike" to march in the streets, Ueland responded that it had once been considered "unladylike" to wear healthy clothes and go to college. The parade drew almost two thousand marchers, many of them university students. The *Minneapolis Tribune* pronounced the gathering to be "a revelation and a bump" to those who had ridiculed the movement because Ueland's marchers were "not a bevy of hopeless spinsters" or "unhappily married women ... [with] nothing else to do." A legislator who supported suffrage congratulated Ueland on recruiting "the best people in Minneapolis."

Liquor interests in Minnesota had opposed the suffrage movement from its outset from fear that women would be "dry" voters, and, by chance, the temperance movement climaxed in the same year that the suffrage movement adopted more aggressive tactics. (The two may have been connected, but there is no direct evidence for it.) County option was the central issue in the fall election of 1914; both Democratic and Republican candidates for governor (gubernatorial candidates were allowed to claim party affiliation) promised to sign into law any reasonable temperance measure. The "drys" won, and county option went into the statute books in February 1915. By mid-summer voters in forty-three counties had chosen to ban saloons; only eight counties remained wet.

Although the battle over liquor occupied most of the legislative session, Clara Ueland, who had become president of the Minnesota Woman Suffrage Association, was determined that the suffrage question be given proper attention. In January 1915, early in the session, the senate elections committee held hearings on a bill to grant women the vote. Ueland organized a battery of six women and two university professors to give testimony. An equally formidable group of six women opposed to the vote joined the rhetorical contest. The "antis" argued that men and women had equal capabilities but operated in separate spheres. Women served in the home, which was "the core of civilization," while men functioned in the public sphere. Women were capable of good works but would only be corrupted by entering the field of politics. Ueland, in response, scoffed at the idea that women would be diminished by being enfranchised. She reminded the senate committee that in Scandinavian countries, ancestral home to many Minnesotans, women had full legal rights, including the right to vote. Perhaps the main result of the debate was that male senators came away with a new respect for the intellectual and oratorical abilities of women. When the bill reached the senate floor in March 1915, it was defeated by a single vote. Ueland promptly announced plans to increase the number of pro-suffrage legislators in the 1916 election.

In December 1915, the National Woman Suffrage Organization elected Carrie Chapman Catt as president, and she brought to the office both a gift for organization and a "winning plan." She rejected the confrontational tactics of Alice Paul and the Congressional Union but welcomed Paul's strategy of focusing on the adoption of an amendment to the U.S. Constitution. By that date twelve states had granted women the vote (although the twelfth, Illinois, allowed them to vote only in presidential elections), and Catt asked women in those states to use their political muscle to create blocks of pro-suffrage legislators in both Congress and the states.

Ueland embraced Catt's strategy, and in June 1916, a presidential election year, she led a delegation of Minnesota suffragettes to put pressure on the Democratic National Convention, which was meeting in St. Louis. At Catt's urging, five thousand women had descended on St. Louis from all over the country, and each day of the convention, wearing yellow hats and sashes, they formed a "Golden Lane" twelve blocks long through which delegates had to pass to get from their hotel to the convention hall. The tactic attracted a great deal of journalistic attention, but it failed to work. The Democrats, fearful of alienating "wets" in the urban Northeast, adopted a platform plank that favored suffrage but left implementation up to the states. The Republicans adopted a nearly identical plank that year, and suffrage remained on the political back burner.

When the United States entered the war in Europe in April 1917, Carrie Catt, who had previously abhorred war in general, persuaded the national women's suffrage convention to adopt a resolution pledging support for the war and offering the services of women if needed. She reasoned that the suffrage movement would gain respectability by flowing with the tide of national patriotism. In Minnesota, Clara Ueland fully agreed with this strategy and induced her state organization to break its ties with Alice Paul's militants, now reconstituted as the National Woman's Party. Paul's followers had begun picketing the White House early that year, and this disruptive behavior during the national war emergency had brought down a heap of journalistic scorn on the entire suffrage movement.

More important than either Catt's tractable approach or Paul's militancy was the contribution of women to the war effort. They went to work in factories and farms, relieving men for military duty. In Minnesota Ueland and other suffrage leaders made front-page news with their offers to replace men in mills and factories and to increase food production with backyard gardening. Governor Joseph A. Burnquist placed Ueland on a food production committee where she recruited young women for summer farm work. The ability of women in Minnesota and elsewhere to perform "equal work" in taking the jobs held by men melted male resistance to their demand for equal political rights.

Seven more states granted women the vote in the course of 1917, and Congress, though controlled by Democrats, could read the script on the wall. The liquor industry, which had waged a mighty battle to prevent New York from granting women the vote, was disarmed when Congress in December 1917 sent to the states a constitutional amendment (the Eighteenth) authorizing the nationwide prohibition of alcoholic beverages. A few weeks later the U.S. House of Representatives gave the necessary two-thirds approval to a suffrage amendment (the Nineteenth). Although President Woodrow Wilson backed the amendment as a means of uniting the nation and rewarding women for their war efforts, the amendment failed when it came up short by two votes in the Senate. Minnesota's senators, Knute Nelson and Frank Kellogg, both voted for the amendment.

By the time of the fall congressional election that year women had gained the vote in fifteen states, and they helped bring about an electoral revolution in which Republican "drys" gained control of Congress and would hold it for the next twelve years. In May 1919, the House again passed the Nineteenth Amendment, and the Senate at last mustered the needed two-thirds votes for approval. Governor

The League of Women Voters swears in new members, keeping its numbers strong after the 1920 passage of the Nineteenth Amendment.

Burnquist promptly issued a call for a special session of the legislature to meet on September 8 to ratify the amendment. The state senate invited the board members of the Minnesota suffrage association to seats on the senate floor the day the legislature convened. The vote took only thirty minutes as both houses approved the measure by overwhelming majorities. Women, who had jammed the galleries, broke into cheers while a band struck up "The Battle Hymn of the Republic." Mrs. Ueland, the *St. Paul Pioneer Press* reported, "radiant and beautiful as usual, was the center of congratulating men and women." Said she, "It is my happiest day."

In the meantime, in January 1919, the states approved the Eighteenth Amendment, which merely authorized nationwide prohibition and left the details to Congress. That duty fell upon the shoulders of Andrew J. Volstead, a Republican "dry" from Granite Falls, Minnesota, and chair of the U.S. House Judiciary Committee. The resulting Volstead Act was one of the most poorly crafted pieces of legislation in American history. It defined intoxicants as including any beverage with more than one-half of one percent alcohol, which alienated beer and wine drinkers who might otherwise have supported "temperance" legislation. Worse, it prohibited only the manufacture and sale of alcoholic beverages, not the consumption. In economic terms, the act restricted supply but not demand—and seldom in history have the laws of classical economics been so well confirmed by popular behavior. The resulting Prohibition Era—symbolized by speakeasies, flappers, jazz, and bathtub gin—marked the demise of social and political reform, the end of a reform-minded age that had begun among a handful of Minnesota farmers some sixty years before.

VISITING HISTORY

Homes of reformers are spread across the state, showing both continuing interest in their ideals and the breadth of their reach.

American Swedish Institute

2600 Park Ave., Minneapolis; 612/871-4907. Exhibits on Swedish culture and the local Swedish American community in a fine mansion built in 1908.

Andrew J. Volstead House

163 9th Ave., Granite Falls. The residence (1894–1930) of the U.S. congressman who drafted the Volstead Act, setting out the rules for Prohibition.

Comstock House

.5 mile north of the I-94 exit on MN Hwy. 75, Moorhead; 218/291-4211. Guided tours of the house built by Solomon Comstock, a banker who helped develop the community and the Great Northern Railway.

Harkin Store

8 miles northwest of New Ulm, on Cty. Hwy. 21; 507/354-8666. An 1870s general store in West Newton, preserved when the railroad passed by the community.

Ignatius Donnelly's Nininger City Home historic marker

Co. Rds. 42 and 87, 3.5 miles northwest of Hastings. Site of the famous politician's home from 1856 to 1901.

John Lind House

622 Center St., New Ulm. Queen Anne brick-and-stone home of Minnesota's fourteenth governor, built in 1887.

Knute Nelson House

1219 S. Nokomis St., Alexandria. Home of the state's first foreign-born governor and long-time U.S. senator.

Oliver H. Kelley Farm

2.5 miles southeast of downtown Elk River on U.S. Hwy. 10; 763/441-6896. Costumed guides labor on an 1860s farm, with heirloom plants and animal stock; visitors can help. Interpretive center with exhibits.

State School Orphanage Museum

540 W. Hills Cir., Owatonna; 507/451-2149. Records, artifacts, and personal stories of children who grew up between 1886 and 1945 in the State School, a progressive institution for its day.

The Atlantic Crossing: An Immigrant's Story

Aslak Haukom came to America in 1887 at the age of twenty-two. He never explained why he made the move, but he was no doubt drawn by the good fortune of his older brother Olaf Haukom, who had come to America sixteen years earlier. Both young men adopted their surname upon beginning their new lives across the Atlantic; it was the name of their family farm in Norway's Telemark Province. Olaf made the move in 1870 after his family—indeed, the entire country—endured poor harvests and went hungry through the late 1860s. After several years in America he attended the Augsburg Lutheran Seminary in Minneapolis and by 1886 was an ordained minister with a parish in Manvel, North Dakota. This sort of success story was rare in Norway, where farming was the only occupation for a rural youth and the land was poor. Aslak Haukom followed his brother to America.

Accompanying Aslak were two of his sisters, a brother-in-law, and an infant nephew. From Liverpool on June 23, 1886, Aslak wrote his parents:

> We are now God be praised in good safety arrived in Liverpool. We have had fine weather the whole time, except from Skien to Kristianaia [Oslo]; then we had not so little storm, from which we all were more or less seasick. ... We have nothing to complain about except the coffee and the disorder which was allowed on board across the North Sea, when namely, boys and girls could unchallenged lie with each other in their bunks. We will be finished with this disorder across the Atlantic Ocean.

After landing in New York and traveling by train to Minneapolis, Aslak passed along through a network of Norwegian families and quickly found a job on a farm near the village of Audubon in Becker County in northwestern Minnesota. His sisters went on to live with Olaf in North Dakota. From Audubon on July 10 Aslak wrote his parents a description of the voyage across the Atlantic on the steamship *Adriatic*:

> [Early on the morning of departure] we had to go to the railway station so that each should take his things out of the huge heap of suit-

cases and mattresses and bedding there. It was a serious business: all crept and crawled in the heap after his own like ants in an anthill, suitcases tumbled down from the top and burst open so Lefse and Butterboxes rolled out the dock; then they were loaded on a large wagon all together and driven on the dock. There again was a pulling and tugging after mattresses and suitcases. Then, overloaded as we were, we were herded together like sheep on board a boat which would take us on board "Adriatic." All this running between stations and docks had taken a long time, so it was late in the afternoon before we got organized on board. We were therefore horribly hungry before we got any food; we got a small piece of meat with a few potatoes; this was naturally not enough so we were dissatisfied and demanded more; we got also a few biscuits with much scolding....

As you can imagine there was much annoyance and uproar among so many nations. There were not many Norwegians, perhaps about 40, but there were many Swedes. There were also many other nations; Russians, Finns, Poles, Germans, yes even Prussians. It is said there were about 500 Irish. Most of them are intolerable, and impudent folk.... Altogether there were over 1,000 people on board the Adriatic....

Saturday afternoon the 3rd of July we came to New York; we stayed on board that night also, which I shall not soon forget. Then we really felt we had come to Hot America. We lay and sweated in our bunks so we almost couldn't sleep. Sunday morning we were up at 3 o'clock and immediately we were in the mob with each other with mattresses, bedclothes and suitcases.

When we finally got on land we had to go on board a steam ferry which took us to Castle Garden [New York's immigrant processing center]. What we went through there I cannot easily describe. We were chased from one room to another with all our stuff, from one ticket clerk to another continually and all were angry and tired. The people at Castle Garden (agents and ticket clerks) all seemed to have fun making it difficult for the immigrants.

In 1887 Olaf moved to Polk County, Minnesota, and became pastor of three small Lutheran congregations in the vicinity of Mekinock, North Dakota. Aslak joined him there and took over management of the farm that supported the parish minister. During the summer Aslak taught in the "Norwegian school." Quite pleased with his prospects, Aslak wrote his parents:

Here money is not as scarce as in Norway, even if it is "hard times" here, too. I have not heard much talk about foreclosures, forced auctions, summons, and that sort of thing here. What a bad condition Norway is in, with all its Public Functionaries, one can first see after coming away from it. All that kind of thing one sees nothing of here, everything seems to work out and by itself, if one only works. It is remarkable what effect it has, when one sees the fruit of one's work. Hans [a friend he had met aboard ship] and I are thinking of taking up land soon in the spring. It depends on finding some that we like.

Within another year Aslak had a farm of his own, probably acquired under the Homestead Act, and his parents had come to live with him. Aslak coupled farming with school teaching and apparently prospered. In 1930 he visited Norway to research his family's history. He wrote a biography of his grandfather, who had purchased the farm, Haukom, and paid four hundred kroner to have the book printed in Oslo. Aslak died in 1939 and was buried in Badger, Roseau County, Minnesota.

Immigrants
*Aslak Haukom was one of many Scandinavian immigrants
who made their way to Minnesota in the 1880s.*

Wood relief by Peter Wedin, 1930 [detail]

8

The Birth of a Liberal Tradition

By 1916 it was apparent that the United States was sliding inexorably into the maelstrom of the European conflict. Germany instituted a blockade of the British Isles that submarines enforced, and President Wilson announced that Germany would be held responsible for any American lives lost. After the Germans sank the British passenger liner *Lusitania* in May 1915 with the loss of 1,195 lives, including 128 Americans, Wilson's protest notes were so bellicose that they occasioned the resignation of Secretary of State William Jennings Bryan. To Bryan and several members of Congress the obvious solution was to discourage Americans from traveling on vessels belonging to belligerents. In early 1916 Congress took up the Gore-McLemore resolution, seeking to warn Americans against traveling on merchant vessels bound for war zones. Although the resolution, which Wilson opposed, was defeated, every member of Minnesota's House delegation voted in favor of it, as did one of the state's two senators. That vote reflected widespread opposition in Minnesota to the United States' entry into the war.

People of German descent in the farming communities of central and southern Minnesota had little sympathy for the English and the French, and they rejected the Allies' propaganda claims of German barbarity. Conservative by nature, they demanded a national policy of "strict neutrality." At the other end of the political spectrum, Socialists, who were prominent in the labor unions of Minneapolis and St. Paul, blamed American war preparations on capitalists who hoped to profit from food and munitions exports. Feeding upon this anti-war sentiment was the germ of a farmer-labor political alliance. It first took shape as the Nonpartisan League.

The Nonpartisan League and Wartime Repression

Arthur C. Townley was a native of west-central Minnesota who drifted westward and began farming with his brother in North Dakota. The pair eventually accumulated eight thousand acres that they devoted exclusively to growing flax. Townley, a charismatic man with a knack for publicity, proclaimed himself the "Flax King of North Dakota." His dreams ended in disaster when drought, an early frost, and a collapse of flax prices in 1913 forced him into bankruptcy. Turning to politics, he made the acquaintance of a handful of talented men who had drifted from Populism into socialism and were advocating state ownership of grain elevators, flour mills, and farm-credit banks. Realizing that North Dakota farmers, who habitually voted Republican, looked with suspicion on anyone calling himself a Socialist, in 1915 Townley formed a Farmers' Nonpartisan League (NPL) with a modest program of state-owned grain terminals and meat packing plants. His objective was to gain control of the dominant Republican Party. After a massive recruiting effort in which his organizers crisscrossed the state in Model T Fords, Townley's candidates carried the Republican primaries in 1916, and in the general election that year the Nonpartisan League won the North Dakota governorship and a majority of the legislature.

In 1917 Townley moved the league's national headquarters to St. Paul where he hoped to broaden his farm organization to include urban radicals (Minneapolis had elected a Socialist mayor in 1916) and the left-leaning labor unions of the Iron Range. Within a month he claimed twelve thousand Minnesota adherents, and by mid-1918 his Model T–driven organizers tallied fifty thousand enrollees. Townley planned to set up a challenger to Republican Governor Joseph A. Burnquist in the 1918 Republican primary. Minnesota's German and Scandinavian farmers were initially skeptical of an alliance with urban Socialists, but the United States' entry into the war in April 1917 and the federal government's heavy-handed insistence upon loyalty to the war effort drove the two disparate interests into each other's arms.

Within a few days after Congress approved a declaration of war, the Minnesota legislature created a Commission of Public Safety with power to register all aliens and silence anyone who spoke out against the government, the war, or military enlistments. With nearly dictatorial powers, the commission banned German language teaching in public schools, jailed the editors of antiwar newspapers, and planted listening devices in the classrooms of professors at the University of Minnesota. Although Townley's league officially declared its support for the war, its prewar pacifism and criticism of "capitalist warmongers" attracted the attention of the loyalty commission, which sent agents to break up NPL rallies and arrest its organizers. After the Bolshevik takeover in Russia in November 1917, the activities of the Min-

The Nonpartisan League recruited members directly, using a fleet of wagons and Model Ts. Theodore G. Mattson poses with his wagon box in Little Falls, 1918.

nesota commission became part of a national "Red Scare" that sought to purge the country of radical speech and undesirable aliens.

Ironically, the commission's loyalty crusade was utterly unnecessary. Despite prewar misgivings about President Wilson's policies, the people of Minnesota responded to the nation's wartime demands with speed and energy. About forty thousand young men volunteered for military service, which was very close to the percentage of eligibles who stepped forward in the first year of the Civil War; a total of 118,000 (including draftees and national guard units) saw service in the war—about half of the state's men of military age. (In 1920, the state's population numbered 2,387,125. Assuming that about ten percent were males aged 18 to 35, the population of military eligibles was about 238,700.) Twenty thousand Minnesota women were organized for war work, including selling bonds in the government's four Liberty Loans; Minnesota's investment in the nation's war debt totaled $450 million. Minnesota's farmers—often women driving the tractors and harvesters—grew bumper crops of cereal grains that helped feed American armies and a substantial part of western Europe.

Birth of the Farmer-Labor Party

The political fallout of the loyalty hysteria alienated German American farmers and urban labor leaders from the mainstream Republican and Democratic parties and led to some new thinking about a farmer-labor third party. The Nonpartisan League, however, did not consider itself a third party, and in the primary elections of June 1918 it adhered to Townley's plan of gaining control of the state Republican Party. Its candidate for governor in that Republican primary was Charles Lindbergh, Sr., a Progressive congressman, longtime critic of the nation's banking system, and opponent of military intervention. Lindbergh traveled the state addressing county farmers' meetings, enduring threats to his life, thrown vegetables, and the arrest of his campaign officials. Turnout for the Republican primary exceeded the 1916 presidential vote, and the party's own candidate, Burnquist, won with 54 percent of the vote. However, Lindbergh and other NPL candidates received twice as many votes as were cast in the Democratic primary; thus, the NPL appeared to be a viable third-party alternative.

In the fall election the NPL joined with Twin Cities labor unions to field candidates for governor and attorney general. When the Minnesota attorney general ruled that the candidates had to have a party designation, the alliance chose "Farmer-Labor," although it would be another four years before the association was officially organized. (It never formally referred to itself as a "party.") Republicans retained control of state government in 1918, but the gubernatorial contest was a harbinger of the future: Burnquist was reelected but received only 45 percent of the vote, while the Farmer-Labor candidate—a small-town merchant and farmer named David H. Evans who had never run for public office—received 30 percent, and the Democratic candidate trailed with 21 percent. Prohibitionists garnered most of the remaining votes.

Arthur Townley never abandoned his dream of replicating his success in gaining control of North Dakota's Republican Party, but he lost Minnesota's Republican primary again in 1920 and shortly thereafter resigned as head of the Nonpartisan League. A Democratic offer of fusion in 1922 alarmed both the NPL and its urban labor allies and triggered at last the formation of the Farmer-Labor Party. By 1922, the recovery of European agriculture led to a collapse in world cereal grain prices and initiated a farm depression that would last for the next twenty years with only brief periods of respite. In the hard times Scandinavian as well as German farmers, who had habitually voted Republican, turned to the new party for relief. Their wrath centered on U.S. Senator Frank B. Kellogg, who was up for reelection in 1922 and who seemed indifferent to the woes of farmers.

As it happened, an attractive candidate emerged from the Farmer-Labor ranks to oppose Kellogg—Henrik Shipstead, a Glenwood dentist who had been the NPL's candidate for governor in 1920. Shipstead was a Progressive in the La Follette tradition, and he shrewdly avoided any contact with the NPL advocates of public ownership. Seeking support from the "farm bloc, the labor bloc, the small businessman's bloc, the soldier's bloc," and (for good measure) "the mothers' bloc," he pledged to cooperate with the La Follette–Norris Progressives in Congress and bring about a "New Deal" for the American farmer. Shipstead won the election, and the Farmer-Labor Party also elected two congressmen, though Republicans retained control of the state government. The following year Knute Nelson's death occasioned a special election for his U.S. Senate seat, and again the Farmer-Labor Association put forth an attractive candidate—homespun and earthy Magnus Johnson, who delighted farm audiences by climbing on a manure spreader and claiming it was the first time he had ever stood on a Republican platform. He joined Shipstead in Washington, and the Farmer-Labor Association became a fixture in Minnesota's political life. In the meantime, Kellogg became Secretary of State under President Calvin Coolidge and later won the Nobel Peace Prize for negotiating the Kellogg-Briand Pact of 1928, by which the major powers of the world (including the United States, Germany, and the Soviet Union) renounced war "as an instrument of national policy."

Progress and Poverty in the Booming Twenties

History books commonly place the Industrial Revolution in America in the middle decades of the nineteenth century when the economy "took off" into self-sustained economic growth led by such industries as steel making and railroad construction. Despite such apparent historical precision, one should remember that industrialization—or perhaps more accurately, modernization—is an ongoing phenomenon, and the advances of the 1920s were as "revolutionary" as those of the earlier period. The classic Industrial Revolution had been powered by coal and steam, featured new industries such as steel and oil refining, and had been driven by railroads and steamships. In the 1920s hydroelectric power and the gasoline engine began to replace coal and steam; glass, aluminum, and reinforced concrete diminished the importance of steel; and automobile manufacturing and housing construction drove the pace of economic growth.

In fact, automobiles and housing nourished one another because the automobile encouraged movement to the suburbs, a population migration that began with the advent of the streetcar in the late nineteenth century. With even greater mobility provided by the automobile, families moved out of the central cities' crowded tenements and row houses and built in the outskirts new, more commodious dwellings surrounded by lawns and trees. The gasoline engine also changed life in rural communities. Tractors and combines enhanced the productivity of labor but required capital input; hence farms became fewer and larger. At the same time market towns drew farther apart. With an automobile or a truck a farmer could drive twenty-five miles to a market town in the same time that he had once driven a horse-drawn wagon three miles. Grain storage and mercantile services that had once been dispersed in small towns five or six miles apart became concentrated in county seats or multicounty trade centers like Rochester, Mankato, and St. Cloud.

In 1920 Sinclair Lewis, who had grown up in the Stearns County village of Sauk Centre, published a satirical account of small-town life in his novel *Main Street*. The novel's Gopher Prairie became the epitome of the midwestern small town, with its social conformity and boring, uncultured people. Railroad tracks divided the "good" from the "bad" parts of town, and the merchants of Main Street, which formed a T with the railroad, were a money-grubbing collection of strident boosters. Lewis's stereotypes left an indelible image on American thinking about small towns, but the automobile, radio, and a modern highway system would soon render "Gopher Prairie" unrecognizable.

Wanted: better roads.
A Minnesota State Automobile Association car mired in mud in 1927.

In 1919 Congress began appropriating money for highway construction, and in 1921 it passed the Federal Highway Act, which established the modern, numbered, U.S. highway system. Congress appropriated seventy-five million dollars to state highway commissions, directing them to set up highway systems that would connect with one another in a national grid. Minnesota was already planning such a system. In 1920, voters ratified an amendment to the state constitution that set up seventy prescribed routes in the state for construction and improvement and imposed a tax on motor vehicles (and later on gasoline) to finance the highway projects. Marketing, salesmanship, and resource development became more mobile and more widely diffused as a result of a highway system that connected every community in the state, as did information, culture, and entertainment. The highway system spurred a social revolution every bit as important as that instigated by the railroads a half-century before.

The growth of ever-larger business conglomerates was another product of the economic boom of the 1920s, just as the rise of "big business" had been one of the features of the revolution of the previous century. In Minnesota two future giants, Honeywell and 3M, passed from adolescence to maturity in the 1920s. Each followed a pattern of product diversification through merger, research and development laboratories, and the professionalization of management. (The landmark between nineteenth-century entrepreneur and twentieth-century corporate executive was the founding of university business schools, beginning with Harvard in 1908.)

Minneapolis Heat Regulator Company, founded under another name in 1885, manufactured thermostats for coal-fired home furnaces and factory boilers. It dominated the field until the 1920s, when homeowners began switching from coal to oil furnaces. This required a different thermostat technology, and a smaller, yet aggressive, competitor, Honeywell Heating Specialties of Wabash, Indiana, challenged Minneapolis Heat. In 1927, with help from investment bankers, the two firms merged, taking the name Minneapolis-Honeywell Heat Regulator Company, with headquarters in Minneapolis. The merger not only ended competition between the two in the thermostat business but allowed company executives to expand generally into the area of heating controls. In 1931 Honeywell acquired a small firm that had patents on a line of heating and refrigeration controls as well as automobile radiator thermostats. With other acquisitions Honeywell was, by the end of the 1930s, the nation's leading producer of heating and cooling devices for homes, commercial buildings, and schools. By diversifying its products and giving substantial authority to divisional managers Honeywell remained in sound condition through the 1930s depression. The number of its employees in Minneapolis rose from 1,000 in 1928 to 3,300 in 1936.

Minnesota Mining and Manufacturing Company (3M) was founded in 1902 by businessmen in Two Harbors who planned to make sandpaper from locally mined corundum. The corundum proved inadequate, and the company moved first to Duluth and then St. Paul, importing garnet to provide the abrasive coating on sturdy paper. The company struggled until 1916 when a newly installed research and development laboratory designed an abrasive cloth that automobile and machine tool manufacturers found useful in sanding metal parts. During the 1920s 3M's research lab developed a paper masking tape, and in 1930 it invented a cellophane tape, the famous Scotch brand. During the 1930s the company diversified into rubber and resin products, developing among other things a sun-resistant, artificially colored roofing shingle. Like Honeywell, 3M evaded the national depression and managed to expand its product line, enlarge its labor force, and pay regular dividends to its stockholders.

Flour milling, the industry that built Minneapolis, peaked in 1916 and thereafter declined due to competition from other milling centers. Buffalo, New York, benefiting from low freight rates on the Great Lakes and favorable tax treatment, became the new milling capital of the nation. Washburn-Crosby, the most imaginative of Minneapolis milling companies since the 1870s when Cadwallader Washburn introduced a process for milling spring wheat, battled the milling decline with new ready-made products and resourceful advertising. In 1924 it introduced a new breakfast cereal, Wheaties, which it advertised using sports heroes, calling it "the breakfast of champions." Three years earlier the company ran a contest to promote its Gold Medal flour; a fictitious food "expert" named Betty Crocker answered letters from contestants.

In 1928 Washburn-Crosby became the centerpiece of a holding

company, General Mills, which maintained a controlling interest in twenty-six other milling companies nationwide and thereby became the world's largest miller. Executives of the new company, whose headquarters remained in Minneapolis, retained the fictitious Betty Crocker to answer letters from thousands of women who used "Kitchen Tested" Gold Medal flour and requested recipes and cooking advice. By 1936 when General Mills first portrayed Betty Crocker in its advertising, she was second only to Eleanor Roosevelt as the best-known woman in America. Initially depicted as a motherly, gray-haired homemaker, her image would be revised every decade thereafter—she became more youthful, with hair and clothing reflecting the fashion of the day. Executives of General Mills continued to experiment with new products, introducing Bisquick in 1931, Kix breakfast cereal in 1937, and Cheerios in 1941.

While Minnesota business prospered in the 1920s and grew ever more sophisticated, organized labor, which had seemed so viable and self-assured on the eve of the war, went into a steep decline. The Red Scare of 1919–20 rendered Socialists and Communists national enemies in the public mind; such radicals had been the most energetic and effective of union organizers. In addition, the exodus to the suburbs broke up ethnic neighborhood subcultures in the Twin Cities that had provided the core of union strength. Hundreds of African Americans who had come north during the war looking for jobs moved into their rundown neighborhoods. Labor unions generally excluded African Americans, and the small community (there were only 8,809 blacks in the entire state in 1920) was confined to service jobs as janitors, cooks, barbers, and railroad porters.

Union membership fell from a peak of five million in 1920 to less than three million a decade later. The nation's umbrella labor organization, the American Federation of Labor (AFL), did nothing to reverse the decline. An organization of trades unions, the AFL ignored the workers in mass industries that required little skill, such as flour milling, lumbering, and iron mining. The AFL also purged the labor movement of radicals in the 1920s and discouraged strikes. In 1926 AFL President William Green visited Minneapolis, a city that had elected a Socialist mayor ten years earlier, and declared: "I know of no other city today where there is as little unrest and agitation." In industries such as 3M and Honeywell, which depended upon semi-skilled workers, company executives co-opted unionization by developing "employee representation" plans, which were essentially company-dominated organizations that served as a safety valve for worker grievances and kept employees content with vacation time and pension plans.

In the state legislature the sole spokesman for labor interests was Myrtle Cain, elected in 1922 from a district of factories and railroad yards in northeast Minneapolis. A suffragette who had picketed the White House in 1917, Cain was a member of the National Woman's Party and campaigned on a platform of "equal rights and no favor" for women. Although her equal rights bill failed in the legislature, during her single two-year term she helped pass laws restricting the activities of the Ku Klux Klan and conferring legal rights on illegitimate children. Cain's isolation reinforced the fact that Republicans remained in solid control of the state government throughout the decade. It would take an economic crisis in the form of a nationwide depression to revive the fortunes of both organized labor and the state Farmer-Labor Association.

The Depression, the New Deal, and Farmer-Labor Leadership

The people of Minnesota, including business executives and journalists knowledgeable in market affairs, did not see the Wall Street crash of October 1929 as much of a threat to their own investments, much less as a harbinger of nationwide depression. One day after October 29 ("Black Tuesday"), when more than sixteen million shares changed hands in the stock market and the value of U.S. Steel (owner of most of the Iron Range) shares fell from 262 to 22, a Minneapolis newspaper carried the headline "Leaders Find Business Good in Northwest. General Situation Fundamentally Sound, Bankers and Others Report. Farmers Are Optimistic." The last statement ought to have been a clue. Farmers—perhaps with good reason—are rarely, if ever, optimistic.

Even if the "general situation" was not "fundamentally sound," the journalist was correct in implying that the stock market crash was, in itself, little more than a Wall Street speculators' problem. The market, in fact, recovered in spring 1930 and by May had reached the level of the previous year (that is, the level prior to the manic speculation of the summer of 1929). The stock market's behavior was a symptom of depression, rather than a cause, and the hard times fell gradually upon the nation as year after year—1930, 1931, 1932—manufacturing production declined and unemployment rose. The causes of the depression were many and complex, but one—especially applicable to Minnesota—rates discussion here. With the help of the U.S. Department of Commerce, headed by Secretary Herbert Hoover, U.S. businesses in the 1920s standardized their products, eliminated waste, and shared technological innovation. The result was a gigantic leap in productivity, but the rewards were not shared with the labor force because of the weakness of organized labor, nor were they shared with the public in the form of reduced prices. The profits instead went to stockholders, and this helped sustain the great bull market that began in 1924. As a result, consumers could not afford to buy all the goods that factories could produce: after 1929, prices fell, factories closed, and people were thrown out of work. "Overproduction" was the analysis of the time; in fact, it was "underconsumption." Minnesota, with its "open shop" mills and mines, commitment to industrial peace, and long-suffering farmers, helped bring about the crash and shared in the general economic decline.

As a protest movement from its inception the Farmer-Labor Party stood to benefit from the widespread distress, but that was not immediately apparent. Senator Henrik Shipstead, the party's most prominent member of Congress, had created a personal organization quite independent of the Farmer-Labor apparatus, and his public addresses played on the theme of voter independence and nonpartisanship. He was reelected in 1928 after blaming the farm depression on Republican policies, while Minnesota's ticket-splitting voters gave their presidential ballots to Herbert Hoover. The Republicans retained the state executive offices and majorities in the legislature.

Minnesota's two-year term for governors and legislators occasioned another state election in 1930, and the onset of hard times brightened the prospects of the Farmer-Labor Party. Although the party still contained radicals who blamed the depression on unbridled capitalists and favored public ownership of utilities and other public service corporations, Shipstead had provided the model for electoral success. The party convention that met in March 1930 was in the firm control of moderates, and its choice for governor was one of the most colorful politicians of the age, Floyd B. Olson.

Raised in the working-class tenements of north Minneapolis—the same neighborhood that produced Myrtle Cain—Olson was imbued with a lifelong sympathy for the down-and-out. After spending several years as a seasonal worker on the West Coast, he returned to Minnesota and worked his way through law school. Fresh from a successful term as Hennepin County attorney, he ran for governor in 1924 on the Farmer-Labor ticket. The Republican candidate won that election by capitalizing on the alleged radicalism of the Farmer-Labor Party and accusing Olson of consorting with Communists. Profiting by this experience, Olson adopted the Shipstead model when he was again nominated for the governorship in 1930.

The platform that the Farmer-Labor convention approved in 1930 would have been acceptable to most Democrats and even some Republicans. It endorsed the St. Lawrence Seaway project, which promised to open Minnesota's lake ports to world commerce; approved the federal McNary-Haugen farm relief program, which had been vetoed by both presidents Coolidge and Hoover; opposed the use of court injunctions against labor; and favored a moratorium on farm mortgage foreclosures. Absent were the once-common planks calling for public ownership of utilities and the confiscation of excess wealth. In promising to restore the fundamentals of good government, Olson warned his own party that he would not stoop to political patronage and would make his appointments on the basis of merit rather than party service. A forceful public speaker, Olson laced his addresses with skillfully told dialect jokes that poked fun but never seemed to offend. To attract the support of Democrats he formed an Olson "all-party" volunteer committee that functioned independently of the Farmer-Labor Party organization.

The looming depression had not, as yet, sufficiently alarmed Minnesota voters in fall 1930, and Olson's victory was largely a personal one. Republicans remained in control of the other state offices, held nine of ten congressional seats, and had a solid majority of the officially nonpartisan legislature.

Sworn into office in January 1931, Olson, not surprisingly, attempted to put together an all-party coalition administration. Although the legislature delayed creating a merit-based state civil service until the end of the decade, Olson sought to redeem his campaign promise of making appointments by merit, rather than by party service. The policy disappointed many of the Farmer-Labor faithful, and as statewide unemployment worsened, it became a major headache for the governor. When the legislature assembled that spring, he asked it to adopt the main features of his campaign platform, and, to combat the deepening depression, he proposed a state old-age pension system and state building projects to provide relief for the unemployed. As a state response to the depression, Olson's program was comparable to that of Progressive Phillip La Follette in Wisconsin and Democratic Governor Franklin D. Roosevelt in New York.

Not surprisingly, given the Republican majorities in the legislature, Olson's success that year was limited. The centerpiece was a fifteen million dollar bonding authorization for new highway construction that was expected to provide work for the unemployed. By executive order Olson required contractors on state projects to provide an hourly wage of forty-five cents for up to forty-eight hours weekly—a stab at minimum wage legislation that would not be adopted by the federal government until 1938. Olson could do little more for unemployment relief because Minnesota's constitution prohibited the state from going into debt, and the state had neither an individual income tax nor a state sales tax. Olson nevertheless created for himself a public image of a hard-working governor who was concerned about public distress. He would gain more adherents as the depression deepened over the next two years.

By 1932, when unemployment gripped nearly a quarter of Minnesota's work force, the radicals in the Farmer-Labor Association grew more vocal. The Hennepin County Association, which included much of Minneapolis, demanded state ownership of banks, railroads, and utilities; a six-hour workday; and creation of a state department of public works. When the party convention met that spring, however, Governor Olson was in firm control. Addressing the convention, he attacked President Hoover but disappointed the party's left wing by hinting at support for Franklin Roosevelt should Roosevelt win the Democratic nomination for president. The Farmer-Labor platform that spring bore Olson's stamp: it proposed a state income tax, a graduated tax on national chain stores (JCPenney's; Sears, Roebuck & Company) to help save small business, low-interest farm loans, and state unemployment insurance. (This last proposal anticipated Roosevelt's Social Security Act by three years.) Olson also fended off a proposal by the party's left to publicly reject Roosevelt and commit the party to a national Socialist ticket.

The depression's impact on Minnesota voters was at last evident in the fall general election. Olson was reelected with nearly 50 percent of the vote; the Republican candidate earned 32 percent and the

As the depression takes its toll in Minnesota,
out-of-work men gather at Gateway Park, Minneapolis.

Minneapolis Star Journal photo, 1937

Democrat 16 percent. The Farmer-Labor Association gained three other state executive offices and five of the state's nine seats in Congress and became the largest bloc in the nonpartisan state legislature (though it would have to ally with Democrats to form a majority). In the presidential contest Roosevelt carried the state with a landslide 60 percent of the vote. For the first time since 1916 the state also sent a Democrat to Congress. Roosevelt's popularity in the state boded well for the Democrats, but the state party continued to lack imagination and leadership, leaving the liberal void to be filled by Olson and the Farmer-Laborites. Roosevelt and his advisers seemed to recognize this, for they consulted Olson on federal patronage and encouraged Minnesota Democrats to defer to Farmer-Labor leadership in the legislature.

In the 1933 legislative session Olson deftly put together a coalition of Farmer-Laborites, Democrats, and a handful of Republican Progressives and achieved many of the goals set forth in his platform. The result was a response to the depression that no other state could match: a moratorium on mortgage foreclosures, reduced property taxes on farmers and homeowners, a state income tax, a progressive tax on national chain stores, a program for farm land "retirement" to take it out of production, tavern reform (anticipating the repeal of Prohibition) that authorized municipally owned retail liquor stores, a limitation on the weekly working hours of women, ratification of a national child labor amendment, initiation of a state old-age pension system, and the first steps toward preserving the boundary waters wilderness.

That legislative session was the high point of Floyd Olson's political career, and it left him and his party well positioned for the 1934 election. But ill health and the seemingly unending depression began to dog him. He developed chronic ulcers, which sapped his energy and (some thought) robbed him of his political savvy. As the depression dragged on, the party radicals became ever more vocal and the party faithful ever more insistent on obtaining patronage jobs. While Olson suffered from the aftereffects of an appendectomy in summer 1933, personnel directors in the state's major executive departments opened the floodgates to patronage appointments, and, by seeming to yield to "machine" politics, in the long run damaged

*The bartender at Schiek's serves the restaurant's first beer
after the long-awaited repeal of Prohibition, 1933.*

the democratic-spirited, nonpartisan public image of the Farmer-Labor Association.

By the end of 1933, Olson, ill and under increasing pressure from the political left, expressed growing sympathy for the principle of public ownership. He felt, it appeared, that the free enterprise system had failed and that the nation's recovery depended on nationalizing key industries. At the same time he hailed the federal programs initiated in the New Deal's first "Hundred Days," though it was not clear whether he viewed them as patching up the capitalist system or paving the way toward socialism. Capitalizing upon Olson's apparent drift to the left, the radicals dominated the Farmer-Labor convention in spring 1934 and drafted a platform calling for state ownership of mines, hydroelectric power plants, banks, and all factories not cooperatively owned. It even proposed state publication of all school textbooks.

While Olson struggled to regain control of his party in summer 1934, Minnesota's long-docile labor unions turned militant. The National Industrial Recovery Act, passed during the New Deal's first "Hundred Days," offered incentives to American businesses to enter into agreements to limit production and hence reduce surpluses, but it also required businesses who joined the National Recovery Administration (NRA) to adopt "labor codes" that recognized unions as collective bargaining agents. In the nation's coal fields United Mineworkers president John L. Lewis told miners, "The President wants you to join a union." Union organizers everywhere spread variations of this half-truth, and union membership soared. In Minneapolis, General Drivers Local 574 had survived the 1920s as a craft union embracing a handful of truck drivers. After passage of the NRA, the local organized the coal yard drivers, and in February 1934 it went on strike, halting all coal deliveries in the city. Having won a victory, the local organized more than three thousand drivers of all kinds throughout the city. When employers refused a collective bargaining agreement in May, the drivers went on strike and brought truck traffic to a halt citywide. The strikers built a kitchen to feed people walking their picket lines, published a newspaper, and established a women's auxiliary to serve in the commissary and raise funds. On July 20 city police surrounded a group of union picketers and opened fire, killing two and wounding over fifty. Governor Olson called out the National Guard, and twenty thousand outraged working people turned up at a funeral of one of the victims. Yielding to the pressure of public opinion, Minneapolis trucking firms agreed to a union contract. It was the first labor victory in Minnesota since before the war, and it inspired further militancy.

In the fall election a chastened Olson dropped all references to public ownership, reinterpreted the party platform to demand nothing more than a Cooperative Commonwealth (whatever that meant), and wholeheartedly endorsed the New Deal. Olson's brief flirtation with radicalism, however, had frightened rural and small town voters, and support for Farmer-Labor candidates declined from its 1932 height. Olson and Shipstead were reelected, but Republicans regained control of the legislature and elected five of the state's eight congressmen.

The ideological split between governor and legislature doomed the state to political drift in 1935, and labor militancy dominated the newspaper headlines. One of the Twin Cities' most important industries was the manufacture of clothing. It employed around five thousand workers, nearly 75 percent of whom were women. The International Ladies Garment Workers' Union (ILGWU) was one of the nation's few labor unions organized on a "mass" basis—that is, by factory, rather than by craft or skill. In late 1935, David Dubinsky, its head, would be instrumental in forming the Congress of Industrial Organizations (CIO) as first an offshoot and later an independent rival of the American Federation of Labor. Although men dominated

Called out by Governor Floyd Olson,
National Guard officers are at the ready during the 1934 truckers' strike.

Dubinsky's national organization, the Minneapolis local was controlled by women who built a network of support in the working class neighborhoods of the city.

Working conditions in the garment industry were abominable. Work was seasonal, insecure, and ill paid. In the depths of the depression two-thirds of the workers were unemployed or worked a shortened week. Women sat at sewing machines and were paid as little as thirty-five cents a dress. The speediest worker could make about eight dresses in a day. When the national garment industry joined the NRA and approved a code containing minimum wage and maximum hour standards, ILGWU organizers in St. Paul and Minneapolis publicized code violations and encouraged workers to join the union. The successful truckers' strike of 1934 showed garment workers the worth of union solidarity, and it created a culture of interunion cooperation in the working class wards of the two cities.

In summer 1935 the Strutwear Knitting Company plant in Minneapolis became the focal point of the garment workers' unionization drive. Although the selection of Strutwear was more by chance than planning, it proved a compelling target because of the company's utter ruthlessness. Strutwear employed 580 female and around 200 male workers engaged in the knitting and seaming of stockings. Men held all management positions. During the 1920s Strutwear kept unions out of its plant by forcing workers to sign "yellow-dog contracts" (that is, agreeing never to join a labor union) as a condition of employment and by maintaining an all-male company union.

In June 1935 a group of knitters visited a unionized hosiery plant in Milwaukee and were impressed with the higher pay and better working conditions. They returned to Minneapolis and persuaded most of the male workers at Strutwear to form a local of the national Hosiery Workers union. When Strutwear officials dismissed eight workers for union activity in August, the local called a strike. Nonunionized female workers joined the picket lines around the factory, and the neighborhood community provided food and vocal support. The strike lasted for eight months and eventually mobilized the entire labor community of the Twin Cities. Other unions organized dances to keep up the strikers' morale, staffed a strike commissary, and donated to a strike fund. In December the truck drivers of Local

574 double-parked their vehicles at the company's gates, obstructing the movement of Strutwear's products and services. Strutwear management finally agreed to most of the union's demands in April 1936, and the strike was won. By then five hundred women had joined the Hosiery Workers Local, and unions throughout the Twin Cities' garment industry were rushing to recruit female workers.

The role of women in the Strutwear strike and their ability to generate community support sent ripples throughout the state's political system. In the 1936 fall election campaign the Farmer-Labor Association formed a Women's Cavalcade, which toured the state by motorcars mounted with loudspeakers. Their message to women—that families lacked enough to eat because farms were failing and city workers were out of jobs—placed a veneer of unity over the age-old divisions within the Farmer-Labor movement.

Floyd Olson died of cancer that summer, and the association turned to Elmer Benson as his successor. Benson, who lived all his life (except for his years in the governor's mansion in St. Paul) in the house where he was born in the Minnesota River valley community of Appleton, was immersed in the small town values satirized by Sinclair Lewis in *Main Street*. He brought to the governorship the prairie-populist's suspicion of business oligarchies, and, though a friend of the urban worker, he mistrusted the "racketeering" tactics of big labor unions. Although a forceful public speaker, Benson was a poor politician, too grimly certain of his rectitude, too outspoken, and too quick to condemn those who disagreed with him.

Elected in 1936 with 58 percent of the popular vote, the largest margin of any Minnesota governor to that time (in the presidential contest Roosevelt swept the state with 60 percent), Benson went before the 1937 legislature with an ambitious program—sharply graduated income taxes, work relief, state aid for schools, compulsory workers' compensation, state-regulated interest rates, liberal state employee benefits, party designation of legislators—that would prove to be a blueprint for Minnesota liberalism for the next twenty years. Unfortunately, he lacked the political skill to steer it through an evenly divided legislature. His truculence and impatience alienated even leaders of his own party.

Of further damage to Benson was his tolerance of Communists in the Farmer-Labor Association. Communists, who looked to Moscow for ideological guidance, stood on the periphery of Minnesota politics through the early 1930s, despite the distress caused by the depression. However, Adolf Hitler's rise in Germany and the support given by both Hitler's Germany and Benito Mussolini's Italy to the Fascist revolution in Spain from 1936 to 1939 made Communists more respectable in both western Europe and America. The Soviet Union, equally alarmed by the spread of Nazism and Fascism, urged American Communists to cease revolutionary activities and join in the Popular Front with U.S. Socialists and left-leaning liberals. Benson, believing that the days of "Red Scare" were over, welcomed them into the Farmer-Labor organization and became a nationally known spokesman for the Popular Front policy of allying the United States with Britain and France against Germany and Italy.

Benson thus resurrected the ancient rivalry between moderates and radicals in the Farmer-Labor movement, and he stirred new anger among Farmer-Labor members who opposed U.S. involvement in foreign wars and looked back on American entry into World War I as a mistake. In 1935, congressional hearings in a committee chaired by North Dakota Senator Gerald Nye reinforced the isolationist attitudes of the Farmer-Labor Association and of Minnesota voters generally. The Nye committee concluded that American entry into the war had been driven by bankers and munitions makers—"merchants of death" in Senator Nye's memorable phrase.

With a divided party and facing voters visibly tired of the bickering between governor and legislature, Benson and the Farmer-Labor Association seemed highly vulnerable as the election of 1938 approached. As it happened, they also faced a newly invigorated opponent, a Republican Party remodeled by a thirty-one-year-old newcomer to the political stage, Harold Stassen.

Harold Stassen and New Model Republicanism

Minnesota-born and educated at the state university, Stassen was a South St. Paul lawyer who, after being chosen a delegate to the 1936 Republican National Convention, became head of Minnesota's Young Republican League. This organization of mostly young, middle-class business and professional people rejected the standpat conservatism with which the stalwarts in the party had battled the New Deal. Stassen preached a gospel of "enlightened capitalism," by which he meant acceptance of the major social reforms of the New Deal—Social Security, the minimum wage, banking regulation, a labor relations act, farm price supports, unemployment compensation, and relief for the unemployed. Stassen and the Young Republicans claimed they could manage these programs more honestly and efficiently than the Democrats, without engaging in "machine" politics or using work relief to "buy votes" (an accusation that had been leveled at the New Deal's centerpiece relief agency, the Works Progress Administration).

After winning the Republican primary in 1938, Stassen struck at the vulnerable Benson, accusing him of coddling Communists in his administration and using political patronage to advance the Farmer-Labor "machine." He called for a civil service law for state employees and establishment of a state labor relations act that would both recognize and regulate unions. The election that fall reflected a massive shift in voter alignment, as Stassen, with 59 percent of the vote, exceeded the margin by which Benson had won two years earlier. The Republicans also won eight congressional seats, all the state offices, and control of the legislature. The sweep gained Stassen national recognition, and in 1940 the Republican National Convention made the thirty-three-year-old governor its keynote speaker.

Far from a rejection of liberalism, the Republican landslide of 1938, which ushered in a decade of Republican rule in Minnesota, was a confirmation of the liberal tradition that had its roots in prewar Progressivism. The popular base of Stassen's Young Republican movement was the state's Scandinavian population (progressive Republicans frequently pictured Lutheran churches in their campaign brochures), the same element that had been the political base for Wisconsin's La Follette family since the beginning of the century. Such voters were independent-minded, earnest, moralistic, conservative, but with a sense of social justice. The victory of the progressive Republicans thus reflected a general acceptance of the nation's response in the first half of the twentieth century to the problems posed by the rise of big business, the mechanization of factories and farms, and the growth of cities with attendant problems of poverty and crime.

VISITING HISTORY

Minnesota's political identity was born in farms and small towns and big cities, in hard times, and through hard work.

Floyd B. Olson House

1914 W. 49th St., Minneapolis. Brick-and-stucco 1922 bungalow residence of three-term governor, political reformer, and leader of the Farmer-Labor party.

Frank B. Kellogg House

633 Fairmount Ave., St. Paul. The home of the statesman, diplomat, and Nobel Peace Prize winner who, as U.S. secretary of state (1925-29), signed the Kellogg-Briand Pact outlawing war.

St. Paul Gangster Tours/Mill City Mob Tours

651/292-1220. Bus tours given by costumed guides to the haunts of gangsters who inhabited the Twin Cities in the 1930s.

Sinclair Lewis Boyhood Home

820 Sinclair Lewis Ave., Sauk Centre; 320/352-5359. The author's home from 1889 to 1902, restored to that period, offering guided tours.

Steamboat Minnehaha

Minnesota Transportation Museum, 328 Lake St., Excelsior; 952/474-2115. Rides on Lake Minnetonka in a restored streetcar boat, one of seven that plied its waters from 1906 to 1926.

God's Fault or the Railroads'?
The Cloquet Fire of 1918

By the time of World War I the great pine forests of northeastern Minnesota were virtually exhausted. Logging continued, but it was largely confined to second-growth pine and pioneer hardwoods, such as aspen and birch. Cloquet, some ten miles up the St. Louis River from Duluth, was the milling center of the region. It boasted three large sawmills, a paper mill, and factories that produced furniture and shipping crates. With a population of about nineteen thousand, it was also a marketing center for farmers who had moved onto the cutover lands. The 6,366 barns that burned in the calamity of 1918 testify to the mixture of agriculture and forestry in the region. With so much of the land devoted to pasture and potato fields people ceased worrying about forest fires. Farmers battled localized fires almost every summer, but a wildfire that consumed thousands of acres seemed a figment of the past.

Northern Minnesota had suffered a drought since 1916, and the summer of 1918 was hot and dry. The brush of the second-growth forest and the slash-and-litter of past logging rendered the region a tinderbox. Farmers battled small fires throughout the last days of summer. On the afternoon of Thursday, October 10, a passenger train on the Great Northern tracks from Duluth to Hibbing stopped on a siding near Milepost 62. After the train departed a nearby farmer noticed smoke rising from grass along the tracks. He and his neighbors fought the fire for the next two days, containing it but not quenching it entirely. On Saturday, October 12, strong winds came up and blew the fire out of control, burning barns and haystacks in the area. At four o'clock in the afternoon fire swept through the village of Brookston, some ten miles up the St. Louis River from Cloquet. The same winds that afternoon blew small fires into large ones along the Soo Line tracks between the towns of Bain and Moose Lake to the south and west of the Milepost 62 fire.

After reducing Brookston to ashes, the Milepost 62 fire jumped the St. Louis River and swept through the Fond du Lac Ojibwe Indian reservation. At about five o'clock that evening, a relief train carrying refugees from Brookston arrived at Cloquet, and an hour later fiery ash began falling on the city. Sirens summoned volunteer fire brigades, but the fire was on them before they could get organized and deployed.

Propelled by sixty-mile-an-hour winds, the fire reached the Northern Lumber Company yard on the west side of Cloquet about eight o'clock in the evening. The yard was filled with neatly stacked boards of drying lumber that quickly blazed. In the ensuing firestorm burning boards flew into the air and set fresh fires around the city. Alerted by telegraph operators in Brookston, the railroads held four passenger trains in Cloquet and were able to pack in about eight thousand refugees. In addition, automobiles streamed out of town loaded with

View of downtown Cloquet after devastating forest fire, 1918.
Despite the fast-moving flames, thousands managed to escape to safety.

Photo by Hugh McKenzie

other refugees, many of them returning to take on more passengers. Street Commissioner Archie Campbell alone made three trips between Cloquet and the Duluth suburbs. By early Sunday morning only a few factories remained along the riverbank in Cloquet. By then the fire had raced on and was consuming the northern suburbs of Duluth. Firemen and a National Guard unit stopped the fire at the crest of the Duluth hill and saved the city's center.

The fire damage of October 12–13, 1918, was the worst in Minnesota's history. The Milepost 62 and related fires cut a swath of destruction forty miles long and twenty miles wide. The separate Moose Lake–Kettle River fire left a patch of scorched earth thirty-one miles long and fourteen miles wide. Total deaths numbered 453, although, because of the stupendous relief effort, fewer than half a dozen people died in the city of Cloquet.

Early in 1919 the first of what would ultimately amount to more than fifteen thousand lawsuits was filed against the Northern Pacific, Great Northern, and Soo Line railroads. Nearly everyone in northern Minnesota believed that the fires had been started by sparks from train engines. The civil actions were complicated because the federal government had taken over railroads during the war. To coordinate rail traffic in the war emergency Congress created the Railroad Administration, which assumed technical ownership and responsibility for the rail lines while leaving actual operation in the hands of the original management. Minnesota lawyers lost no time in naming the U.S. government a defendant in the lawsuits, and the legal department of the Railroad Administration remained a participant even after 1920, when Congress restored the railroads to their original owners.

The railroads' defense rested on the argument that some of the fires, particularly in the Moose Lake region, were of unknown origin and thus may have been started by lightning or some other "act of God." Even if some property had been damaged by sparks from a railroad train, they argued, it stood in the path of a fire caused by an act of God and therefore had no value for which the railroad could be held liable. A Minnesota district judge disagreed and instructed the jury that if it found that a fire caused by a railroad engine was a "substantial element" in causing a plaintiff's damages, the railroad was liable even if its fire mingled with a fire of unknown origins. The

Minnesota Supreme Court affirmed this decision and it became a landmark in American tort law. A few months later, another district judge, after hearing the testimony of farmers living near the Great Northern's Milepost 62, had "no difficulty in assigning the origin of the fire at Mile Post 62 to the defendant railway company." That judgment resolved the liability issue for the suits filed at Brookston, Cloquet, and Duluth.

Following these decisions and the determination of damages in several hundred suits, the U.S. government in 1925 offered to settle all the claims with a payment of 50 percent of the property loss. The original claims had totaled $73 million; a Minnesota court judged the total damages to be about $29.7 million; and the federal government paid $12.7 million to the fire sufferers. Utterly dissatisfied with that result, the fire claimants formed an organization to lobby Congress for the unpaid balance of the court-determined damages. Minnesota congressmen introduced relief measures annually, but not until 1935 did Congress finally pass a bill appropriating ten million dollars. The *Cloquet Pine Knot* declared "The DEBT is PAID," and people danced in the streets of the rebuilt city.

VISITING HISTORY

Carlton County History and Heritage Center

406 Cloquet Ave., Cloquet; 219/879-1938. Includes exhibits on the 1918 Cloquet Fire.

9

Maverick in the Mainstream

American politics in the latter half of the twentieth century followed a cyclical pattern, oscillating between an activist liberalism and a conservatism that within itself fluctuated between passivism (on matters of economic welfare) and activism (on enforcing patriotic loyalty and a moralistic social agenda). In the 1930s and '40s New Deal liberals sought to use government to ameliorate some of the harsher aspects of free enterprise capitalism with a social welfare system and support programs for farmers and working people. After a red scare that stifled political dissent and an interlude of relatively passive government under President Dwight D. Eisenhower in the 1950s, liberalism experienced a rebirth in the 1960s, but with different goals. Liberals of the Kennedy-Johnson era retained some New Deal economic-class rhetoric (Lyndon Johnson's War on Poverty, for instance), but the principal thrust was toward equal rights for racial minorities and women. Racial violence in the late 1960s, coupled with busing and other affirmative action programs, produced a backlash among middle-class whites and a new era of conservatism in the 1970s and '80s. In the last decades of the century religious conservatives abandoned political passivism and sought government action on social issues such as contraception and abortion, while Republican presidents pursued a more proactive, go-it-alone foreign policy (interventions in Grenada, Panama, Nicaragua, and Kuwait) culminating, at the beginning of the twenty-first century, in President George W. Bush's doctrine of preemptive war.

Minnesota shared in these national trends in the second half of the twentieth century, but the state's moral political culture* and assortment of compassionate liberals (Hubert H. Humphrey, Eugene McCarthy, Walter Mondale, Orville Freeman, Paul Wellstone) and voluble conservatives (Walter Judd, Jesse Ventura) produced some variations that reinforced the state's reputation—earned in the first half of the century—as a political maverick.

The story of Minnesota's slideslip down the mainstream begins with the state's response to trouble brewing in Europe.

World War II

Throughout the late 1930s Minnesotans shared the national desire to avoid becoming involved in another European war. The state's congressmen unanimously supported neutrality legislation allowing belligerents to purchase munitions in the United States only on a "cash and carry" basis. Although the congressional delegation voted in favor of war after the Japanese attack on Pearl Harbor, members remained generally isolationist during and after the war with respect to the efforts of Franklin D. Roosevelt and Harry S. Truman to effect international agreements on tariffs, trade, and world governance. Henrik Shipstead, elected to the U.S. Senate in 1922 as an antiwar Farmer-Labor candidate, turned Republican in 1940 in opposition to Roosevelt's military preparations. Shipstead, who fought the president's efforts at postwar international agreements until he left the Senate in 1947, was an authentic, if somewhat singular, voice of Minnesota.

Governor Harold Stassen, on the other hand, was an avowed internationalist before the war. At the 1940 Republican National Convention he worked as floor manager for the candidacy of Wendell Willkie, who supported Roosevelt's efforts to aid the allies in their war with Hitler's Germany. Inaugurated for a second term as governor in January 1941, Stassen predicted that the United States would be drawn into the "horrible hammering of war" and asked Min-

---

* A major political scandal of the 1990s involved a group of legislators who spent a winter weekend in Duluth paid for by the city. Only in Minnesota would anyone regard a weekend in Duluth in January as a lavish political junket.

nesotans to support the president's efforts to build up national defense. The attack on Pearl Harbor the following December roused the state, as it did Americans generally, and Minnesotans threw all their energy into the war effort. More than 300,000 Minnesota men and women served in the armed forces; more than six thousand lost their lives in combat.

Defense contracts stimulated Minnesota's economic recovery even before the United States entered the war. Minneapolis-Honeywell retooled its thermostat production line to build airplane control systems and periscope sights for submarines and developed the proximity fuse for anti-aircraft shells. Between 1940 and 1941 Honeywell added one thousand men and women to its work force (a 50 percent increase). The U.S. government built the Twin Cities Ordnance plant (TCOP) to produce munitions. When it opened in 1941 it employed 8,500 workers, more than half of them women. Military recruitment created a shortage of male workers during the war, so Minnesota companies adapted their hiring strategies and workplace conditions to attract

Manufacturing ammunition, Twin Cities Ordnance Plant, Arden Hills. The war opened employment opportunities for women and minorities.

Minneapolis Star Journal photo

women. They were most successful in the Twin Cities area, where more than sixty thousand women entered the work force between 1940 and 1945. These women took positions in factories and machine shops that had been held by men or were newly created by technological change. The TCOP, for example, had nearly seventeen thousand female employees by 1945. African Americans and Native Americans, gravitating toward Minnesota's cities, also benefited from wartime workplace shortages, as local defense plants offered opportunities that had previously been unavailable due to employer discrimination.

In June 1941, six months before the United States entered the war, President Roosevelt issued an executive order forbidding racial discrimination in defense industries. To enforce the order he created the Fair Employment Practices Committee, the first federal civil rights agency. In Minnesota nondefense industries such as the Hamm's, Schmidt, and Grain Belt breweries continued their practice of refusing to hire African Americans, but the newly built TCOP gracefully conformed to the law. It not only employed black workers; it assigned them positions commensurate with their skills, education, and training. By the end of the war the ordnance plant employed about one thousand African Americans.

While wartime opportunities accelerated the migration of Indians from reservations to cities, inspired higher expectations among black workers, and offered women the option of working outside the home, employment gains during the war failed to survive the return of peace. Southern congressmen scuttled the federal Fair Employment Practices Committee in 1946, and the Roosevelt-Truman administration, fearful of the return of 1930s-style unemployment, encouraged women to leave the workplace and return to homemaking. The GI Bill, which guaranteed veterans their prewar employment positions and offered financial aid for education, also helped to squeeze women out of the work force and higher education. As millions of male veterans opted for college education, schools tightened admission requirements for women and elbowed them into secretarial and home economics courses. By the mid-1950s the percentage of female students in American colleges (35 percent) was actually less than it had been in the 1920s (47 percent). The author of a history of the University of Minnesota in the 1950s offered this portrait of a typical

PhD candidate on graduation day: "His wife will be there to see his investiture and along with her there may be a son or daughter." Recalled one Minnesota woman of the postwar decade, "We married what we wanted to *be*. ... If we wanted to be a lawyer or doctor we married one."

Hubert Humphrey and the Democratic-Farmer-Labor Party

Harold Stassen won a third term as governor in 1942, but the following year he resigned to join the navy. He would not again be a factor in Minnesota politics, and after serving a term as governor of Pennsylvania, he would spend much of the rest of his life in a fruitless struggle to win the Republican nomination for president. Stassen's lieutenant governor, Edward Thye, took over as chief executive and was reelected in 1944 by a huge margin. The Farmer-Labor Association, still led by the hapless Elmer Benson, was riddled with Communists and incapable of offering voters a reasonable alternative to the dominant Republicans. The long-dormant Democratic Party had been rejuvenated by the New Deal, but it needed the Farmer-Labor constituency to challenge the Republicans. In 1943 Franklin Roosevelt, who regarded Minnesota as a crucial "swing state" in the approaching president election, urged Minnesota Democrats to seek a merger with the Farmer-Laborites. In that same year Russian dictator Joseph Stalin abolished the Comintern, the Leninist agency that for decades had promoted worldwide Communist revolution. After Germany attacked the Soviet Union in June 1941, Benson and the Farmer-Labor Popular Front supported the United States' entry into the war. Thus, Stalin's seeming abandonment of world Communism allowed Minnesota's Communists to pose as domestic radicals, rather than as agents of a foreign power. Moderates in the Farmer-Labor movement had long desired to merge with the Democrats; Benson and his radical followers now gave their blessing to the idea. The final catalyst was a young Minneapolis politician, Hubert Humphrey.

Born in 1911, Humphrey grew up in Doland, South Dakota, the son of the town's druggist. His mother was a devout Methodist, and his father, Hubert Humphrey, Sr., was active in the Dakota farmer-labor movement. Hubert Humphrey, Jr., was thus raised in a household that was intensely moral, compassionate, and politically liberal. Expected to take over his father's business, Humphrey attended pharmacy school in the early 1930s and worked for a time in his father's store, by then relocated to Huron, South Dakota. That experience and a later stint at college teaching would be the only nongovernmental employment of his life. After telling his father that he could no longer "peddle pills," Humphrey moved to Minneapolis with his wife, Muriel (also a native of South Dakota), to continue his education at the University of Minnesota. After graduating in 1937 he went to Baton Rouge to do graduate work in political science at Louisiana State University. He wrote a master's thesis on the political philosophy of the New Deal, but the most lasting impression carried home from his brief sojourn in the South was that of racial prejudice and the social injustice of segregation. Inviting black students from a nearby school for "bull sessions" in his apartment, he learned of the deep mistrust that Louisiana African Americans had for whites generally, and particularly for authority figures such as bill collectors and policemen.

By 1940 Humphrey was working for the New Deal's Works Progress Administration. Deferred from military service because of his government job, he oversaw the vocational training of Minnesota's unemployed and helped channel them into defense factories. His job brought him into contact with the Twin Cities' labor leaders, and he developed an electrifying speaking style at union meetings and civic affairs. In 1943, at the urging of moderates in the Farmer-Labor Association who were looking for "new blood," Humphrey ran for mayor of Minneapolis. He lost to the Republican candidate by a mere six thousand votes, and the *Minneapolis Star Journal,* a Republican sheet, marveled that he had "come dashing out of nowhere to stage a colorful fighting campaign."

After the election, which by Minnesota law was officially nonpartisan, the editor of the *Star* invited Humphrey to become a Republican. "Look," he reportedly told Humphrey, "we'll make you governor, we'll make you senator. We have the power in the state to make a man of your capabilities anything he wants politically. But we'll only do this if you become a Republican. If you won't, we'll break you." Muriel Humphrey later recalled that Hubert was much torn between the temptation of political and financial security (especially after the Republicans threw in the offer of a lakeside home valued at over $35,000) and the emotional tug of his parental upbringing. After a day or two he went back to the editor and said, "I can't do it—I am a Democrat."

Humphrey realized, however, that political success—whether as city mayor or member of Congress—depended on fusion with the Farmer-Labor Association. In July 1943 he used the family's seventy-dollar nest egg to take a bus to Washington, DC, for a personal appeal to Democratic Party leaders. A family friend from South Dakota gained him access to Postmaster General Frank Walker, the Democratic national chairman. Walker, aware of the president's concern for Minnesota's electoral votes, agreed to "send a man out to work with you." Labor leaders in the Twin Cities were enthusiastic about the idea of a merger. When the time came for discussions with Farmer-Labor leaders, Humphrey injected a prudent reminder. Both the Roosevelt administration and local Democrats thought only of absorbing the Farmer-Laborites. Mindful of Farmer-Labor's long history in Minnesota and hard-core constituency of 200,000 votes, Humphrey suggested, "Let's call it the Democratic-Farmer-Labor Party." And so it was agreed. A fusion committee worked out the details, and in early 1944 conventions of the two parties accepted the merger. That summer Humphrey was a delegate to the Democratic National Convention in Chicago, where he opposed Roosevelt's decision to drop Henry Wallace as his running mate in favor of Harry Truman. Wallace, Humphrey thought, was more closely aligned with "Populist liberals, Farmer-Laborites, . . . and ardent New Dealers." Under Humphrey's leadership, the Minnesota DFL would be on the liberal wing of the national Democratic Party.

Hubert Humphrey and Civil Rights

Humphrey supported his family by teaching at Macalester College in St. Paul and groomed himself for another shot at the Minneapolis mayor's office. He already had the support of the city's labor leaders, and he wooed the tiny black community with a promise of a city civil rights commission modeled on the federal Fair Employment Practices Committee. To appeal to the city's white middle class he gave talks on civic virtue—half sermon and half stump speech—in church basements and conducted a Sunday evening class in the city's largest Methodist church. He reminded Lutherans that his grandparents were Norwegian and that he had been baptized in a Lutheran church in rural South Dakota. He was elected mayor in 1945 by the largest margin in the city's history to that time.

Immediately upon taking office, Humphrey proposed a city ordinance making racial discrimination by employers subject to a fine. Opposition of businessmen and organized labor held up the law for a year. Adopted in early 1947, it created the nation's first municipal Fair Employment Practices Ordinance. Although the commission actually leveled few fines and its directives were generally ignored, the city's larger banks and department stores saw the public relations value in civil rights and began hiring blacks in increasing numbers.

Humphrey also recognized that racial and ethnic prejudice on the part of police was a source of urban unrest and not to be tolerated in a democratic society. Informed that Minneapolis police regularly stopped black men on the street when they were accompanied by white women, the mayor put a stop to the practice. He also suspended without pay two policemen who had made anti-Semitic remarks. He instructed the police chief to have his men on the beat in minority neighborhoods work with the clergy, the schoolteachers, the shopkeepers, and other citizens who had the neighborhood's respect. The effect of these efforts was to redefine the issue of prejudice in the United States. It was a problem to be solved, rather than a fact of life to be taken for granted.

The strides made in Minneapolis on civil rights drew national attention. The liberal magazine *New Republic* described Humphrey as "the most interesting phenomenon in the liberal skies of the Northwest" and "the most extraordinary politician that Minnesota has produced in fifty years." Humphrey received more than 150 inquiries from cities across the country seeking advice on establishing civil rights commissions, and in 1947 he received an invitation to join in forming the Americans for Democratic Action (ADA), an organization composed of intellectuals and New Dealers (including Eleanor Roosevelt and the theologian Reinhold Niebuhr) who believed that civil rights was the next step in establishing social and economic justice in America. Elected to the group's executive committee, Humphrey eventually became a vice-chair.

Humphrey won reelection as mayor in 1947 by a vote of slightly more than 102,000 to his opponent's 52,000—a nearly two-to-one margin that set another record in Minneapolis city elections. The most prominent Democrat in the state, he was casting his eye on a seat in the U.S. Senate when he faced a full-scale revolt by the Farmer-Labor element in the DFL coalition. The issue was not civil rights but foreign policy. President Harry Truman had responded to the onset of the Cold War and the Soviet occupation of Eastern Europe with financial aid to Greece and Turkey and the Marshall Plan for the economic recovery of Western Europe. Seeming gestures of benevolent generosity, the plans were, in reality, an attempt to block the spread of Communism, and hence Soviet influence, in Western Europe and the Middle East.

Henry Wallace, Roosevelt's one-time vice president, regarded these measures as unnecessarily belligerent, and in December 1947 he left the Democratic Party to form the Progressive Citizens of America. In Minnesota, Elmer Benson and the Farmer-Labor radicals sided with Wallace and schemed to take over the DFL party organization in order to make Wallace, rather than Truman, the DFL candidate for president in 1948. Humphrey, who had already parted ways with Wallace on the issue of the Soviet threat to Europe, got wind of the Benson strategy and countered it by mobilizing DFL moderates, particularly young people who had not been part of the Farmer-Laborites' flirtation with Communism. The climax came at the party's state convention in June 1948, where Humphrey's followers seized control and evicted Benson and the radicals. The party then went on to nominate Humphrey for the U.S. Senate in the fall election.

Joining ranks with Humphrey in his climactic battle with the old-time leftists was a new generation of aspiring politicians, a group of exceptionally able men and women who would provide leadership for the Democratic-Farmer-Labor Party in decades to come. Orville Freeman, Humphrey's classmate and best friend at the University of Minnesota and a decorated veteran of the Solomon Islands campaign, was a DFL county chair in 1948 and helped organize the moderates at the June convention. He would emerge from the convention as a member of the party's central committee and Humphrey's campaign manager for the fall election. Eugene McCarthy, a St. Thomas College sociology professor whom Humphrey had put in charge of organizing the St. Paul precincts for the June convention, was elected to the U.S. House of Representatives in the fall election. Eugenie Anderson, a delegate to the June convention from Red Wing and member of the DFL executive committee, was named by the convention to the Democratic National Committee, and in 1949 President Truman made her ambassador to Denmark. She was the first American woman to be given that diplomatic rank. Finally, a newcomer to DFL ranks in 1948, twenty-year-old Walter Mondale, son of a Methodist minister and a student at Macalester College, worked the floor of the DFL convention, caught Orville Freeman's eye, and became a Humphrey campaign organizer for southern Minnesota in the fall election.

A month after his June convention coup Humphrey was on his way to Philadelphia as a delegate to the Democratic National Con-

Native sons and Farmer-Democratic-Labor leaders
Walter Mondale and Hubert H. Humphrey, 1975

vention. Expecting to make his civil rights record in Minneapolis a focal point of his Senate campaign, he carried to the convention a draft of a strong civil rights plank for the national party platform. The party's 1944 platform had contained nothing more than some pious affirmations, and Truman was again content with that in 1948. Facing a Republican Congress and a Wallace third-party candidacy, the president did not want to alienate the southern white supremacists in his party. Although Humphrey secured a seat on the platform committee, he was completely outnumbered. At a committee session that lasted until four o'clock in the morning, he denounced the administration plank as "a bunch of generalities." "Who does this pipsqueak think he is?" asked Scott Lucas of Illinois, one of the titans of the U.S. Senate.

Orville Freeman and Eugenie Anderson, with help from the ADA, rounded up delegates for a floor fight on the platform, but on the eve of the vote they counted only one hundred fifty sure votes and one hundred probables for a minority report at a convention of more than a thousand delegates. It was nevertheless agreed that Humphrey would submit a minority civil rights plank and support it with a short speech. The ADA continued its lobbying and gradually convinced party leaders in the northeastern states that the African American vote might be crucial in the election. The next morning, after the majority completed its report to the convention, Humphrey stood up to give a short eight-minute address. He began by calling attention to the Berlin airlift, by which American planes were flying food into Berlin over the Soviet blockade, and he pointed out that the attempt to preserve democracy in western Europe would fail if the United States could not guarantee democratic rights for its own citizens. "There can be no hedging," he cried as delegates began applauding every sentence, "no watering down. To those who say that we are rushing this issue of civil rights—I say to them, we are 172 years late."

Humphrey sat down, and Orville Freeman tallied the vote. Rising hopes turned to high drama when Humphrey's father stood up to cast all eight of South Dakota's votes in favor of civil rights. A few minutes later Wisconsin cast its votes unanimously for the minority plank, and the issue was decided. The final tally was six hundred fifty-one and a half votes in favor to five hundred eighty-two and a half votes against.

Although the delegations of four southern states bolted the convention and later nominated Dixiecrat Strom Thurmond as a fourth-party candidate in the election, the platform fight rejuvenated party regulars. Truman's victory in the fall election was the biggest political upset of the century, and his margin came from urban blacks and liberals who had otherwise been leaning toward Wallace. Civil rights was now placed on the masthead of the Democratic Party, and Humphrey, the sometime druggist and college professor, was a political figure of national stature.

The Ebb and Flow of a Liberal Consensus

When Humphrey took his seat in the U.S. Senate in January 1949, his freshman class included Lyndon Johnson, Estes Kefauver, and Paul Douglas. *Time* magazine nevertheless singled out Humphrey for its cover, characterizing him as a "glib, jaunty spellbinder with a 'listen-you-guys' approach who talks and looks like a high school teacher who coaches basketball on the side." The Minnesota senator, *Time* predicted, would hit the Senate with "the cyclonic attack of an ad salesman." If Humphrey shared *Time*'s enthusiasm, he was doomed to disappointment. The Senate was still very much a gentlemen's club, dominated by southern elders, whose lily-white Democratic electorate returned them to office every six years. Because of the Senate's seniority rule, these men held most of the committee chairs and thus controlled the flow of legislative business. As a freshman and an outsider—he was, after all, the first Democrat Minnesota had ever elected to the Senate—Humphrey was expected to bury himself in respectful silence on a back bench. He went to Washington with an armload of civil rights measures—everything from fair employment practices to black voting rights—which he annually dropped into the legislative hopper. His bills were either ignored or drowned in a southern filibuster when an effort was made to bring them to the floor. Though popular enough in Minnesota to be reelected in 1954, throughout the decade of the 1950s Humphrey had little or no impact on the national political scene.

While the turmoil within the DFL attracted public attention to Minnesota in the late 1940s, Republicans quietly managed the state government for a decade after the war. Although Harold Stassen had left the state, his concept of "enlightened capitalism" remained a central feature of the Republican creed. Luther W. Youngdahl, governor from 1947 to 1951, was the scion of a large Swedish American Lutheran family and, in the phrase of his biographer, a "Christian in politics." He set up a Youth Conservation Commission to provide state-supervised employment for minors convicted of crimes. He obtained a law that made slot machines illegal and another investing liquor control officers with powers of arrest. He improved the state's mental health system, authorized municipalities to build low-rent housing, and opened the state's National Guard to African Americans. When Youngdahl resigned to become a federal district judge, his successor, C. Elmer Anderson of Brainerd, pursued the same social and moral policies. While Americans generally were preoccupied with Senator Joseph McCarthy's efforts to weed Communists out of the federal government in the early 1950s (a crusade in which Minnesota Congressman Walter Judd actively participated), the state's Republican Party seemed content with Governor Youngdahl's dictum that politics is the "machinery by which society makes its moral decisions."

The DFL finally captured the state's chief executive office when Orville Freeman was elected governor in 1954, but his six years in the office (1955–61) were little more than a continuation of the moral humanitarianism of Youngdahl and C. Elmer Anderson. The legislature finally enacted a fair employment practices law in 1955, and under Freeman's prodding legislators increased aid to education and reorganized the state bureaucracy. When Freeman left to become President John F. Kennedy's secretary of agriculture, Republican Elmer L. Andersen succeeded him; two years later, Andersen lost to DFL candidate Karl Rolvaag in an election so close that the courts had to do the counting. After several months the courts declared Rolvaag the winner by ninety-one votes. The state parties remained evenly balanced for the next decade, trading places in the governorship and the legislature, while the voters in presidential elections went from Eisenhower to Kennedy and Johnson and, in 1972, to Richard Nixon.

African American sit-ins and civil rights marches organized by Martin Luther King, Jr., and other black leaders in the early 1960s brought civil rights to the forefront of national politics. In summer 1963 President Kennedy sent to Congress a comprehensive bill that was essentially a collation of the ideas that Hubert Humphrey had been placing before the Senate for fifteen years. It prohibited racial segregation in public facilities, barred racial, gender, and age discrimination in employment, and empowered the attorney general to help register individuals who had been denied the right to vote. The bill was before the House of Representatives when Kennedy was assassinated in November 1963; with President Lyndon Johnson's support the House passed the measure in early 1964. Johnson and Sen-

The battle for civil rights comes to St. Paul as NAACP members picket outside Woolworth's and Grant's stores for integrated lunch counters, 1960.

St. Paul Dispatch & Pioneer Press photo

ate Majority Leader Mike Mansfield gave Humphrey the job of steering it through the Senate. Humphrey deftly gained enough Republican support to overcome the white segregationists among Southern Democrats, waited out a seventy-five-day filibuster, and won passage of the bill in June 1964. In his memoirs Humphrey called the Civil Rights Act "my greatest achievement," and no doubt it was. Credit might also be given to the moral political culture of Minnesota that had nurtured Humphrey's idealism.

In the presidential election that year Johnson asked Humphrey to be his vice presidential running mate, and Humphrey resigned his seat in the Senate. Governor Rolvaag appointed Walter Mondale to fill the seat. Mondale had served three terms as Minnesota's attorney general and was widely known as an advocate of consumer rights. He was elected to a full term in the Senate in 1966 and reelected in 1972 even though Minnesota cast its presidential vote for Nixon in that year.

The vice presidency was four years of trial and humiliation for Humphrey. When he voiced doubts about the wisdom of Johnson's bombing of North Vietnam in 1965, Johnson cut him out of all policy meetings. Humiliated, Humphrey sought to compensate by publicly defending the president's conduct of the Vietnam War, which only earned him the scorn of liberals, who by 1967 had come to oppose the war. It also put Humphrey on a collision course with his old friend, Senator Eugene McCarthy, who entered the 1968 presidential primaries as an antiwar opponent of Johnson. In April 1968, after Johnson declared that he would not run for reelection, Humphrey announced his candidacy. It was too late in the season for Humphrey to enter any primaries, but he won the nomination in the Democratic convention anyway.

Nixon won the fall election by vaguely promising to end the Vietnam War and by focusing on the restoration of "law and order"—a reference to the racial violence that had swept U.S. cities from 1965 to 1968 and the destructive vandalism of antiwar demonstrators on college campuses. Hubert Humphrey had brought on his own ruin. He had hunkered down too long, had made too many personal sacrifices in his pursuit of the nation's highest office. He returned to the Senate in 1971 (taking the seat vacated by Eugene McCarthy) and entertained hopes of winning the Democratic nomination in 1976, though Jimmy Carter, the eventual nominee, dismissed him as a "has-been." Humphrey died of cancer in 1978.

Nixon's election in 1968 and reelection in 1972 was largely the product of a white, middle-class backlash against the urban violence of the 1960s and affirmative action programs, such as court-ordered busing of schoolchildren to create racial balance in public schools. Reinforcing this trend in Minnesota was the breakup of the old ethnic neighborhoods in the Twin Cities, as good wages allowed blue-collar workers (Mayor Humphrey's constituency in the 1940s) to move to the suburbs. Running for reelection to the Senate in 1972, Walter Mondale commissioned a confidential survey of popular opinion. "We are surprised," his pollster told him, "to find so much anti-black sentiment in a state like Minnesota, which has a miniscule black population." (The state's black population at the time numbered fewer than thirty thousand.) The pollster attributed sentiments to a tax revolt among suburban voters. "Lashing out in anger," he thought, "many pick on one tax expenditure that they see no benefit in to themselves—blacks on welfare." Although Mondale won reelection, a comparison with his 1966 vote revealed that he had slipped badly in the Twin Cities' suburbs. A sobered Mondale later reflected, "It made me realize how begrudging progress is. You had to be modest in your expectations about what government intervention could do to fundamentally affect the life opportunities of millions of children."

Although New Deal–style liberalism was fading nationally, the DFL in Minnesota remained, for the moment, alive and well. "New Left" liberals, many of them fresh from college campuses, flooded into the party ranks and brought with them a new agenda—antiwar, reduced military spending, equal rights for women, and strong environmental regulation. In 1970 Wendell R. Anderson, a "second-generation" DFL leader who had no ties to Humphrey and the 1948 coup, was elected governor. In a two-year battle with a split legislature, Anderson managed to push through a far-reaching tax and school-finance reform plan that shifted the source of public education financing from local property taxes to state sales taxes and included a "sin tax" on liquor and cigarettes. Dubbed the "Minnesota Miracle," the tax reform proved immensely popular and enabled the DFL, for the first time, to win control of the legislature in 1972. Retaining control in 1974, Anderson and the DFL majority enacted the entire agenda of the "new liberalism": a 1973 law that allowed elected officials to identify themselves by party (ending the nonpartisan experiment that had begun in 1913), an extension of the governor's term in office from two to four years, ratification of the Equal Rights Amendment (for women) to the U.S. Constitution, strong environmental laws, generous increases in workers' compensation and unemployment benefits, elimination of income taxes for the working poor, and the assignment of party offices on an equal basis to women.

The new public interest in the rights of women and racial minorities encouraged a resurgence of ethnic pride among Minnesota's In-

Amid growing educational opportunities on Indian reservations and in universities, Governor Wendell Anderson signs an American Indian Week proclamation in 1971.

dian tribes. Indian children, previously relegated to reservation schools or church missions, entered the state's public schools in greater numbers, and many went on to college. State colleges and universities developed Indian studies programs, paralleling the African American studies programs that had emerged a few years earlier. The federal Indian Education Act of 1972 provided money for Indian counselors and language teachers in the public schools.

Indian communities nevertheless became dissatisfied with the failure of public schools to hire Indian teachers and with the high dropout rate among Indian children. As a result, several communities decided to establish all-Indian schools. Staffed by college-trained Indian educators, the schools combined a conventional curriculum with courses in Indian history and culture. The Bug-O-Nay-Ge-Shig School on the Ojibwe Leech Lake Reservation became one of the largest tribal schools in the country. Operating under the direction of tribal governments, other schools were founded at the Cass Lake, White Earth, Mille Lacs, and Fond du Lac reservations. Not content with Indian studies programs in mostly white colleges, tribal leaders founded Indian community colleges in Cloquet and at Leech Lake and White Earth reservations. The "No Child Left Behind" concept, coined by politicians at the turn of the twenty-first century for largely political purposes, had long since been pioneered by Minnesota people truly interested in education.

The moral humanitarianism of Minnesota politics—which stood in stark contrast to the growing problems of President Nixon with the Watergate scandal—and the state's consistent ranking near the top in quality-of-life surveys attracted national attention. On the cover of its August 13, 1973, issue *Time* pictured Governor Wendell Anderson, garbed in a plaid shirt and standing on a dock on a Minnesota lake holding up a nice-sized northern pike. Its story was titled "Minnesota: A State That Works." In addition to extolling Anderson, whose future, *Time* predicted, "may be larger than Minnesota," the article focused on intangibles that produced a "quality of life"—crystalline lakes and well-kept farms, a cultural climate (Guthrie Theater, Minnesota Symphony Orchestra, Walker Art Center) that rivaled any city on the eastern seaboard, and a vibrant economy spearheaded by banks and insurance companies. Although *Time*'s effusiveness was clearly exaggerated, the notion of "a state that works" seemed to fit the humane and orderly political system that Anderson and the DFL had created by the mid-1970s.

Despite *Time*'s suggestion that Anderson might be destined for national office, Democratic candidate Jimmy Carter chose another Minnesotan, Walter Mondale, as his running mate in 1976. Then the DFL leadership committed a political blunder that cost it control of state government. When Mondale resigned his Senate seat, Anderson turned the executive office over to his lieutenant governor, Rudolph Perpich, who dutifully named Anderson to the vacant Senate seat. Minnesotans were horrified by this seeming bit of party nepotism. Two years later, when Hubert Humphrey died, Perpich failed to allay public suspicion when he named Muriel Humphrey to fill out her husband's term in the Senate. Meanwhile, Minnesota Republicans distanced themselves from the Watergate scandal by renaming their party the Independent Republicans. The public ax fell in fall 1978, an election dubbed by the media as the "Minnesota Massacre." The Independent Republicans captured both Senate seats and the governorship.

The national trend of waning liberalism and rising conservatism finally reached maverick Minnesota in the late 1970s. The Stassen legacy among Minnesota Republicans had faded, and many were now supporting a more limited social and economic role for government and looked to California conservative Ronald Reagan for future presidential leadership. Religious conservatives began speaking out against the supposed liberal excesses of the late '60s and early '70s with respect to gay rights, abortion, and leniency toward criminals and drug users. The state nevertheless voted loyally for the Carter-Mondale ticket in 1980, and the DFL retained control of both houses of the legislature.

The governorship of Rudy Perpich, who held the executive office from 1976 to 1979, and again from 1983 to 1991, reflected the independence of Minnesota voters. A native of Hibbing, he was the first Minnesota governor to come from the Iron Range, the first Roman Catholic governor, and, in a state long dominated by Scandinavians, a second-generation Croatian. A loyal DFL partisan when he took office in 1976, he returned to politics in 1982 as an independent who disregarded the DFL party apparatus. He won reelection in 1986 after making peace with the DFL, which maintained its majority in the state legislature.

The unconventional Perpich fit no ideological category. He appealed to religious conservatives by favoring legislation limiting abortions, yet he named more women to government offices than any other Minnesota governor. In 1977, during his first term (prior to the "Minnesota Massacre"), he named Rosalie E. Wahl to the state supreme court. She was the first woman to serve on that body. By the time Perpich left office in 1991 women were a majority on the court. Marlene Johnson, his running mate in 1982 and again in 1986, was the first woman to serve as lieutenant governor. Perpich made attracting business to the state one of his main goals. He was not always successful. One of his goofier ideas was to wed Minnesota's timber supply with China's unending demand for eating utensils by building a chopsticks factory on the Iron Range. Unfortunately, pine is not a suitable wood for chopsticks, and, in any case, no one in Minnesota knew how to make them. Perpich was more successful in attracting Canadian financing to build a huge retail and entertainment complex in the Twin Cities area. Opening in 1992, the Mall of America in Bloomington would attract more out-of-state tourists by the mid-1990s than did Minnesota's lakes and parks.

Rudy Perpich's ideological independence preserved Minnesota's reputation as a political maverick, for the national trend in the 1980s was a drift into conservatism under presidents Ronald Reagan and George H. W. Bush. The nation's rejection of DFL-style liberalism was most evident in Walter Mondale's disastrous presidential bid in 1984. It is likely that no Democrat could have defeated the glib and photogenic Reagan in that year, but Mondale had no chance at all. His choice of Geraldine Ferraro of New York as a running mate proved to be an unfortunate one. Although she was the first woman placed on a presidential ticket by a major party, she proved to be a poor campaigner and a liability among traditionalists, male and female alike.

An ill-at-ease public speaker lacking in stage presence, Mondale read his speeches from a teleprompter in an accent as flat as the Min-

nesota prairies. He refused to review tapes of his television performances or to subject himself to media coaching. "I'm not interested in
the remake artists or what they have to say," he once remarked. "If I
have to be a movie star to be a good politician, then I don't want to be
a politician."

In addition to lacking any sense of theater—so necessary in the age
of television and fifteen-second sound bites—Mondale lacked a message for the 1980s. "Mr. Mondale is one of the few major figures on
the American scene," remarked one newspaper columnist, "whose
political style and vocabulary fit comfortably in a world of Al Smith,
Franklin Roosevelt, and Harry Truman." He did have the courage to
remind Americans that they could not go on incurring budget deficits
forever and that the next president would have to raise taxes, but he
never spelled out what taxpayers would get for their money. Mondale
ran an honest and fair-minded campaign that simply was out of tune
with the times. After the election, in which the Mondale-Ferraro
ticket carried only Minnesota and the District of Columbia, the *Washington Post* editorialized that he "made the best fight he could for his
party" and emerged from the campaign "with honor and with his
reputation enlarged."

The Ultimate Maverick

Whatever the merit in *Time* magazine's original encomium, Minnesota in the 1990s clearly deserved the title "A State That Works." A
few statistics should suffice. In 1987 Minnesota became the first state
to establish a publicly subsidized health insurance program for children who had no access to private systems. Subsequent legislation
provided state-subsidized coverage for the roughly half-million low-
income citizens of the state, and the result, by the beginning of the
twenty-first century, was coverage of an estimated 95 percent of state
residents (versus a national average of 84 percent). The investment in
health produced results. Residents of Minnesota were found to live
longer lives, on average, than residents of any other state, except
Hawaii. (Unfortunately, there was no ready statistic on the number of
Minnesotans who spent their winters in Hawaii.) Minnesota ranked
number one, ahead of Hawaii, in longevity for women.

Perhaps because of the state's generous social programs, the Twin Cities became centers for new immigrants in the 1990s. Hmong people who had fought for the United States in the mountains of Laos became refugees after the Vietnam War; by 2005, St. Paul held the largest urban concentration of ethnic Hmong people in the world. Immigrants from the Somali diaspora built a large community in Minneapolis. New arrivals from Central and South America, from other parts of Africa, and from Asia have also moved to smaller communities across the state.

Minnesota's moral culture and political conscientiousness appeared in other statistics. The state placed at or near the top in such areas as voter turnout at elections, high school graduation rate and student rankings for ACT and SAT scores, rankings among states as a healthy place to live, and corporate philanthropy. Garrison Keillor, the popular host of Minnesota Public Radio's *A Prairie Home Companion,* based his stories on the mythical town of Lake Wobegon, where "all the children are above average." Statistics suggested that all of Minnesota might have been above average.

Minnesota voters continued to split their tickets in the 1990s. From 1991 to 1999 the state had a Republican governor, Arne Carlson, and a DFL majority in both houses of the legislature. Carlson's political ideology never went beyond trimming the size and expense of the state government—this continued even when national prosperity produced annual budget surpluses. He agreed with the legislature that giving tax incentives to parents would allow them freedom of choice among public schools, but he vetoed any suggestion of improvements in health and welfare. Carlson, in fact, vetoed more bills than all of his predecessors of the past half-century put together. The political standoff between governor and legislature opened the way, in 1998, for the emergence of the ultimate Minnesota maverick, Jesse Ventura.

His given name at birth was James Janos. He grew up in Minneapolis and served six years in the navy (some of it in Vietnam). After a stint at a California community college, he became a professional wrestler and adopted the stage name Jesse "The Body" Ventura. At the end of his wrestling career Ventura returned to Minnesota and in 1990 was elected mayor of Brooklyn Park, a suburb north of Minneapolis. After his term as mayor he became a talk-show host on a Twin Cities radio station.

Ventura entered the gubernatorial race in 1998 as a candidate of the Reform Party, the organization created by Ross Perot in the early 1990s to advance his third-party presidential bid. Already well known to Minnesota radio listeners, he campaigned as an outsider, benefiting from the fact that the other candidates included the sons of Walter Mondale, Orville Freeman, and Hubert Humphrey. In televised debates his opponents would, in Minnesota fashion, explain their programs in exhaustive detail. Ventura would then confess little knowledge of the issues, promise an open mind, and leave the impression that intimate knowledge of the workings of government was a drawback, especially because his opponents could not agree on anything. One of the few proposals he made during the campaign was for a unicameral legislature—on grounds that it was simple, would save the state money, and would reduce the number of politicians. Because the balloting was split among three candidates, Ventura won the fall election with a mere 37 percent of the vote.

In his first State of the State message in 1999 Governor Ventura proclaimed that "the free ride is over" for Minnesotans, implying that he planned to cut back drastically on social spending. When college students later asked him if this meant an end to loans and student aid, Ventura told them: "If you're smart enough to go to college, you're smart enough to figure out how to pay for it." During the election campaign he expressed the view that state-supported preschools were "terrible for children" because they undermined parental authority. Despite all these statements, Ventura approved the 1999 legislature's large increases in Minnesota's already sizable expenditures on preschool and college student aid. And, despite his verbal scorn for governmental expertise, he surrounded himself with highly respected advisers and departmental administrators, both Republicans and Democrats.

Ventura was clearly a pragmatist and that certainly fit Minnesota's political culture, but his tendency to make ill-considered and often off-color remarks embarrassed many Minnesotans. A hound for publicity, he gave an interview to *Playboy*, appeared on national TV talk shows, and hosted a weekly radio call-in show of his own, *Lunch with the Governor*. His flippant remarks were sometimes funny and often insulting. He claimed that drunken Irish workmen laid out the crooked streets of St. Paul. He criticized fat people for lack of willpower and unwed mothers for not anticipating the problems of child rearing before they hopped into bed. And he dismissed organized religion as a crutch for weak-minded people—an ironic parallel to Karl Marx's famous dictum that religion was "the opiate of the people." Minnesotans nevertheless, like most Americans during Bill Clinton's presidency, were able to separate job performance from personal peccadilloes. In early 2000 opinion polls indicated a job approval rating of 70 percent for the governor.

In that presidential election year Ventura left the national Reform Party and formed a new Minnesota third party, the Independence Party. Ventura had been the only state executive elected by the Reform Party, and he suspected that the party had become little more than a vehicle for Ross Perot's personal ambitions. Ventura, however, did not attempt to build an organization for his new state party. His political career rested, after all, on antiparty rhetoric. As a result, he had no political vehicle of his own and had to win support for his programs from regular Republicans, who controlled the state House of Representatives, and Democratic-Farmer-Laborites, who controlled the state senate. These leaders understandably cooperated with the governor only when it was in their own interest, while seeing to it that nothing was done that would be of political advantage to Ventura.

In 2002 Ventura declined to run for reelection, saying that he was tired of partisan bickering and warfare. Republicans in that year won the governorship, control of the legislature, and a majority of the state's congressional delegation. Since that result coincided with the national political mood in the first years of the twenty-first century, one might ask if maverick Minnesota had at last joined the mainstream. Possibly. But don't bet on it.

```
╔══════════════════════════════════════════╗
║           VISITING  HISTORY                ║
╚══════════════════════════════════════════╝
```

Through service in wartime and in modern political life, the state's people have surprised the rest of the country—and sometimes, themselves.

Humphrey Forum at the Hubert H. Humphrey Institute

301 19th Ave. S., Minneapolis; 612/624-5893. Exhibits and collections on Minnesota's famous U.S. senator and vice president (1965–69).

Minnesota Military Museum

Camp Ripley, 15000 Hwy. 115, Little Falls; 320/632-7374. Indoor and outdoor exhibits on military history and Minnesotans in all branches of the service.

Minnesota State Capitol

St. Paul; 651/296-2881. A working masterpiece of public architecture, restored with original furnishings; guided tours, portraits of the state's governors, rathskeller café.

St. Louis County Heritage and Arts Center

506 W. Michigan St., Duluth; 218/727-8025. Includes Veteran's Memorial Hall, operated by the county's historical society in the Duluth Depot.

10

Minnesota Exceptionalism

Historians who venture into the field of state and local history encounter a problem when the narrative reaches the twentieth century. In the past century the federal government, through its regulatory and taxation powers, has touched nearly every facet of American life. Of local decision making there is not much of a story for the historian to tell. Similarly, the development of a mass media and instantaneous communications have tended to homogenize American society, leaving only traces of once-colorful local variations in speech, customs, manners, and dress.

Minnesotans, nevertheless, have managed to retain their self-image of exceptionalism, and they have developed a number of institutions that lend the state a special character. Let us, then, conclude our excursion through Minnesota's past with a look at several of these distinctive developments of the past century.

The Mayo Clinic

William Worrall Mayo, a graduate of the University of Manchester with a degree in chemistry and physics, moved to the United States in 1845 and completed medical studies at the University of Missouri. St. Paul's spectacular growth attracted him to that city in the 1850s, and after serving as an army surgeon in the Civil War, Mayo settled

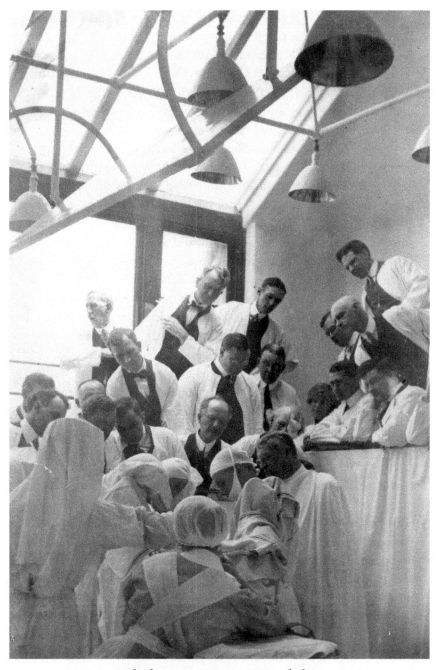

*Dr. Charles Horace Mayo operates and educates
at the Mayo Clinic, Rochester, 1913.*

in Rochester with his wife, Louise Abigail, also of English ancestry. Rochester in 1863 was the momentary terminus of the Northwestern Railroad, which was laying tracks into Iowa and South Dakota, and the city held the promise of future growth. The Mayos had two sons, William ("Will"), born in 1861, and Charles Horace ("Charlie"), born in 1865. Will later recalled of his childhood, "We were reared in medicine as a farm boy is reared in farming."

When the Dakota War of 1862 resulted in the trial and hanging of thirty-eight Dakota leaders in Mankato, Dr. Mayo dug up one of the bodies, which had been buried in a sandbank on the Minnesota River, and painstakingly salvaged the bones. With this skeleton he taught his sons osteology. In 1866 he made a small abdominal incision in a female patient to drain an ovarian cyst, and the operation, new to Rochester, was reported in the local newspaper. Dr. Mayo soon found himself swamped with female patients who suffered from a variety of uterine disorders due to frequent childbearing.

His sons, growing into adolescence, attended the operations and learned how to apply ether, which had recently replaced chloroform as an anesthetic. Will studied medicine at the University of Michigan and graduated in 1883. Charlie graduated from the Chicago Medical College five years later. Both became partners in their father's medical practice. By the late 1880s the Mayo family had the largest medical practice in southern Minnesota.

Surgery had long been held in disrepute because any physical invasion of the body almost invariably led to infection and, often, death. Barbers had performed surgery since the Middle Ages, although in more modern times armies and navies had developed specialists for treating bullet wounds. In the early 1860s a French chemist, Louis Pasteur, theorized that infections were caused by germs, microscopic organisms that covered the body and lived in the surrounding air and earth. He published elegant proofs of his theories, and in 1865 a Scottish physician, Joseph Lister, having read Pasteur's work, began cleaning his patients' surgical wounds with gauze dipped in antiseptic carbolic acid. The mortality rate among his patients fell dramatically. Lister then discovered that sterilizing his hands, his surgical implements, and even the air in the operating room dropped the rate of postsurgical infection even lower. He published his findings, and the Lister "antiseptic method" became widely used in Europe.

The method found a more skeptical reception in America, in part because it involved a lot of effort. Sterilizing the air of the operating room, for instance, involved setting out pans of carbolic acid, the fumes of which often made both doctor and patient ill. Will Mayo's instructors at the University of Michigan wanted nothing to do with it, although later in the decade Charlie found that most of the surgeons at Chicago were converts to Listerism. The Mayos, father and sons, were by nature experimental. They not only embraced the antiseptic method, they improved on it. They discovered, for instance, that it was not necessary to fill the air of the operating room with carbolic acid fumes, as Lister had; antiseptic cleansing of clothing and implements was sufficient. An improved survival rate, in turn, encouraged them to undertake operations that always had proved fatal—removal of a diseased appendix, for instance, and stomach surgery for peptic ulcers.

Impressed by the success of the Mayo family, a Catholic order of nuns, the Sisters of St. Francis, offered to raise money to build a hospital in Rochester. Dr. Mayo resisted, thinking the town not big enough to support such an institution, but the Sisters persisted and with financial help from the Catholic Church finished the first unit of St. Mary's Hospital in 1889. Dr. Mayo was appointed physician-in-charge, and his sons received staff appointments. It was the beginning of an institution that would become known as the Mayo Clinic, a name first applied in 1905 to a growing complex of Mayo-owned and church-affiliated hospitals.

By that date a half-dozen physicians had joined the Mayo brothers, including an optometrist and an anesthetist. Word of the Mayos' quality care had spread beyond the boundaries of the state, and passenger trains daily disgorged patients from Wisconsin, Iowa, and South Dakota. Hotels sprang up in the vicinity of the clinic to house patients and their kin. By 1911, when the elder Dr. Mayo died, the clinic was performing four thousand surgical operations a year.

Always eager to keep abreast of new developments, the Mayo brothers frequently attended surgical conferences in eastern cities.

In one conference in Boston a world-renowned surgeon explained his technique for removing gall bladders, based on nine operations that he had performed. When he finished, Will Mayo stood up in the back of the room and described a procedure he used that got far better results. When the speaker demanded to know his credentials, Will explained that he and his brother had performed 123 gall bladder procedures in the past nine months. To an easterner that sounded as if these prairie-practitioners were removing every gall bladder in Minnesota.

Skeptical about such claims, doctors flocked to Rochester from all over the country to see for themselves and came away with the feeling that the Mayos, if anything, were *understating* the traffic through their clinic. The visiting surgeons ended up extending the reach of the Mayos' influence, for whenever they encountered in their own offices a particularly serious or unusual illness, they referred the patient to Rochester.

A visiting surgeon almost always remained long enough to watch an operating procedure, and both of the Mayo brothers encouraged observers. Indeed, they had been giving informal instruction to medical students for some time. By 1910 they had thirty-six Fellows undertaking postgraduate study at the clinic, although they had no formal curriculum and granted no degree. The University of Minnesota established a medical college in 1888 and by 1914 was considering a graduate program for physicians wishing to specialize in certain fields. This aim coincided with the Mayo brothers' growing interest in a teaching facility. And they had money for such a program at hand. Although the fees at the clinic were low—the very poor, about 25 percent of the patients, paid nothing for their care and another 30 percent paid the bare cost of their treatment—the Spartan work habits of the brothers allowed them to accumulate large amounts of money. Funding a graduate program of the university with facilities in Rochester was a natural solution.

In 1915 the brothers incorporated the Mayo Foundation for Medical Education and Research and funded it with a gift of $1.5 million. Rochester businessmen became trustees of the foundation. The Mayos' idea was to formally link the foundation to the university.

Graduate students from the medical school would go to Rochester for further training in specialties, with opportunities for gaining hospital experience and doing their own research. The foundation would appoint a committee of scientists to administer the program.

The idea unfortunately suffered the fateful maxim that no good deed goes unpunished. Physicians in the Twin Cities objected to the prospect of Rochester becoming the medical center of the state, and members of the legislature objected to placing the state's graduate medical school in the hands of a private foundation. Eventually the parties reached a compromise whereby the school facilities would be in Rochester but the university's board of regents would control the foundation and its income. The compromise worked, and students from all over the world began coming to the Mayo Clinic for specialized study. The "affiliation" continues to the present day, but the feeling of trust and cooperation that the Mayo brothers had originally envisioned never really developed.

One result of the university affiliation, however, was that following World War I the clinic began recruiting staff in medical fields outside of surgery. New technology and new skills forced the subdivision of surgery itself. During the 1920s the clinic established departments of neurosurgery; orthopedic surgery; eye surgery; ear, nose, and throat surgery; and plastic and reconstructive surgery. The brothers retired in 1928 and 1929 respectively, and both died within weeks of one another in 1939. Charlie's son "Chuck" Mayo continued the family tradition of medical practice and remained active on the clinic staff until his death in 1965. He was the last of the Mayos to be associated with the clinic.

St. Mary's Hospital added new wings in 1920, 1940, and 1952. During these same years the foundation built new hospitals for specialized surgeries and one, the Curie, for the new science of radiation treatment. At the beginning of the twenty-first century, the Mayo Clinic employed more than forty thousand people, including two thousand physicians. A pioneer in the concept of integrated group practice of medicine, it is one of the premier medical facilities in the world.

"Which Way Is Ireland?" Lindbergh's Flight Across the Atlantic

Although humans had been flying heavier-than-air machines for only eleven years when World War I broke out, the infant aircraft industry made giant strides during the war in enhancing the speed, strength, and firepower of machines that were little more than collections of glued sticks and lacquered cloth. But the one-on-one dogfights between enemy craft and the international celebrity of aces, such as Germany's "Red Baron" von Richthofen and the American Eddie Rickenbacker, captured the public imagination. Britain alone manufactured fifty thousand planes during the war, and commercial aviation began as soon as peace returned in 1918.

By the end of the war improvements in aircraft power, range, and endurance led to dreams of intercontinental flight. In May 1919 Raymond Orteig, a French-born American who owned hotels in Manhattan, offered a prize of twenty-five thousand dollars for any aviator who would fly nonstop from New York to Paris or Paris to New York. Because of doubts about engine performance for such a distance and problems of gasoline storage, it was seven years before anyone took up the challenge. In 1926 France's wartime ace, Rene Fonck, traveled to America and joined forces with a syndicate willing to build a suitable craft. The syndicate produced a three-engine biplane to be handled by a four-man crew. The cockpit included a bed so that crew members could take turns resting. Loaded with gasoline and ample amounts of food, the plane taxied down the runway of Roosevelt Field on Long Island and never got off the ground. It disappeared into a gully at the end of the runway and exploded, killing two of the crew members.

By spring 1927 a half-dozen syndicates were drafting plans for capturing the prize. All but one of them involved a two- or three-motored craft with two or three crew members. The exception was the plan of twenty-five-year-old Charles Lindbergh, Jr., who thought that a single-engine plane with a lone pilot had the best chance of making the transatlantic leap. The son of a Progressive Minnesota congressman, Lindbergh dropped out of the University of Wisconsin in 1922 to attend a flying school. He later joined the Army Air Service Reserve Corps and received military flight training in San Antonio. By the time he graduated in 1925 a frugal Congress had virtually eliminated the air service. Lindbergh then joined the barnstorming circuit and by 1926 was flying for a government airmail contractor in St. Louis.

With credentials that included flying skill and a well-known name, Lindbergh persuaded a group of financial backers from St. Louis to give him fifteen thousand dollars to build a plane to his specifications. The plane, built by a San Diego aircraft company, was ready for testing by the middle of April 1927. Building a plane from scratch meant that Lindbergh could supervise every detail and become intimately familiar with its workings. Throughout the building process workers noticed that Lindbergh always referred to himself in the plural, "we." After his flight made him an international hero, the publisher of his hastily written autobiography gave it the title *We*, implying the union of aviator and machine. For the rest of his life Lindbergh insisted that the plural referred instead to his St. Louis sponsors.

The finished plane was twenty-seven feet, eight inches long, with a wingspan of forty-six feet and a nine-cylinder, air-cooled motor of 223 horsepower. Made of wood and metal struts, held together by bolts and glue, the skeleton was covered with a cotton fabric, strengthened and waterproofed by a coating of cellulose acetate dope of silver-gray. On the nose was stenciled the name Lindbergh had chosen for his craft, *Spirit of St. Louis*. In the cockpit night-flying equipment, even a parachute, was sacrificed to save weight. His emergency landing equipment consisted of a small rubber raft, flares, matches, a knife, fishing tackle, and chocolate rations. His flying suit, ordered from New York, was one piece, lined with wool, and weighed only nine pounds. While Lindbergh tested his craft during the middle weeks of April, three potential contestants for the Orteig prize crashed on takeoff, and Lloyd's of London established ten-to-one odds against any successful flight across the Atlantic in 1927.

On Tuesday, May 10, 1927, Lindbergh left California for St. Louis. On the previous Sunday, May 8, two French aviators took off from Paris and were expected to capture the Orteig Prize on Monday in New York. They were never heard from again. Lindbergh flew on to New York on Thursday, May 12, and then was held up by a week of rain. As he crossed the country the nation's press picked up the story of the lone aviator who planned to brave the North Atlantic. Reporters by the hundreds hounded his hotel and the airfield in New Jersey where he parked his plane. On Thursday, May 19, Lindbergh received word that skies were clearing over New England, and he announced plans to leave the next morning. Because the flight was expected to take more than thirty hours, what he needed most was a good night's sleep. Aides and other visitors continually interrupted that, and at 2:30 AM he gave up and put on his flight suit. The *Spirit of St. Louis* was towed to Roosevelt Field.

Roosevelt Field's three-thousand-foot grass runway was dotted with puddles from the week-long rain. Prudence dictated a delay of a day or so to let the field dry out, but Lindbergh couldn't afford to wait because navy commander Richard E. Byrd, who had flown over the North Pole the previous year, was scheduled to take off for Paris later that day or the next. At a little before eight o'clock Lindbergh's aide spun the prop, and the Whitney engine coughed to life. Revving the engine to maximum speed, Lindbergh sloshed down the runway. With only two thousand feet of runway left, he finally felt the wings take hold and the plane begin to rise. Twice it plopped back onto the ground until it finally rose into the air just short of the end of the runway. The crowd cheered as the telegraph line from London crackled the news that Lloyd's was not quoting odds on Lindbergh because "the risk [was] too great."

On his charts of the Atlantic Lindbergh had marked off checkpoints on his route, each representing a change in the magnetic compass. When he passed over Nova Scotia, he was pleased to note that he was only six miles off his mark. Twilight was descending as he flew over Newfoundland. He departed his flight path and flew low over its capital, St. John's, so the populace could report his progress. Because he was flying into the sun, Lindbergh had only about two hours of total darkness that night before the east became etched with the first light of dawn. Near sunrise he encountered a wave of thunderstorms that batted the plane about and forced him off course. The compasses ceased to function properly, probably, he thought, because he was flying through a magnetic storm. Fighting sleep and hallucinating about ghosts in the cabin, the lone pilot could only aim his plane eastward into the rising sun. He eventually lowered his plane to within two hundred feet of the ocean's surface.

Minnesota's most famous son, Charles A. Lindbergh,
with his Spirit of St. Louis, *1927*

Finally, at midmorning, Lindbergh spotted fishing boats on the sea below. Within fifty feet of the water, he circled the boats, stuck out his head, and shouted, "Which way is Ireland?" The fishermen could not hear him over the roar of his motor, so again he aimed his plane generally eastward. A few minutes later he spotted land, his charts confirming that it was the Dingle Peninsula on the southwest corner of the island. He followed the coastline of Ireland and England and crossed the English Channel to Cherbourg. Night was again falling when he spotted the lights of Paris. Lindbergh knew that Le Bourget airport was somewhere north of the city, but he had trouble locating it. Flying over a black patch that appeared to be a runway, the weary pilot was confused by a string of lights that extended all the way to the city. He flew on, found nothing, turned back, and flew lower over the black patch. Realizing then that the field was lit by the headlights of hundreds of automobiles awaiting his arrival, Charles Lindbergh put the *Spirit of St. Louis* down on the ground at 10:24 PM Paris time, thirty-three and a half hours after he had left Roosevelt Field. A crowd of 150,000 people waited at the airfield that evening, and a mob converged on his plane. He was carried off on the shoulders of worshipers and finally escaped with the help of some quick-thinking French citizens who placed his helmet on an American reporter's head for a diversion and led him to one of their own cars for a getaway. Lindbergh would remain an international celebrity, through good times and bad, for the rest of his life.

Novelist F. Scott Fitzgerald, chronicler and critic of the Jazz Age and a native of St. Paul, put Lindbergh's triumph in perspective:

> A young Minnesotan who seemed to have nothing to do with his generation did a heroic thing, and for a moment people set down their glasses in country clubs and speak-easies and thought of their old best dreams.

Words and Music in the Twin Cities

Irish-born Tyrone Guthrie was one of the most prominent theatrical producers in New York City, and one of the unhappiest. He was a maverick who got little joy out of producing and directing another Broadway hit. He had several complaints about the American theater, in addition to the fact that it was centered in New York. He objected to the design of American theaters, which separated the players from the audience, with an orchestra pit between stage and seating emphasizing the gap. Because of the distance between players and audience, the scenery and settings of the stage were as important as the actors, and stage technicians as powerful as the director. Guthrie wanted a playhouse that would thrust the stage into the audience, which would enable players and audience to interact while cutting the expenses of production. "The theater after all," said Guthrie, "is a two-way traffic between the audience and the stage."

Guthrie also objected to the Broadway system of producing single plays that could be either smash hits or dismal flops. If a flop, the actors were out of work; if a hit, they were subjected to tedious repetitions, day after day for a year or more. Guthrie wanted a repertory theater where a group of actors could master a series of plays, from Greek classics to Shakespeare to modern drama. Such a theater could survive without the need for smash hits, and it would enliven the cultural environment of its site while guaranteeing players a living wage and a chance to develop their potential. Said Guthrie, "What a young actor needs is to play a number of ... parts in the quickest possible succession, under experienced direction with an experienced company and before the public. This is exactly what Broadway no longer offers."

Guthrie's prestige enabled him to break free of the system that bound directors and actors to the Broadway-Hollywood axis. *New York Times'* drama critic Brooks Atkinson inserted a note in his column to the effect that Guthrie wanted to move out of New York; Atkinson invited interested cities to respond. Seven did so, and Guthrie, accompanied by fellow producer Oliver Rea, set off, so he later wrote, "with spears and blow pipes, with pretty beads, bright shells ... to bribe the native chieftains."

In a decision announced in May 1960, the pair ultimately selected Minneapolis, even though several other cities, including Detroit and Milwaukee, offered more financial backing. In explaining his decision Guthrie dwelt at length on the drama of the Mississippi River as a backdrop for his theater. But his associates (to whom he left the final decision) were probably swayed by more mundane considerations, such as the history of theater in the Twin Cities, dating back to old Fort Snelling, the quality of the drama department at the University of Minnesota, and the level of education in the community.

Although the T. B. Walker Foundation donated property in Minneapolis for the theater, it took $2.2 million and three years to complete the project. Architect Ralph Rapson found working with Guthrie both "wonderful" and "traumatic." The producer was, said Rapson, "always surrounded by this great entourage of people" who would wait until Guthrie ventured an opinion on design "and then they'd all pounce on the Midwest architect." Rapson approved the idea of a thrust stage, but he disagreed violently with Guthrie's desire for all-blue seating. Rapson wanted multicolored seating and won out by delaying the order for seats until a few weeks before the theater was scheduled to open. By combining a thrust stage with semicircular seating Rapson designed a theater that accommodated 1,437 people with no seat farther than fifty-two feet from center stage. Because Guthrie hated orchestra pits but liked to use music, Rapson placed the orchestra near the ceiling on the left side of the stage. Orchestra members called it "the birdcage." Rapson's summation of Guthrie: "I found him to be an exciting, invigorating, dynamic, arrogant, obnoxious bastard."

Public interest in the experiment rose as the opening drew near in spring 1963. A volunteer organization of seven hundred women, "The Stagehands," sold season tickets in every city in the state, eventually reaching a record 23,305 season subscriptions. The theater opened on May 7 with Guthrie's modern-dress production of *Hamlet,* and, according to *Newsweek* magazine, attracted out-of-town drama critics "as thick as the smelt running in the northern streams." The remainder of the first season featured *The Miser* (Molière), *The Three Sisters* (Chekhov), and *Death of a Salesman* (Miller). "The Tyrone Guthrie Theatre is a cause for celebration," enthused the *New York Times,* "Affluence, a high educational level and civic leadership, combined with the spirit of a small town in the midst of a metropolis, have set the stage for Sir Tyrone Guthrie's triumphant entrance." *Newsweek* called it "the most pleasurable theater-going experience in the United States."

The following year the Guthrie began building an audience for the future by offering special low-price tickets for students and sending preparation kits to teachers who ordered tickets for their classes. By 1967 the Guthrie had obtained state and federal funding that paid for theater tickets and transportation for thirty-three thousand students during the school year. The following year the Guthrie management opened a separate theater in St. Paul and an experimental theater called The Other Place on Harmon Place in Minneapolis. Many of the players at The Other Place were from the university's drama department, and a journalist described the atmosphere as "no gowns, no tuxes, no champagne.... It seemed to be about 80 percent theater people."

Tyrone Guthrie made it clear from the outset that he would serve as director of the theater for only three years. When he retired after the 1965 season, the University of Minnesota appointed him a visiting professor. For the next few years Guthrie conducted student workshops and an occasional play. In declining health he retired to his home in Ireland and died in 1971. For the next decade the Guthrie Theater struggled under a succession of directors, often operating at a loss. By the 1980s, however, it had become a civic treasure, as important to civic pride as the Minnesota Twins baseball team, the Minnesota Vikings football team, and the University of Minnesota.

In 1976 the Minneapolis Chamber of Commerce created the Five Percent Club (since renamed the Keystone Program) to formalize corporate philanthropy. With such commercial giants as Target Corporation and the St. Paul Companies (now the St. Paul Travelers Companies)—all examples of the growing diversification of Minnesota's economy—devoting five percent of their earnings to charity, by the 1990s the *Chronicle of Philanthropy* judged the Twin Cities to have the highest level of corporate philanthropy of any metropolitan area in the United States. An important beneficiary of this gift giving, the Guthrie Theater would remain a permanent feature of the Twin Cities' landscape.

The Minneapolis Symphony Orchestra (since 1968 the Minnesota Orchestra) is another civic treasure of national renown. It was born in 1903 when a private choral group, the Philharmonic Club, decided to establish its own orchestra instead of relying on freelance accompaniment. The symphony's first conductor was German-born and

Paris-trained Emil Oberhoffer, who arrived in the Twin Cities as a member of a Gilbert and Sullivan touring troupe. The orchestra numbered fifty musicians when Oberhoffer's baton waved the first downbeat on November 5, 1903. In nineteen seasons at the podium Oberhoffer built the symphony into one of the best known in the Midwest. Realizing that he could expand his audience and revenue by touring, out of his own pocket he financed appearances in various Minnesota and Wisconsin cities beginning in 1907. When the tours made money, the board of directors approved funds for travel. The symphony made

*Members of the world-famous Minneapolis Symphony Orchestra
"fiddling around" in 1934*

its debut in Chicago in 1911 and reached New York the following year. By 1917 when the orchestra traveled to California it had become known as the "Orchestra on Wheels." A western correspondent of the national magazine *Musical Courier* declared that "those who have heard other traveling orchestras do not hesitate to place the Minneapolis Symphony Orchestra in the category of the few really great orchestras in the country."

In 1931 the institution took another giant step toward national recognition when it hired Eugene Ormandy as conductor. A Hungarian immigrant, Ormandy had directed the orchestra of the Capitol Theatre in New York when he came to national attention with a sensational debut in conducting the Philadelphia Orchestra as a substitute for the great Arturo Toscanini. Minneapolis's alert orchestra board promptly brought him west and signed him to a contract. Ormandy combined a conducting style of "a lashing and athletic elasticity" with a genius for adapting symphonic pieces to the demands of a 78 rpm phonograph record. During the 1920s jazz musicians made the recording industry into a national "big business." Americans spent more money on records than on any other form of entertainment—the phonograph cabinet became a standard piece of furniture in middle-class living rooms. In his five-year tenure as director (before returning to Philadelphia) Ormandy gave the Minneapolis Symphony a national audience with his phonograph recordings.

When Ormandy departed in 1936, the board replaced him with Dimitri Mitropoulos, widely thought to have been the most inspiring conductor the orchestra has ever had. Born in Greece and educated at the Athens Conservatory, Mitropoulos made his American debut in 1936 as a guest conductor of the Boston Symphony. The Minneapolis board offered him a contract, and his debut on January 29, 1937, was a sensation. "The Orchestra," enthused one critic, "under the flying fists and the shaking, quivering, and yet completely poised figure of Mitropoulos, evoked a splendor of tone, an incandescent brilliance of technique it has never summoned in the past." Mitropoulos remained with the Minneapolis Symphony for twelve years (before departing to become director of the New York Philharmonic), and elderly concertgoers still regard it as a golden age.

By 1980 the Minnesota Orchestra was the largest nonprofit organization in the state serving both the Twin Cities metropolitan area and the entire Midwest. It benefited financially from the establishment of the Five Percent Club and particularly from the benefactions of Kenneth Dayton, the department store retailer whose family enterprise evolved into the giant Target Corporation. At its hundredth anniversary season in 2002 the Minnesota Orchestra had ninety-five musicians and an annual budget of thirty million dollars. An "Orchestra on Wheels and Wings," it had, in the first century of its existence, made appearances in 658 cities in twenty-two countries. Blending musical excellence with democratic instinct, its appearances ranged from forty-three performances in New York's Carnegie Hall to twenty-nine in Appleton, Wisconsin; eighteen in Albert Lea, Minnesota; and twenty-six in Aberdeen, South Dakota.

The State Park System

In 1872, when Congress established Yellowstone as the nation's first national park, the westward movement was still in high gear, and a conservation ethic lay in the distant future. The legislation established Yellowstone as a "public park or pleasuring ground," perhaps inspired by landscape pioneer Frederick Law Olmstead's vision of Central Park as a fragment of wilderness in the middle of New York City. The legislation further specified, however, that Yellowstone's unique natural features be left "in their natural condition" for future generations. Congress thus unconsciously endorsed a potential conflict—recreational use versus preservation—that would bedevil the development of national and state parks from that day to the present.

In the 1870s Scottish-born and Wisconsin-bred John Muir refined the conservation ethic and intensified its internal conflicts with a series of articles and books on California's Yosemite Valley. Influenced by the writings of Ralph Waldo Emerson and Henry David Thoreau, Muir viewed nature as mystically divine, its pristine innocence worthy of preservation for its own sake. In 1890 Muir, with help from a New York magazine publisher who had camped in Yosemite, persuaded Congress to turn the valley into the nation's second national park. Muir then helped found the Sierra Club to guard the park's unsullied virginity by keeping out loggers and sheep ranchers. This was the status of the nation's fledgling conservation movement when Minnesota began experimenting with state-owned parks.

In 1885 New York became the first state to set up a state park when it set aside a forest preserve in the Catskills that eventually became part of Adirondack Park. It was hardly a model for other states, however, for the park was established primarily for the prosaic purpose of ensuring a water supply for the Erie Canal. It nevertheless helped inspire Jacob V. Brower, who had camped on Lake Itasca and surveyed it for the Minnesota Historical Society, to propose a park safeguarding the Mississippi River's headwaters. Wrote one of Brower's associates in 1889, "Why cannot we ... have a real wild park, one far from the hum and bustle of large cities, like the National Park of the Yellowstone ... [or] the Adirondack region in New York?"

The Minnesota Historical Society endorsed the idea, and the legislature established Itasca State Park in 1891. The next year Congress transferred the federally owned lands in the region to the state, and Brower, named park commissioner, negotiated the purchase of lands owned by railroads and lumber companies. Land acquisition went on for a decade; by the time of Brower's death in 1905 the park contained 16,117 acres. With further state acquisitions in the 1920s the park reached its present size of approximately thirty-two thousand acres (fifty square miles). It remained the gem of the Minnesota state park system into the twenty-first century.

During the 1890s the state acquired a few acres on historic sites of the Dakota War (Camp Release and the battlefield at Birch Coulee), but these remained roadside monuments rather than becoming state parks. The next state park was established in 1895 at the Dalles of St. Croix, where the river plunged through a canyon of ancient basaltic rock. Renamed Interstate, the park contained only 167 acres (the Wisconsin state park on the other side of the river was thirteen hundred acres), but that limited area included the most important geological features. Because of its proximity to the Twin Cities, Interstate became one of the most heavily used of Minnesota's parks. Except for some durable rock cliffs, its pristine character has been lost.

Between 1900 and 1920 the legislature established fifteen small parks, half of them historic monuments and the remainder of local interest and for local use—such as Minneopa, on the edge of Mankato, Alexander Ramsey in Redwood Falls, and Horace Austin in Austin. Jay Cooke, on the shores of Lake Superior near Duluth, originated as a local enterprise, but it underwent a huge expansion in the 1930s and '40s. It became the state's sixth largest park, rivaling Itasca for its blend of wilderness preserve and camping facilities.

By 1925 Minnesota had a total of twenty-three parks and monuments but lacked a centralized administration. The parks were under the general control of the state auditor, whose duties left little time for park management. Wisconsin and several eastern states had by this time established state park commissions staffed by experts. Minnesota also lacked a philosophy governing the acquisition and development of parks. State officials, however, were beginning to address this latter issue. In 1927 an official in the auditor's office thought a distinction should be made between local parks in or adjacent to cities, which might be improved by adding playgrounds and planting shrubbery, and state parks, which were of historic and scenic value and should be "kept as nature made them." From that distinction the idea developed over the next few years that each state park ought to represent a particular type of landscape (or biocultural region). That meant establishing new parks in regions that had nothing more than local recreational facilities, notably in the counties bordering Iowa and the Dakotas.

In 1933 Franklin D. Roosevelt's New Deal established the Civilian Conservation Corps (CCC) as a relief agency to provide jobs for men aged eighteen to twenty-five. The men lived in army-style camps with barracks and mess halls. Bugle calls sent them to bed at night and wakened them in the morning. In addition to room and board, the men received thirty dollars a month, of which twenty-five dollars automatically went to their families. The CCC worked on reforestation and water-quality improvement in both state and national parks; the National Park Service (NPS) made many of the decisions with respect to such improvements. Because the NPS preferred to channel its federal largesse through trained parks administrators, Minnesota and other states that lacked parks commissions felt obliged to establish them. Minnesota did so in 1935 by creating a division of state parks within its Department of Conservation. By that date Minnesota had fifteen CCC camps in operation, nine of them in state parks.

The New Deal also contributed to the nation's evolving parkland philosophy when Congress created Everglades National Park in 1934. All earlier parks had been established to preserve "great mountains, deep canyons, and tumbling waterfalls." The Everglades was preserved because it was a unique, albeit flat and undifferentiated, land-

Lake Itasca as seen from Douglas Lodge, 1955.
Minnesota's first state park preserves the headwaters of the Mississippi.
Photo by Donald Holmquist

scape that had certain plant and animal species in need of protection. This initiative would have reinforced Minnesota's dawning interest in preserving prairie landscapes on its southern and western borders if the state had had the money. Unfortunately, through the remaining years of the depression and World War II, it did not.

In 1940 the director of state parks tried to shame the legislature into appropriating more money for park acquisition and maintenance by pointing out that its annual appropriation amounted to only $2.22 an acre, while Michigan was spending $2.63 an acre and Wisconsin $5.44. There was little response, however, and while the state built sixteen more parks over the next decade, all were small—half of them amounted to little more than highway waysides. Finally, in 1953 the legislature approved a law requiring vehicle owners entering a state recreation area of more than fifty acres to purchase a windshield sticker. At long last, state parks could generate revenue of their own.

Over the next few years the state established small parks that protected the superb scenery along the North Shore of Lake Superior (at the mouths of the Manitou, Cascade, and Temperance rivers), and, in 1957, a park on the western side of Mille Lacs. This site, called Kathio, had been a focal point of the Dakota culture for hundreds of years, and it contained mounds of religious significance dating back five hundred to a thousand years. At 10,500 acres it became the fourth largest in the state system and was noteworthy for the informational tours conducted by park rangers.

The state purchased Fort Snelling from the U.S. Veterans Administration in 1960 and in 1969 turned its management over to the Minnesota Historical Society. In 1963 the legislature passed a major appropriation bill that allowed a vast expansion of some existing parks, such as Traverse des Sioux on the Minnesota River, and establishment of new ones in the southern and western extremities of the state. Most important of these—and fifth largest in the system—was Maplewood in lake-studded Otter Tail County, some fifty miles southeast of Moorhead. Located in the transition zone between northern woodlands and southern prairies, the park was a naturalist's dream, blending glacial lakes and wetlands, hardwood forests, and abandoned farms.

During the 1970s the parks division experienced the first public resistance to the establishment of new parks. A tract of land just west of the undeveloped Baptism River State Park on the North Shore had been logged over at the turn of the twentieth century and then managed for the next seventy years by a succession of private owners as a wilderness retreat. In 1975 the state's effort to buy the tract, which amounted to about ten thousand acres, ran into strong opposition from Lake County residents. They feared that removal of the land from the county's tax base would increase their own property taxes. After years of contention, the Nature Conservancy in 1979 sidestepped the opposition by persuading the owner to sell about half the tract to it. The legislature then passed a bill erecting Tettegouche State Park and reimbursing the Nature Conservancy for its outlay.

While the bill worked its way through the legislature the head of the state park system promised the residents of Lake County that "This will be the last new state park in the program." Though the commissioner later amended the statement to read "while he was commissioner," the fact remains that Tettegouche was the last important park to be set up in Minnesota. In the growing public conservatism of the last decades of the twentieth century the preservation ethic yielded to a rising concern that land, whether agricultural or woodland, be kept in productive use. Those who wanted to preserve John Muir's legacy (known then as "deep ecology") had to turn to the Nature Conservancy or other private nature-reserve organizations.

The Boundary Waters

In 1890, the U.S. Census Bureau announced the end of the American frontier. (In the census that year, the bureau found no significant region of the country with fewer than two people per square mile—its definition of "frontier." It clearly was not counting Indians in this calculation. This announcement inspired University of Wisconsin Professor Frederick Jackson Turner's essay on "The Significance of the Frontier in American History," which argued that American democracy emerged from the frontier experience.)

In 1891, Congress approved a Forest Reserve Act, which authorized the president to set aside (that is, take off the market) forested public lands (later called national forests).

Benjamin Harrison, president at the time, ordered the enclosure of thirteen million acres of wilderness lands, followed by Grover Cleveland, who set aside five million acres. Nothing further was done until Theodore Roosevelt became president. Roosevelt, who camped with John Muir for three days in Yosemite (and thought the experience was "bully"), placed the Bureau of Forestry, established in 1898, in the agriculture department to enhance its status. The head of the bureau, dubbed "Chief Forester" by Roosevelt, was Gifford Pinchot. Roosevelt then added millions of acres to the national forest system.

Pinchot, who coined the word "conservation" as applied to natural resources, was the quintessential Progressive. He set up offices and commissions, staffed them with geologists, hydrologists, foresters, and engineers, and made conservation a profession. His objective was not simply the preservation of natural resources, but the scientific management of their use. He allowed lumbering in the national forests, provided it was under the supervision of government foresters. To John Muir's horror, Pinchot allowed California sheep ranchers to run their animals ("hoofed locusts" to Muir) into the Sequoia National Forest adjacent to Yosemite. The nation's fledgling conservation movement was thus deeply divided within itself when the first voices were heard in Minnesota asking for preservation of the land of the voyageurs, the beautiful landscape of lakes and rivers along the international border between Lake Superior and Lake of the Woods.

In 1902, Christopher C. Andrews, who held the position of forestry commissioner in the state auditor's office, persuaded the federal land office to withdraw from sale some 500,000 acres around the headwaters of the Brule River in far northeastern Minnesota. Because the land had suffered a series of forest fires in the last half of the nineteenth century, lumbermen had passed it over. Andrews thought the lakes and second-growth forest might be a valuable "fish and game preserve." Three years later, after a canoe trip along the Rainy River, he persuaded the land office to withdraw another 141,000 acres along beautifully timbered Crooked Lake and Lac la Croix. In February 1909, just before leaving office, President Roosevelt converted all the federally owned public lands in northeastern Minnesota into Superior National Forest. Nudged by Minnesota, the Canadian province of Ontario responded in kind, establishing Quetico Provincial Forest Reserve on its side of the Rainy River border. Quetico became a provincial park in 1913.

When Andrews died in 1922, Superior National Forest was already becoming known as spectacular canoe country. The best way to see the land, advised a forest service pamphlet, was by canoe, and the Duluth and Iron Range Railroad obligingly published a map of canoe routes and portages. Unfortunately, the public lands that Roosevelt had converted to national forest were a collection of parcels broken up by private holdings, most owned by lumber companies. The region was still being logged in the early 1920s, and logging roads, such as the Gunflint Trail from Grand Marais to Gunflint Lake, allowed automobiles to penetrate the forest reserve. By the mid-1920s resorts had appeared on the more accessible lakes. John Muir died in 1914, but his preservationist philosophy had been absorbed by the Izaak Walton League, whose Minnesota branch urged the forest service to buy up the private holdings and ban all roads. That action was bitterly opposed by the merchants and resort owners of towns bordering the reserve, such as Ely and Grand Marais.

In 1928 a group of preservationists formed the Quetico-Superior Council to present their point of view to Congress and the forest service. The council's leading figure was Ernest Oberholtzer of Davenport, Iowa, who had studied at Harvard under the father of landscape architecture, Frederick Law Olmsted. Though much of the council's funding came from Twin Cities businessmen who had canoed the boundary waters, its members included representatives from the Izaak Walton League, the American Legion, and the General Federation of Women's Clubs. The council gained the attention of U.S. senator Henrik Shipstead, who drafted a bill to curtail logging, dam building, and road construction in a huge region extending from Lake Superior on the east, to Rainy Lake on the west, and south to Lake Vermilion and Birch Lake. The proposal applied to four thousand square miles of landscape, including the Superior National Forest's twenty-five thousand square miles. Congress passed the act in 1930, and the Quetico-Superior Council concentrated thereafter on consolidating and expanding the federally owned lands.

Ironically, the depression helped. Logging operations ceased in the late 1920s, and the sawmills at Duluth and Cloquet shut down. Millions of acres of cutover and tax-delinquent property came on the market early in the depression. The forest service under President Herbert Hoover was rather timid, however, and only about 400,000 acres were added to the Superior National Forest prior to 1933. The State of Minnesota tried to help near-bankrupt northeastern counties by purchasing tax-delinquent lands within the area protected by the Shipstead Act, but it made the lands into state forests rather than turning them over to the federal government.

In 1934 President Franklin D. Roosevelt set up a special committee to study the Superior-Quetico issue, and the committee delighted Oberholtzer by adopting his program of extending the national forest to cover the entire region from Rainy Lake to the mouth of the Pi-

Preservation in the BWCA yields scenic views and tranquil canoe rides.
Photo by Peleaux, 1970

geon River. By the end of the 1930s Superior National Forest grew to 3.5 million acres. The forest service, however, could not afford the acquisition of private developments or old logging roads that allowed motor vehicles to penetrate the forest reserves. That would remain a problem for the next decade.

Federal funds for land acquisition vanished during World War II, but in 1948 Congress appropriated money for the purchase of lands and resorts adjacent to the national forest, with extra funds to reimburse St. Louis, Lake, and Cook counties for their lost tax revenues. This was a major step in the growing philosophy of a wilderness reserve, for it enabled the forest service to remove nearly all the roads—and hence motor vehicles—from the region. Pontoon-equipped airplanes remained a problem, but in 1949 President Harry Truman signed an order preserving the airspace above the roadless area to a height of four thousand feet. Merchants and resort owners in Ely and other communities on the edge of the protected area contested the order, but the federal courts held that resort owners had no vested rights in airspace and that the federal government had the power to regulate air travel.

Around this time, writer and conservationist Sigurd F. Olson resigned as dean of Ely Junior College to follow a new career that would take advantage of his graduate degree in ecology and his passion for Minnesota's canoe country. He served the Izaak Walton League as a wilderness ecologist and on other committees as a consultant. A gifted writer, Olson described the bounty of the northland and offered philosophical reflections on the relationship of wilderness to human values.

Articles touting the beauty of Minnesota's boundary waters appeared in national magazines during the 1950s, and usage rose dramatically. And so did the problems. Portages northward out of Ely became cluttered with trash, stored fishing boats, motors, and wheeled trailers for pulling boats across portages. Canoeists who went north seeking silence and solitude grumbled about motors on the lakes. The roadless areas that motorboats could not reach were given the name Boundary Waters Canoe Area (BWCA) in 1958.

In 1964 Congress approved the Wilderness Act that at last made John Muir's preservationist philosophy a matter of national policy.

Drafted by Senator Hubert Humphrey, the act authorized the president to designate as wilderness certain public lands (most of it already national forest land) "where the earth and its community of life are untrammeled by man, where man himself is a visitor who does not remain." Not surprisingly nearly all of the public lands that qualified as wilderness lay in the West. In approving the act Congress recognized that the BWCA presented a special problem. Having been logged once and subjected for years to motorized traffic, it hardly qualified as wilderness. Consequently, the act directed that management of the area follow regulations established by the secretary of agriculture and that the regulations permit lumbering in certain areas and the use of motorboats on lakes that already had them.

Secretary of Agriculture Orville Freeman sought a compromise between the competing interests. He divided the protected region into two zones. An inner zone of the BWCA, some 600,000 acres, would be free of lumbering and motorboats, preserved as wilderness for canoeists. The outer portal zone would be open to lumbering under federal supervision and its lakes open to motorboats. Freeman prohibited the storing of boats on federal property and use of motorized equipment on portages. Intended to placate all special interests, the compromise satisfied no one, and for the next decade the forest service was hauled into court by environmental groups, such as the Sierra Club, seeking expansion of the wilderness zone and by fishermen and resort owners seeking more range for motorboats.

Although the dispute was conducted with considerable heat, it is worth noting that each side had a reasonably defensible position. Motorboat enthusiasts pointed out that they were not trying to exclude anyone from the BWCA; they wanted the scenic landscape to be available to everyone, including the aged and infirm who could not manage canoes. Canoeists, on the other hand, just as reasonably pointed out that motorized craft were inconsistent with a wilderness experience. The presence of motors would make the BWCA look and feel just like all the rest of Minnesota's lakes. In 1975 the environmentalists notched one small victory when the forest service banned snowmobiles from the canoeing zone.

In 1978, with support from President Jimmy Carter's administration, Congress gave a partial victory to the environmentalists on the question of motorboats. The Boundary Waters Wilderness Act cut in half the water surface area available to motorboats under Secretary Freeman's 1965 regulations. The victory was due largely to a growing public concern for land preservation—reflected in a law passed that same year protecting large parts of Alaska from lumbering and oil drilling. The act also sought to appease resort owners and outfitters by providing funds to compensate for their lost business.

Although no permanent solution to the conflict of interests between canoeists and motorboat users was found, the noise level of the debate seemed to subside in the 1980s and '90s. The purists among canoeists who did not want to pass through motorized lakes to reach solitude chose to cross the border and make use of Quetico Provincial Park's motor-free environment. Indeed, canoeists who prefer Minnesota waters became an important source of income for northern residents. Businessmen in the "jumping off" cities of Grand Marais, Ely, and International Falls built huge canoe supply and rental establishments that became a mainstay of the local economy. One could wish that wilderness preservation always paid such dividends.

The Taconite/Reserve Controversy

Hematite, the soft-earth iron ore mined in open pits with giant shovels, lay near the center of the geologic formation known as the Mesabi Range. The eastern third of the range consisted of a hard flinty rock containing fine particles of magnetic iron, with only a patch here and there of soft hematite. This quartz-like silicate, which a Minnesota geologist named "taconite" in 1892, contained relatively small amounts of iron. Because the earthen ore in the mines to the west contained a much higher percentage of iron and could be mined with steam shovels, Minnesota hematite accounted for more than half of U.S. iron production through the first half of the twentieth century. But there simply was no market for the hard-rock taconite that made up 95 percent of the Mesabi Range.

In 1913 landowners in the logged-over and apparently useless eastern end of the range sent a sample of taconite to the University of Minnesota's School of Mines to see if it had any commercial value. There it was handed over to a recently hired and underused math instructor, Edward W. Davis. Although Davis's training was in engineering, rather than metallurgy, he discovered that the iron was enclosed in the rock in the form of minute magnetic particles, and he hit upon the solution of crushing the rock and extracting the iron with a magnet. Experimental refineries in the 1920s, however, ran into technical problems that made taconite too costly to be commercially viable. Davis nevertheless continued his experiments, becoming the leading figure in the school's taconite research for the next forty years and earning a reputation throughout the mining world as "Mr. Taconite." By the late 1930s he had found a way to reduce the rock to a powder, from which the iron could be extracted with a magnet and then, using a water paste, reformed into a bullet-sized pellet that had a higher percentage of iron than earthen hematite.

Following this scientific breakthrough, two political and military events made taconite processing commercially feasible. In 1941 the Minnesota legislature exempted the Iron Range from local property taxes and U.S. entry into World War II that same year caused the demand for steel (rising since Roosevelt's ship-building program began in 1938) to skyrocket. The steel giants in Pittsburgh, Pennsylvania, and Gary, Indiana, anticipating exhaustion of the hematite deposits, took a new interest in taconite. In 1942 they formed a mining subsidiary, Reserve Mining Company (so named because taconite was still thought of as a long-range backup), to design and locate a processing plant.

Reserve quickly discovered that the refining process developed by Davis created new problems that made site selection difficult. The manufacture of pellets required a great deal of water, and lakes were few on the Iron Range. If a plant were located on one of Minnesota's glacial lakes, it would seriously affect the water level. Because the iron made up only a small portion of the taconite rock, the refining process created a huge amount of waste tailings that required extensive and unsightly settling basins. After discovering that the tailings, when placed in water, settled quickly to the bottom, Davis and other researchers at the School of Mines suggested that the refining plant be located on Lake Superior. The lake provided an abundant source of water for the refining process, and the tailings deposited in the lake would slip into the deep rift at its bottom. Regarding the tailings as chemically and biologically inert, the scientists insisted that they would not pollute the lake, endanger the water supply of Duluth and Two Harbors, or adversely affect the fishing industry.

In 1946 Reserve announced plans to construct a taconite refinery at Silver Bay on the North Shore. It would also build a harbor to accommodate the ore boats and a company town to house its employees. On the basis of Davis's assurances, the Minnesota Department of Conservation and the state Water Pollution Control Commission granted the necessary permits, but they also stipulated that the permits could be revoked if the tailings caused clouding of the lake water or affected aquatic life or municipal water supplies. Reserve proceeded to build a model company town in which company executives lived side-by-side with other employees. It also built a railroad to bring the rock ore down from the Range and completed the refining plant at Silver Bay in 1955. Shipping of taconite pellets to the steel mills of the East began the following year. In the meantime, Erie Mining Company, a subsidiary of U.S. Steel, began building a taconite plant near Aurora, Minnesota, where it planned to acquire water from local lakes and dispose of its tailings on land.

At its inception, the Reserve plant employed twenty-five thousand people, and both state and county officials viewed taconite as the economic salvation of Minnesota's hardscrabble northeast. Through the 1950s and '60s state agencies readily granted permits for increases in Reserve's production capacity; by the late '60s it was producing 10.7 million tons of pellets annually. By that time taconite shipments to eastern steel mills exceeded the earthen iron ore shipments. By then, also, the costs to the environment were becoming evident. Reserve deposited sixty thousand tons of tailings *a day* into Lake Superior, and an unsightly delta built up in the lake adjacent to the plant. It was also apparent that, despite the careful planning that went into its company town, Reserve had made a mistake in rerouting U.S. Highway 61 (the main North Shore highway) through the middle of its operations so that any passing tourist could not fail to see—and be offended by—the tailings delta.

During the 1960s public concern for the quality of the environment grew alongside the civil rights and feminist movements. Rachel Carson's *Silent Spring* (1962), which pointed out the harmful effects

of DDT on wildlife, served as a catalyst for the change in public thinking. Lady Bird Johnson, wife of President Lyndon Johnson, made
cleaning up the nation's roadsides one of her top priorities—that project could not fail to remind Minnesotans of their state eyesore at Silver Bay. The momentum continued into the Nixon presidency and resulted in the creation of the U.S. Environmental Protection Agency
(EPA) in 1970. By that date the federal interior department had issued
a report critical of Reserve's impact on the water quality of Lake Superior, citing specifically a turbid "green water" that extended about

*Evidence of tailings' effects on Lake Superior is apparent in the fan-shaped
deposit visible in this 1962 photograph of Silver Bay's taconite plant.*

eighteen miles out from the tailings delta. In 1969 scientists at the National Water Quality Laboratory in Duluth began testing the lake for pollutants that might affect the city's drinking water. They discovered that the tailings contained a fibrous silicate very similar to asbestos fibers, which were known to cause cancer. They also discovered that the tailings had drifted eastward and could be found off Wisconsin's shoreline.

In 1970 the Minnesota Pollution Control Agency, joined by the state of Wisconsin, filed suit against Reserve in the U.S. district court in St. Paul. They sought an order halting the dumpings. The EPA joined the suit the following year on grounds that the pollution had become an interstate problem. The suit went on for years, as decisions by the district court were appealed to the U.S. Court of Appeals in St. Louis and often modified. By 1973 the central issue in the case was public health, rather than the water quality of Lake Superior, when tailing fibers were discovered in Duluth's drinking water. Minnesota rejected a compromise offer by Reserve to send the tailings by deepwater pipe to the middle of the lake. In 1974 a federal judge ordered Reserve to cease dumping tailings into the lake and to find a site on land instead.

Negotiations between Reserve and Minnesota permit agencies dragged on for another four years. In 1978 Reserve at last agreed to build a pipeline that would send its tailings to a site on its railroad line seven miles inland from Silver Bay. The site, appropriately named Milepost 7, was still only three miles from the lake, and six immense earthen dams had to be built to contain the tailings. Completion of the site in 1980 marked the end of one of the nastiest environmental controversies of the century.

Six new taconite plants were built on the Iron Range during the 1980s, but the economic salvation of Minnesota's northeast was not to be. In the course of that decade, the antiquated steel mills of Pittsburgh and Gary, with their highly paid workers, found that they could not compete in the world market. Steel imports from such unlikely places as Brazil soared in the 1980s, and the demand for Minnesota ores collapsed. The mining of earthen hematite ceased altogether, and by 1990 taconite production was down by a third from what it had been in 1979. In 1986 Reserve itself went into bankruptcy. The steel industry continued to struggle in the first years of the twenty-first century, sustained only by a tariff on foreign imports imposed by President George W. Bush. With or without the tariff, which might be found contrary to international treaties, the future of the industry and its mining subsidiaries remains cloudy.

A postscript: Despite initial fears, in the early years of the twenty-first century, no significant increases in cancer rates appeared in Duluth or other North Shore cities dependent on Lake Superior for drinking water. The aesthetic appearance of the lake was the issue all along. That in itself is not unimportant, however. Because the only outlet to this huge lake is the narrow and shallow St. Mary's River, the lake's water turnover—and hence its powers of self-healing—is glacially slow. It takes five hundred years for a drop of water to migrate from Duluth to Sault Ste. Marie. Retaining a balance between the demands of modern technology and the ideal (with its own economic as well as spiritual values) of preserving the state's natural beauty will remain a central concern for Minnesota's people and politicians in the coming years.

VISITING HISTORY

Minnesota is a state like many others—except for those many things that make it exceptional.

Charles A. Lindbergh House

2 miles south of Little Falls on Lindbergh Dr.; 320/616-5421. The aviator's boyhood home, with original family furnishings and possessions; visitor center with exhibits.

Dorothy Molter Museum

2002 E. Sheridan, Ely; 218/365-4451. Molter, the famed "Root Beer Lady" of the BWCA, was trained as a nurse, then moved to Knife Lake in the 1930s and lived alone there for decades, helping injured canoeists and selling home-brewed root beer to visitors. After her death in 1986, her home and a guest cabin were hauled to Ely for use in this museum.

Guthrie Theater

725 Vineland Place, Minneapolis; 612/377-2224. (The theater moves to its building on the Mississippi River in summer 2006.) Guided backstage tours offered Saturdays.

Hockey Hall of Fame

801 Hat Trick Ave., Eveleth; 218/744-5167. Exhibits on the history and highlights of the game.

Mayo Clinic

Rochester; 507/284-9258. Guided tours of clinic daily operations and of art and architecture; exhibits are in the Mayo Historical Suite on the third floor of the Plummer Building.

Mayowood

3720 Mayowood Rd. S.W., Rochester; 507/282-9447. Originally built in 1911 as Dr. Charles Mayo's summer home, this 48-room mansion housed two generations of Mayos until 1965.

Orchestra Hall

1111 Marquette Ave., Minneapolis; 612/371-5656. Home of one of the country's top orchestras, with exceptional acoustics.

Rabideau CCC Camp

6 miles south of Blackduck on Co. Hwy. 39 in Chippewa National Forest. One of two surviving Civilian Conservation Corps camps in Minnesota, constructed in 1935–41.

SPAM Museum

1937 Spam Blvd., Austin; 507/437-5100. Learn everything there is to know about the famous luncheon meat, presented in humorous, informative, interactive, multimedia exhibits.

Suggestions for Further Reading

There are two very fine general histories of the state: Theodore C. Blegen, *Minnesota: A History of the State* (2nd ed., 1975), and William E. Lass, *Minnesota: A History* (2nd ed., 1998). Both tend to be encyclopedic, and many readers will find them most useful as reference works. Edited collections of articles and essays on Minnesota history include Anne J. Aby, ed., *The North Star State: A Minnesota History Reader* (2002); Clifford E. Clark, Jr., ed., *Minnesota in a Century of Change: The State and Its People Since 1900* (1989); Rhoda R. Gilman, *The Story of Minnesota's Past* (1991); and Stephen R. Graubard, *Minnesota, Real and Imagined: Essays on the State and Its Culture* (2000). Travelers will enjoy using Tim Bewer's *Moon Handbooks Minnesota* (2004), an excellent and detailed guidebook with thumbnail histories of hundreds of communities and highlights of places to visit.

The impact of the glacier on Minnesota is described in minute detail by Richard W. Ojakangas and Charles L. Matsch, *Minnesota's Geology* (1982). Sarah P. Rubinstein, *Minnesota History along the Highways: A Guide to Historic Markers and Sites* (2003), includes texts of the state's sixty geological markers. Roy W. Meyer, *History of the Santee Sioux: United States Indian Policy on Trial* (1993), and Thomas Vennum, Jr., *Wild Rice and the Ojibway People* (1988), offer helpful perspectives on Minnesota Indian cultures. Ignatia Broker's *Night Flying Woman: An Ojibway Narrative* (1983) provides an Ojibwe family's story of the years of transition. Otherwise, the determined reader will have to rely on nineteenth and early twentieth century descriptions that the Minnesota Historical Society Press has recently reprinted: Samuel W. Pond, *Dakota Life in the Upper Midwest* (2002); Frances Densmore, *Chippewa Customs* (1979); and William W. Warren, *History of the Ojibway People* (1984). Grace Lee Nute, *The Voyageur* (1931, reprinted 1987), though dated, is still the best study of the fur trade. Also recommended are two popular treatments by Carolyn Gilman, *Where Two Worlds Meet: The Great Lakes Fur Trade* (1982) and *The Grand Portage Story* (1992).

Detailed, yet quite readable, studies of the founding and economic growth of the Twin Cities are Lucile M. Kane, *The Falls of St. Anthony: The Waterfall that Built Minneapolis* (1987), and Shannon M. Pennefeather, ed., *Mill City: A Visual History of the Minneapolis Mill District* (2003). Volume 58.5–6 (2003) of *Minnesota History* contains excellent articles on the history of Minneapolis. A special issue of *Minnesota History* edited by Anne R. Kaplan and Marilyn Ziebarth contains very interesting essays on early economic and political development: *Making Minnesota Territory, 1849–1858* (1999). Minnesota's two-front Civil War is well told by Kenneth Carley in *Minnesota in the Civil War: An Illustrated History* (1961; 2nd ed., 2000) and *The Dakota War of 1862* (1961; 2nd ed., 1976). Gary Clayton Anderson's biography, *Little Crow: Spokesman for the Sioux* (1986), is thoroughly researched and nicely written.

Scholarly studies of post–Civil War economic developments, sometimes difficult to read, are Allan G. Bogue, *From Prairie to Corn Belt: Farming on the Illinois and Iowa Prairies in the Nineteenth Century* (1963; 2nd ed., 1994); Annette Atkins, *Harvest of Grief: Grasshopper Plagues and Public Assistance in Minnesota, 1873–1878* (1984); Glenda Riley, *The Female Frontier: A Comparative View of Women on the Prairie and the Plains* (1988); Agnes M. Larson, *History of the White Pine Industry in Minnesota* (1949); and David A. Walker, *Iron Frontier: The Discovery and Early Development of Minnesota's Three Ranges* (1979). Albro Martin, *James J. Hill & The Opening of the Northwest* (1991) is an excellent biography of the railroad magnate.

Two biographies are the best introduction to late-nineteenth-century reform movements in Minnesota: Thomas A. Woods, *Knights of the Plow: Oliver H. Kelley and the Origins of the Grange in Republican*

Ideology (1991), and Martin Ridge, *Ignatius Donnelly: The Portrait of a Politician* (1962). Carl H. Chrislock, *The Progressive Era in Minnesota, 1899-1918* (1971), is the standard work on early-twentieth-century reform, and Richard M. Valelly, *Radicalism in the States: The Minnesota Farmer-Labor Party and the American Political Economy* (1989), traces the beginning of the liberal political tradition. Barbara Stuhler tells the story of the woman suffrage movement in *Gentle Warriors: Clara Ueland and the Minnesota Struggle for Woman Suffrage* (1995). Minnesota's best-known citizen in the 1920s is the subject of an excellent biography, *Lindbergh* (1998), by A. Scott Berg.

A pair of scholarly though rather slow-moving works describe depression-born radicalism in Minnesota: Elizabeth Faue, *Community of Suffering and Struggle: Women, Men, and the Labor Movement in Minneapolis, 1915-1945* (1991), and Katherine Jellison, *Entitled to Power: Farm Women and Technology, 1913-1963* (1993). Carl Solberg, *Hubert Humphrey: A Biography* (1984), is a judicious study, while a more recent one, *Hubert H. Humphrey: The Politics of Joy* (1993) by Charles Lloyd Garrettson, is an uncritical paean that rests Humphrey's politics on religious belief. Stephen M. Gillon, *The Democrats' Dilemma: Walter F. Mondale and the Liberal Legacy* (1992), examines the problems Democrats faced when liberalism went out of fashion in the last quarter of the twentieth century.

There is no adequate history of the Mayo Clinic. Helen Clapesattle's *The Doctors Mayo* (1941) is a commissioned work, flattering but informative and well researched; Alan E. Nourse, *Inside the Mayo Clinic* (1979), alternates chapters describing patients' experiences with chapters on the history of the clinic. Frank M. Whiting, *Minnesota Theatre: From Old Fort Snelling to the Guthrie* (1988), is definitive on that topic. Roy W. Meyer, *Everyone's Country Estate: A History of Minnesota's State Parks* (1991), is an exhaustive history of each individual park. R. Newell Searle, *Saving Quetico-Superior: A Land Set Apart* (1977), takes the story from 1902 until the book went to press in the 1970s. James N. Gladden, *The Boundary Waters Canoe Area: Wilderness Values and Motorized Recreation* (1990), focuses on the motorboat controversy of recent times. Robert V. Bartlett, *The Reserve Mining Controversy: Science, Technology, and Environmental Quality* (1980), is judicious but burdened with excessive political science jargon.

Appendix
A Guide to Visiting History

These cities are keyed to the numbered map on page 272. Destinations in each city are listed with the numbers of the pages on which they are described.

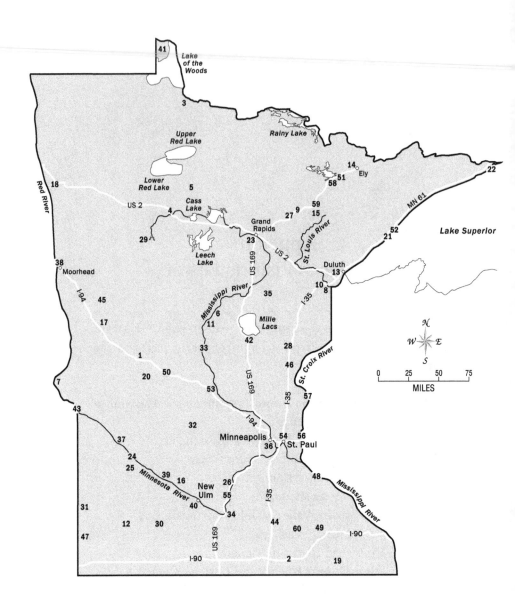

41

Lake
of the
Woods

3

Upper
Red Lake

Rainy Lake

Lower
Red Lake

18

5

Red River

US 2

4

Cass
Lake

27 9

59
15

14 Ely
51
58

22

MN 61

52
21

Lake Superior

29

Leech
Lake

Grand
Rapids

23

US 169

Mississippi River

US 2

St. Louis River

Duluth
13
8
10

38 Moorhead

45

I-94

17

6

11

35

Mille
Lacs

42

28

I-35

33

1

50

20

53

46

US 169

St. Croix River

I-35

57

7

43

32

I-94

37

Minneapolis
36

54 56
St. Paul

24

25

Minnesota River

39 16

48

31

47

12

30

40

New
Ulm

26
55

34

44

I-35

60 49

Mississippi River

I-90

19

US 169

I-90

2

N
W E
S

0   25   50   75
MILES

Index